Axis of Unity

Related Titles from Potomac Books

The War of All the People: The Nexus of Latin American Radicalism and Middle Eastern Terrorism
—Jon B. Perdue

Israel vs. Iran: The Shadow War
—Yaakov Katz and Yoaz Hendel

Iran's Revolutionary Guard: The Threat That Grows While America Sleeps
—Steven O'Hern

Axis of Unity

Venezuela, Iran & the Threat to America

SEAN GOFORTH

Potomac Books
Washington, D.C.

Library of Congress Cataloging-in-Publication Data
Goforth, Sean.
    Axis of unity: Venezuela, Iran & the threat to America / Sean Goforth. — 1st ed.
        p. cm.
    Includes bibliographical references and index.
    ISBN 978-1-61234-015-9 (hardcover : alk. paper)
    ISBN 978-1-61234-016-6 (electronic edition)
    1. Alliances—History—21st century. 2. Iran—Foreign relations—Venezuela. 3. Venezuela—Foreign relations—Iran. 4. Russia (Federation)—Foreign relations—Iran. 5. Iran—Foreign relations—Russia (Federation) 6. Russia (Federation)—Foreign relations—Venezuela. 7. Venezuela—Foreign relations—Russia (Federation) I. Title.
    JZ1314.G64 2011
    327.55087—dc23
                            2011023364

Printed in the United States of America on acid-free paper that meets the American National Standards Institute Z39-48 Standard.

Potomac Books
22841 Quicksilver Drive
Dulles, Virginia 20166

First Edition

10 9 8 7 6 5 4 3 2 1

Empires collapse. Gang leaders
Are strutting about like statesmen. The peoples
Can no longer be seen under all the armaments.

—Bertolt Brecht, "On the Suicide of the Refugee W.B."

For Mom

Contents

Introduction

On Sunday, November 28, 2004, Venezuela's flamboyant president Hugo Rafael Chávez Frías attended the unveiling of a statue of Simón Bolívar, considered the Liberator of South America. Similar depictions of Bolívar are ubiquitous in Latin America. They can be found in every Latin American capital and nearly all large cities, and in almost every pueblo in Colombia and Venezuela, which together formed the colonial territory where Bolívar was born in 1783. Bolívar on horseback is on prominent display in Washington, D.C., and towers aside the 59th Street and 6th Avenue entrance to Central Park in New York City. Many a European metropolis, such as Paris, London, Frankfurt, and Rome, also honor Bolívar with statues. For his dogged vision of an American continent free of imperial control Bolívar is a symbol that resonates throughout the modern democratic world. But on this day, Bolívar's bronzed likening was being introduced to the public at Dialogue Park, in Tehran.

Few at the time noted the statue's arrival; those who did found it a bit odd, if not a tad culturally aloof. And it wasn't hard to imagine how displaying a statue of El Libertador might backfire on Iran's authoritarian government. Furthermore, Iran and Venezuela were worlds apart. There were few historical ties between them, and no cultural ties to speak of. At most, the two nations had maintained proper diplomatic ties over the previous half-century, regularly exchanging ambassadors and the like. In the 1960s and 1970s they found common cause in lobbying for higher prices the

Organization of the Petroleum Exporting Countries (OPEC), of which they were two of the cartel's largest producing members, establishing reputations as "price hawks" among their petro-peddling peers. Beyond that, there was nothing to suggest any sort of kinship.

The obvious explanation for Bolívar's simulacrum in the Iranian capital was that Venezuela merely wanted to return a favor. A year before, Iran had gifted to Venezuela a statue of Omar Khayyám, an eleventh-century Persian philosopher and mathematician, which was placed on the patio of the National Library in the Venezuelan capital of Caracas. Tehran's mayor, Mahmoud Ahmadinejad, declared Caracas and Tehran "sister cities," an innocuous statement of goodwill between nations. At the time Iran was under an era of reform, and Iran's President Mohammad Khatami had sought warmer relations with a slew of nations, Venezuela being one.

Iran desperately needed allies, as the political climate from 9/11 to 2004 had been jarring. Reformists in Iran had quietly helped America bring down the Taliban after 9/11 by providing critical intelligence to the United States, and by encouraging its Afghan allies, the Northern Alliance, to join America's side. In preparation of what would be Operation Enduring Freedom, Iran even volunteered to help rescue downed American pilots.[1] Shortly thereafter the Islamic Republic of Iran was repaid by being branded a member of the "axis of evil," along with Iraq and North Korea.

In 2003, the United States invaded Iraq and toppled Saddam Hussein in three weeks' time, a task that the Islamic Republic's leadership could scarcely fathom in the course of its eight-year conflict with the Iraqi dictator in the 1980s, the bloodiest war between two nations in over a century. American forces now sat as bookends on Iran's borders, Iraq to the west and Afghanistan to the east. Talk quickly spread of a U.S. invasion of Iran, and "best guess" intelligence assessments of Iran's military strength and key bases found their way into major media reports and punditry, fueling widespread suspicions that the Islamic Republic was next. Though it is easy to forget now, for a time President Bush's neoconservative project to spread democracy and eliminate "evildoers" came close to cowing even those hostile regimes that were not invaded.

Still, the Khatami government continued to make overtures to the United States, proposing a "grand bargain"—faxed via the Swiss Embassy in Tehran— that proffered negotiation on every issue distressing U.S.-Iranian relations,

including Iran's nuclear program.[2] Tehran's major request: an American promise not to pursue regime change. Washington didn't respond, driving a final
nail in the coffin of Iran's reformists. Iran's ruling clerics used the presidential
election of Mahmoud Ahmadinejad to signal a decisive end to the political
opening painstakingly created by the country's reformists. Within months of
the bronzed Bolívar's arrival in Tehran, a coterie of hardliners replaced the
closest thing Iran had seen to moderate governance since 1979.

Conditions were only somewhat better for President Chávez and the
"Bolivarian revolution" he sought to create. The magnetic populist came into
office in 1999 with 80 percent of Venezuelans supporting him, but he had so
far failed to deliver on his promises. Poverty and inequality increased in
Venezuela during his first term, and shortages of basic foods were afflicting
ever larger swaths of the country.[3] There were more than twenty massive street
protests against Chávez in response, the worst outbreak of civil disobedience
in Venezuela since the 1950s. Chávez was temporarily toppled in a 2002 coup,
which he blamed on the United States. (No evidence of direct U.S. involvement
has surfaced, but the Bush administration initially made statements in support
of the coup.) By 2003 only 30 percent of Venezuelans approved of his per-
formance. And in 2004 he survived a national recall referendum that some
exit polls indicated he had, in fact, lost by a wide margin. He had cracked
down hard on all forms of dissent to get by, leaving only a few gossamers of
democratic accountability in Venezuela, such as an opposition TV station.

These were all domestic problems. What if the problems ahead involved
a truly hostile U.S. government, not just the one he conjured up to the public? Or what if neighboring Colombia, having recently elected a hawkish
new president keen to sniff out the Revolutionary Armed Forces of Colombia
(FARC) guerillas, acted on the steady stream of news reports and intelligence
that indicated Chávez was providing refuge, and possibly material aid, to
them? The United States and European Union classified the FARC as a terrorist organization, after all, and it was a bad time to be giving sanctuary to
terrorists. Venezuela's only committed ally was Cuba, but it was too poor to
lend much support beyond medical staff.

Luckily for the governments of Iran and Venezuela two seismic changes
were taking hold in the world. Having routed two detestable governments

in two years, the United States, with the help of relatively few allies, assumed the task of remaking Afghanistan and Iraq into democracies with some iota of stability. Although ready to declare "mission accomplished" in Iraq, the Bush administration was not prepared to handle the internecine sectarian divisions there, or the task of nation-building that it assumed. As violence between Sunnis and Shi'ites waxed, support for the war waned. Public opinion shifted distinctly against the war. In America, the president's approval ratings dropped from the highest in polling history in 2002 to the level of President Nixon's during the Watergate scandal by 2008. In much of the rest of the world opposition to the wars turned into derision, and many celebrated the backlash against what they saw as America's "imperial overstretch."

Meanwhile, prices for commodities, especially oil and natural gas, but also gold, copper, silver, steel, timber, rubber, soybeans, fish, beef, rice, cotton, coffee, and chocolate, were soaring. A global economic boom was at hand. But unlike previous eras of heady growth, the economic advances were being driven principally by China, India, and other emerging Asian economies. With an enormous labor pool but relatively few natural resources, "the rise of Asia" meant sourcing commodities from other developing countries in Africa, the Middle East, and Latin America, whirling them into finished products, and exporting them to conspicuous consumers in the West. It was expected that in the future, burgeoning middle classes in Asia would also increase demand for such commodities across the rapidly developing region. This shift meant a huge market was opening for commodity exporters, and, while still important, America no longer represented the exclusive source of demand for these countries' goods.

Amid this backdrop, the tender dalliance marked by the statues of Omar Khayyám and Símon Bolívar would be transformed. After years of going it alone, Iran and Venezuela, each ruled by self-proclaimed "revolutionary" governments, finally bent to history's counsel—a successful revolution requires outside support. As Chávez saw it, "Two revolutions are now joining hands: the Persian people, warriors of the Middle East . . . and the sons of Símon Bolívar, warriors of the Caribbean, free peoples."[4]

The two governments entered into a union, endowed by oil and sanctioned by anti-American fervor. In 2007, Ahmadinejad and Chávez declared "an axis of unity" so that each country "did not need the United States to survive," making official what had been underway since Ahmadinejad came to power two years before. Hundreds of official agreements have been signed by the two nations, including a military pact, while bilateral trade spiked, from less than $189,000 in 2001 to almost $57 million by the end of 2008.[5]

The most visible signs of the partnership can be found in Venezuela, where subsidiaries of Iranian state-owned banks now operate, along with a "VenIran" tractor plant, bicycle factories, petrochemical factories, milk processing facilities, and a host of others. All of these are state-backed initiatives, no private investment is involved, and while a few enterprises claimed to sell their goods at a fair price to the public, many were deemed "social projects" unlikely to ever turn a profit.[6]

But much of the trade claimed to be for "social development" is subterfuge. On hand at the bicycle factory's ribbon-cutting ceremony, Chávez dubbed the conveyances "atomic bikes," a sarcastic retort to allegations made by local Venezuelan newspapers and the likes of the *Wall Street Journal* that the facility was a cover for uranium enrichment. Media speculation withered as the first production run of 4,860 bicycles sold out. Less than a year later the joint venture ground to a halt, its production down 90 percent in 2009. Still, workers continued to show up for work at the factory in a remote town where infrastructure is lacking.

Other examples, discussed in the chapters that follow, are equally baffling at first blush. Iranian auto factories in Venezuela produce six cars an hour. An Iranian bank in Caracas stays in business even though employees admit they have no customers. VenIran tractors—hailed as "agricultural tanks" by President Chávez—were supposed to go from being made with mostly Iranian parts to 100 percent Venezuelan parts, yet the red VenIrans continue to rely on Iranian inputs just as before. The rubric of investment for "social development" is a mask for illicit trade.

There is plenty of reason for doubt. Even if Venezuela and Iran are unified in their criticisms of "the empire" or "Great Satan," the preferred moniker for the United States by each government, this could be nothing more than a hollow partnership. A careful skeptic, recalling the wayward intelligence that led to the 2003 invasion of Iraq, could hardly be blamed for harboring a dollop of mistrust. To others, the idea of a functional alliance between

Venezuela and Iran might sound like a grand conspiracy theory. But a bevy of evidence put forth by the U.S. Treasury Department, U.S. prosecutors including the Manhattan District Attorney's Office, Turkish customs officials, reports by nonpartisan think tanks, unclassified intelligence reports, and leaked government documents detail the lowdown. Iran and Venezuela cooperate on nuclear technology. Venezuela sends gasoline to Iran with the express purpose of helping the Islamic Republic bear the weight of UN sanctions, underlining one of the great ironies of the Islamic Republic's existence—it must import gas because it lacks domestic refineries. Iran uses Venezuela's financial system to carry out transactions prohibited by sanctions, which almost certainly fund Iran's nuclear program. And Islamic terrorists loyal to Iran operate in Venezuela, serving as an advance front for retaliating against the West in the event that the United States or Israel launches an attack on Iran's nuclear facilities.

In this book I argue that *Iran and Venezuela have forged an alliance that frays the American security blanket while constraining U.S. foreign policy on an array of issues.* Although it is an explicitly anti-American alliance, it does not directly target its avowed foe. First and foremost, this alliance threatens the security of Colombia and Israel, key U.S. allies that are located on the front lines of the Western security blanket. A secondary threat to Western security arises because this alliance weakens the effectiveness of UN and Western-backed sanctions against Iran. Finally, the Venezuela-Iran alliance presents a tertiary challenge to Western energy security, as the two countries connive to use oil as a weapon in order to achieve their geopolitical aims.

Chapters 1 and 2 focus on the foreign policy approaches of the Islamic Republic and Venezuela. The purpose of these chapters is to establish that each country has utilized different methods to realize the same end, regional domination. Having elevated their status to that of a regional power—Iran in the Middle East and Venezuela in South America—the two countries forged the Venezuela-Iran alliance, described in chapter 3. Shortly after this alliance developed, Venezuela began to facilitate the spread of Iran's influence into Latin America, which is addressed in chapter 4. As a result, Iran has become a transregional threat to Western security, spreading its influence not only across the Middle East but also into parts of Latin America.

Why can't the West effectively isolate these "rogue states" as it did with Libya or North Korea in the past? Several chapters in the middle portion of this book address that question. In brief, Caracas and Tehran enjoy "great power" support that helps each government stay in power and blunt Western ire. Chapter 5 argues that because of the alignment of anti-Western interests, a destabilizing partnership has been created between Russia, Venezuela, and Iran. This partnership relies on Russia's willingness to transfer arms and nuclear technology to Venezuela and Iran, as well as to provide diplomatic protection to Iran in the UN. Chapter 6 describes how Venezuela and Iran reciprocate, aiding Moscow's attempt to control the flow of hydrocarbons into Europe. To muddle the more suspicious exchanges between these three countries, a web of intermediary states are often involved. Chapter 7 focuses on the use of minion states, particularly Belarus and Syria, to serve as go-betweens for some of the questionable arrangements between Iran, Russia, and Venezuela.

What differentiates China's role in supporting Iran and Venezuela from that of Russia? Chapter 8 takes up China's relationship with Tehran and Caracas. Billions of dollars in Chinese investment have flowed into Venezuela and Iran in recent years, reducing each country's reliance on Western markets and also impelling China's reluctance to slap the Islamic Republic with stiff UN sanctions. In this way, China also enables Venezuela and Iran to defy the West. Still, Russia is a more worrying sponsor of each government. This is because of the offensive nature of its arms sales, current willingness to transfer nuclear know-how, and anti-Western agenda.

Chapter 9 weighs the potential breakdown in cooperation between Iran, Russia, and Venezuela. Although friction increased between Iran and Russia in the months leading up to the June 2010 UN Security Council sanctions against Iran over its nuclear program, the two nations quickly returned to their previous level of collaboration. However, the innate stress between Russia and Iran over control of the Caspian region is a fissure that is likely to widen over time. This chapter weighs these stressors in light of the fall in oil prices since 2008.

Finally, chapter 10 provides policy recommendations for containing the influence of Venezuela and Iran and rupturing the alliance between them. Most of the recommendations adopt a bilateral approach to containing and reducing the influence of Venezuela-Iran alliance in Latin America. However, several specific recommendations call for robust action by the United States against individual governments in order to compel their adherence to international norms.

Iran: A Sphere of Influence by Other Means

Just as stormy weather does not mean perpetual rain, so a state of war does not mean constant war.
—Thomas Hobbes, *Leviathan*

Regional domination has been the objective of the current Iranian and Venezuelan governments from the outset. The Islamic Republic's attempts to control the Middle East rely on encouraging and financing insurgencies that can blossom into popular political movements. In Venezuela the course has been different. Although Chávez hasn't shrunk from backing an insurgency, he has enjoyed more success through political patronage. Each country differs in its methods, a product not of ideology but of political and economic development in the regions where they lie. And so, for the governments of both Iran and Venezuela, building a sphere of influence called not for bald coercion, but for aggravating regional stability and seizing opportunities created by political openings.

Iran's attempts to establish itself as the Middle East's greatest power predate the 1979 Islamic Revolution, by 2,500 years if one takes the long view—and nearly all Iranians do—back to the Persian empire of Cyrus the Great. But more recently it was the Shah, allied to the United States, who sought to redo regional dynamics in Iran's favor. He doggedly pursued modernization in Iran, vowing to make the country "a second Japan" while coupling his appetite for radical change with enormous arms purchases from the United States. It was all meant to advance his case for regional hegemony. Once Britain ceded its last colonial outpost in the region in 1971, the Shah opined that "the safety of the Gulf had to be guaranteed, and who but Iran could fulfill this function?"[1] Instead, the Shah's ambitions and sense of grandeur, which many saw as megalomania, alienated moderate Iranians, ultimately leading to the downfall of his regime.

Ayatollah Khomeini gained widespread support in Iran in 1978, returned from exile after the Shah fell in 1979, and then quickly consolidated his grip on power through use of Hezbollah (the "Party of God") forces, loosely organized to act as a counterweight to newspapers and other opposition voices in Iran. After 1979, the Hezbollahi were given free rein in Iran to assail persons and groups purported to be insufficiently Islamic. Within several months' time every bubble of dissent was burst.

Not long after Khomeini established himself Supreme Leader of the Islamic Republic of Iran, neighboring Iraq invaded. An eight-year-long war between the forces of the Islamic Republic and those of Saddam Hussein followed. Although Iran appeared to be on the offensive for the better part of the war, the country suffered a million casualties, many as a result of hopeless frontal assaults ordered by Iranian leaders and Saddam's use of chemical weapons against Iranian positions. The contest finally ended in a stalemate on August 20, 1988.

History has largely determined this outcome to have been a product of the Iranian leadership's belated recognition that their economy stood on the brink of utter ruin. For the Ayatollah Khomeini, at least, Iran's request for a cease-fire to the United Nations on July 17, 1988, was also a capitulation of zeal to the forces of realism. A fortnight before, the USS *Vincennes*, acting as naval escort to oil shipments through the Persian Gulf (at the request of Kuwait), had exchanged fire with Iranian ships. In the melee between Iran and the *Vincennes*, the American destroyer deemed hostile an Iranian commercial jet and mistakenly shot it down, killing all 290 passengers onboard. To some this wasn't a mistake. Daniel Yergin, in his Pulitzer Prize–winning tome on petropolitics, *The Prize*, writes that much of the Iranian leadership took it as a sign "that the United States was taking off its gloves and preparing to bring its great power to bear in direct military confrontation with Iran in order to destroy the regime in Tehran."[2] In such a weakened state, Iran could not expect to withstand even limited air strikes by the United States. Suing for peace with Iraq left the Grand Ayatollah despondent and vengeful.

He claimed to take "the poison" of peace with Saddam while vowing revenge on the House of Saud and America.

SEEDING THE FERTILE CRESCENT WITH INSURGENCY

Getting bogged down in the war with Iraq did not sap the Islamic Republic's ambitions, but it did dispel important notions of how Iran should best assert itself in the Middle East. Iran had managed to forge an alliance with the regime of Hafez al-Assad in Syria, giving the Republic a tenuous reach on the far side of the Middle East. Together the governments sought to fill a power vacuum created by the civil war ravaging Syria's neighbor Lebanon. With Syrian assistance, Iran exported the Hezbollah model to Lebanon. Iran's Revolutionary Guard, an elite wing of the Iranian army, assumed the task of training the small contingency of Hezbollah in Lebanon. At first Lebanese Hezbollah's raison d'être was to prevent the emergence of a consolidated, independent government in Lebanon, thereby allowing Iran and Syria to use the country as a nether land of regional insurgency. Hezbollah also vowed to "destroy the Zionist entity" of Israel, which remains a cornerstone of the group's rhetoric.

In 1984 Lebanon collapsed; its capital, Beirut, became the embodiment of Hobbesian anarchy. In this setting, "Hezbollah filled the void like water finding its own level, and never stopped appropriating sovereign authority until it became *a state within a state*"[3] (emphasis added). Far from being a pell-mell advance, Hezbollah's spread throughout southern Lebanon marked the first instance of a concerted Iranian strategy to "manage chaos," seizing on the lawlessness both to strike at Western and Western-allied targets, especially Israel, and embed itself into Lebanese social fabric. Hezbollah grew into the social servicer of last resort, building schools and running health clinics and welfare programs mostly funded by Iran. These efforts helped build Hezbollah's rapport in the area. Hezbollah even became an early progenitor of what we now call microfinance. In 1984 it started al-Qard al-Hasan (literally "good loan"), and by 2007 the program offered about 750 small loans.[4] So while Hezbollah is widely regarded as a state within a state, looking back at its initial involvement in Lebanon it might be more fair to deem it "a state in lieu of a state." And throughout its existence, it has also been the projection of another state.[5]

In 1988 Hamas, a Sunni insurgency, was founded in the Palestinian territories. Given sectarian differences between Hamas and the Islamic Republic, Iran initially paid little attention to the group. Iran's support for the Palestinian Islamic Jihad—in direct conflict with Hamas for control over parts of the Palestinian territories—further contributed to the initial coolness between Hamas and Iran. This relationship only began to change after the 1991 Desert Storm campaign rolled back Saddam's invasion of Kuwait. Sensing that its fortunes were improving as Saddam's soured, Iran hosted a Hamas delegation in October 1992. At meetings attended by Ayatollah Khomeini, Iran reportedly pledged Hamas $30 million in annual aid and promised the group weapons and training from the Revolutionary Guard.[6]

By the late 1990s, as each group continued to develop its own leadership and independent identity, Iranian support for Hezbollah remained constant while Hamas was generally considered a vestige of Iran's Middle East strategy. In addition to sectarian and historical affinities for Hezbollah, Tehran's preference was pragmatic: Hezbollah had simply proven more successful than Hamas at attacking Western targets and expanding its base of support in the Middle East. Hezbollah carried out bombings against the Israeli Embassy in Buenos Aires in 1992—considered the first bombing by Islamic extremists in the Western Hemisphere—then a more deadly attack against a Jewish cultural center in the Argentine capital two years later. In 1996 a Hezbollah truck bomb killed nineteen U.S. servicemen and more than three hundred civilians of various nationalities at Khobar Towers in Saudi Arabia. In every case Iran's role in the attacks was clear. Furthermore, pockets of Hezbollah were—and still are—taking hold in other countries, such as Egypt, Jordan, and Azerbaijan. Hamas, meanwhile, had its contingency booted from Jordan in 1999. At the time the group's support in the Palestinian territories was estimated below 20 percent.[7]

This began to change in the new millennium. Over the course of the Second Intifada (2000–2005), Hamas deployed suicide bombers with awesome effect. Although not a new tactic, the scale to which Hamas used suicide bombing had certainly never been seen before. Palestine Liberation Organization (PLO) leader Yasser Arafat called suicide bombers "Palestinian F-16s." To an astonishing degree this weapon of the weak worked, both as a public relations tactic—highlighting the vast inequalities between Palestinians and Israelis—

and as an implement of guerilla warfare. For the first time in the history of the modern Middle East there was talk of "strategic parity" between the overwhelmingly powerful Israeli military and an Arab force, namely Hamas.[8] A Hamas spokesman pointed out to Al Jazeera that Israeli-Palestinian conflicts in disputed territories had, in recent decades, a death ratio of one Israeli for every twelve Palestinians. Indiscriminate rocket attacks simply didn't stand a chance against Israel's tanks, precision-guided missiles, and intelligence network. But by conducting suicide bomb attacks within Israel's 1948 borders— "taking the fight to them," as it were—the ratio changed dramatically: nine Israeli deaths to every one Palestinian.[9] Meanwhile, to address the tremendous turmoil faced by innocent Palestinians caught in the middle, Hamas provided medical care and ran schools, which in turn stoked its popularity.

From 2004 to 2006, Hezbollah and Hamas repositioned themselves. Hezbollah's military strength grew significantly in the wake of Israel's withdrawal from Lebanon in 2000. At the same time, the group mellowed its rhetoric about turning Lebanon into a Shi'ite state and instead advertised itself as a resistance leader against U.S. and Israeli aggression in the Muslim world. Hamas all but ended its suicide bombing campaign and offered a ten-year truce to Israel, ostensibly to advance talks on Palestinian statehood. Its representatives whispered to Western journalists that Hamas accepted Israel's right to exist, even if the group's charter couldn't be changed for "internal reasons."[10] It was a parlous situation for Iran and its proxies. Tehran faced a unique opportunity to project its power through the Middle East, but if Iranian expansionism coursed through the veins of Hezbollah and Hamas, the move could backfire. Grassroots support for Hezbollah in Lebanon and Hamas in Gaza might dissipate if the two appeared to be Iranian hobgoblins. Furthermore, signs of Iranian adventurism might bring Arab powers like Egypt and Saudi Arabia into line against the Islamic Republic, not to mention the looming threat of air strikes or special forces raids by the United States or Israel against Iran.

TERRORIST-CUM-POLITICOS

Having kindled a wide base of support, Hamas and Hezbollah parlayed their insurgent street cred into vibrant political movements, seizing opportunities as they arose. In 2005 former Lebanese prime minister Rafiq Hariri was assassinated. Within Lebanon Syria was widely blamed for Hariri's murder,[11] inciting a popular backlash against Syria's three-decade-long military occupation of Lebanon. Signs like SYRIAL KILLERS sprung up across Beirut. In response to the groundswell, the UN passed an unusually bold declaration ordering Syria out of Lebanon. This produced the Cedar Revolution, a democratic movement that caught the world's attention. Unfortunately, though the West was willing to threaten Syria with sanctions, Western powers did not act to deliver aid or significant support to the foundling Lebanese government.[12] Hezbollah seized the opportunity, transforming itself into a political power in Lebanon and creating a legislative block that could sway—and impede—government action on all fronts. Consequently, Hezbollah is now the most powerful political and military faction in Lebanon.

A political opening also presented itself in the Palestinian territories. After the death of Palestinian leader Yasser Arafat in November 2004, Hamas quickly refashioned itself into a potent political machine, preparing for 2006 parliamentary elections in Gaza. Hamas won the elections by beating the Fatah party that had long ruled the territory, catching the United States off guard. Shortly thereafter Arafat's successor, Palestinian president Mahmoud Abbas, invited Hamas to form a government to rule Gaza. When Hamas rebuffed calls to formally recognize Israel's existence, both the United States and Israel responded by cutting off aid for the Palestinian Authority. Into the budgetary void stepped Iran. That February Ayatollah Khamenei pledged to cover the budget shortfall of the Palestinian Authority that now counted Hamas as its legislative entity in Gaza.[13]

Surprisingly, Iranian support has helped legitimize Hamas and Hezbollah by encouraging a transition from outright terrorist group to important, and respected, political party. On this basis, some argue that Iran has had a moderating effect on the two groups, moving each from the fringes to the mainstream, where they have had to seek policy solutions and compromise with rival political parties. As one example, a 2009 article in *Foreign Affairs* argues that "Western diplomats" should acknowledge Hamas's "reduced aspirations and ideological softening."[14] And now that each group is out of the shadows, they "have an address"; their members travel, and so they are subject to a host of reprisals if they carry out terrorists bombings.

It is broadly true that Hamas in particular has abandoned its heated rhetoric regarding Israel's right to exist. Although Hamas and Hezbollah have become embedded as political actors on Israel's flanks, they still call on their militias to launch rocket attacks or suicide bombings against Israel. Israel's war against Hezbollah in the summer of 2006 came a year after Hezbollah won elections in Lebanon, and many sources viewed the conflict as an Iranian concoction to deflect mounting pressure by Western governments for Iran to stop enriching uranium. Ditto for the brief war between Hamas and Israel in January 2009.

Noting Hezbollah's enhanced capability since the 2006 war, the U.S. Director of National Intelligence's February 2009 report to the Senate states:

> Lebanese Hezbollah continues to be a formidable terrorist adversary with an ability to attack the US Homeland and US interests abroad. Hezbollah is a multifaceted, disciplined organization that combines political, social, paramilitary and terrorist elements, and we assess that any decision by the group to resort to arms or terrorist tactics is carefully calibrated. At the same time, we judge armed struggle, particularly against Israel, remains central to Hezbollah's ideology and strategy.[15]

Iran has managed to seed these insurgencies at arm's length, and over time nourish them into major political actors. As insurgencies they brought a sense of chaos to the Middle East, and international politics. Now as political actors they operate within a more fixed domain, but they weigh most heavily on different parts of Israel's border.

IRAN'S INVOLVEMENT IN IRAQ

Hasty attempts to install a democratic government in Iraq after the U.S.-led invasion brought down Saddam's dictatorship opened yet another front for increased Iranian influence in the Middle East. Early on, intelligence reports suggested Hezbollah members born in Iraq but exiled to Iran or Lebanon as a result of the Iran-Iraq War were gearing up to return to Iraq as soon as America began its "shock and awe" campaign against Saddam. Within a year of his toppling, Iran was inciting Shi'ite extremist activity throughout southern and central Iraq. For more than a year the U.S. military neglected Iraq's border with Iran, a grave mistake in its counterinsurgency campaign.[16]

Hezbollah activities initially alerted the United States to Iran's presence. Regarding improvised explosive devices (IEDs), the largest killer of U.S. coalition forces in Iraq, Bob Woodward wrote in *State of Denial*:

> The Pentagon had a $3.3 billion plan to come up with effective defenses against IEDs. But this was really a multifaceted problem. It was no longer just the lethality of the weapons that was important, but the significance that the weapons were coming from Iran. Some evidence indicated that the Iranian-backed terrorist group Hezbollah was training insurgents to build and use the shaped IEDs, at the urging of the Iranian Revolutionary Guard Corps. That kind of action was arguably an act of war by Iran against the United States.[17]

Probably more damaging to the coalition effort was the involvement of the Quds Force (QF) in Iraq. While many details on the composition of the QF are unknown, the group is regarded as the elite foreign operations wing of the Iranian Revolutionary Guard, with a force strength of around fifteen thousand men (and according to some estimates, tens of thousands more). Many terrorism analysts, such as Richard Clarke, believe the QF takes orders directly from the Ayatollah Khamenei.

From 2005 to 2007 the QF became the most potent instrument of Iranian statecraft in Iraq. Initial news accounts alleged the QF incited civil war by supplying and training Iraqi Shi'ites. By 2006 QF operatives were directly fighting in Iraq. Higher-quality machining and triggering devices used in a type of IED called EFP (explosively formed penetrator), designed to penetrate the undercarriage of Humvees and even tanks, were proving four times more lethal than conventional IEDs. According to U.S. intelligence, the prevalence of EFPs in Iraq could be traced to Iran. This had dire implications for U.S. policy. Again, Woodward's *State of Denial* points to the crux of the problem:

> If all this were put out publicly, it might start a fire that no one could put out. First, questions would immediately arise about the quality of the intelligence. Was this potentially another WMD fiasco? Second, if it were true, it meant that the Iranians were killing American soldiers.

. . . The chief premise of a Republican foreign policy had been tough-ness—no more weakness, no more Carters or Clintons and their pathological unwillingness to use force. Where would that lead them in the dealing with Iran now?[18]

Iran's boldness coincided with the end of the reform era and the election of Ahmadinejad, as well as a growing sense that the United States was "mired" in Iraq, vulnerable, and unlikely to open a new theater in the war on terror against Iran or its allies Syria, Hezbollah, or Hamas. As the United States got caught up in trying to keep Iraq from tearing itself apart while support for the war waned at home, Iran had found a way to constrain the United States from acting on behalf of its national security interests. Plenty of sources pointed to a growing Iranian threat—sponsorship of terrorism in Iraq, a restarted nuclear program, arms and aid to Hamas and Hezbollah, creeping Iranian involvement in Afghanistan—but the United States was stuck, exposed to Iranian attacks but largely unable to act. The "axis" policy had come full circle, adding to the insecurity it sought to rid.

Naming Iran as a direct participant in Iraq's civil war would be awk-ward. But Iran's involvement was confirmed in ample detail by Gen. David H. Petraeus at a press conference in Washington on April 26, 2007:

The Iranian involvement has really become much clearer to us and brought into much more focus during the interrogation of the mem-bers—the heads of the Qazali network and some of the key members of that network that have been in detention now for a month or more. This is the head of the secret cell network, the extremist secret cells. They were provided substantial funding, training on Iranian soil, ad-vanced explosive munitions and technologies as well as run-of-the-mill arms and ammunition, in some cases advice and in some cases even a degree of direction.

After discussing intelligence details on specific Iranian-backed attacks, the general recapped: "And there's no question, again, that Iranian financing is taking place through the Quds Force of the Iranian Republican Guards Corps . . . there are seven Quds Force members in [U.S.] detention as well."[19] While not citing specific military intelligence, President Bush adopted a similarly exacting tone.

In sum, Iran's regional aspirations are abetted by persistent and growing support for insurgents that attack Israel and a growing opportunism in Iraq and Afghanistan. Even despite claims that Iran's longstanding allies Hamas and Hezbollah are "softening" because they now represent viable political parties, each group has fought a war with Israel since gaining a voice in government. Hamas's brief war with Israel—in the last days of December 2008 and through much of January 2009—appeared to be a tactical move endorsed by Iran in order to strengthen its position vis-à-vis the new Obama administration. A recent *New York Times* piece, "Iran Gives Hamas Enthusiastic Support, But Discreetly, Just in Case," quoted Mustafa el-Labbad, a Cairo-based Iran expert: "Iran wants to sit at the negotiating table with Obama with all the cards of the region in hand: Palestine, Lebanon, Iraq, the relationship with Syria."[20]

Iran's growing strength in the Middle East speaks to the refinement of its strategy to incite violence first; "manage chaos" to both weaken rivals and strengthen itself; and then, eventually, support the transformation of the insurgent groups into viable political actors. Its successful use of Hezbollah forces in Lebanon provided a strategic blueprint for later involvements. Hamas trekked a broadly similar course from insurgency to social servicer to political party. Now Iran is adopting this strategy in Iraq. In 2008 U.S. ambassador to Iraq Ryan C. Crocker called it Iran's "Lebanonization of Iraq," which has spread from the level of violence to political control.

In fact, since as early as 2003 an accelerated version of Iran's "chaos" strategy has been visible in Iraq. Hezbollah and the QF employed sophisticated guerilla tactics to stew sectarian violence and attack American and coalition forces, helping erode international and domestic support for U.S. efforts in Iraq. Compared to Lebanon and the Palestinian territories, though, the sustained U.S. presence has allowed Iran to catalyze its process for taking control of the country. Instead of encouraging a social service stage where Iranian proxies build up support to become political parties, the U.S. presence, both by assuming the responsibility for social services, which allows for easy criticism when efforts fall short, and by its insistence on elections, has allowed Shi'ite movements loyal to Iran to jump straight into the political realm. Now

Iran is not only a dominant force in politics in the south of the country but the dominant force in Iraqi national politics.[21]

VACUUM OF POWER

Rising power adores a vacuum,[22] as it creates a vortex of opportunity for established powers to sink into. It's a lesson that Iran knows well. Throughout its history, the Islamic Republic has cultivated a variety of terrorist organizations to attack its opponents and capitalize on any Western response by encouraging the very same terrorist groups to provide social services in the absence of state control. As a result, the West has repeatedly been left worse off while Iran has extended its influence. Iran's key proxies, Hezbollah and, to a lesser extent, Hamas, have seized intermittent opportunities in the Middle East to legitimize their power, becoming influential political parties, while the Quds Force, a shadowy wing of the Revolutionary Guard, incites conflict against the West and works to arm groups like Hezbollah.

Once in power, Hezbollah and Hamas have become irritants to political cohesion, ready to launch attacks to unsettle any progress that could lead to democratic consolidation in Lebanon or Gaza. This process is now being repeated in Iraq. Insofar as there has been a lull in violence because of the Surge, the abatement also evidences Iran's steadying control over the country. Bombings are down in recent years, but that doesn't mean Iraq is necessarily more stable.

2

The Hugo Sphere

Chávez is a prophet in search of disciples. He seeks to present Venezuela as a more moral world power, uniting Latin America and poor countries everywhere in a socialist alliance. He has invented a new kind of socialism, which he calls Bolivarian socialism, named for the independence hero Simón Bolívar: a little Marx, a little Jesus, a little anti-imperialism and a lot of the whim of Hugo Chávez, dedicated to the "comprehensive, humanist, endogenous and socialist development of the nation." His is a gospel greased by oil, which is financing his transformation of Venezuela.

—Tina Rosenberg, "The Perils of Petrocracy," *New York Times Magazine* (November 4, 2007)

abriel García Márquez came away ambivalent after interviewing Venezuela's new president in 1999. On the one hand, Hugo Chávez Frías might just have had the brio "to save his country." But "Gabo," as Márquez is affectionately known across Latin America, thought Chávez equally likely to turn out "an illusionist, who might pass into history as just another despot." That aversion, dubbed the "enigma" of Chávez, became a common sentiment throughout the region during Chávez's first years in office. Certainly there were signs that Venezuela's president had authoritarian instincts; he quickly passed a new constitution through Venezuela's National Assembly, a body which he installed because the preexisting Congress had too many entrenched opponents. He also regularly lambasted the United States, though that was hardly a new tactic for rallying support among Latin America's working classes. Fuel prices were low, and Chávez's popularity cratered in the gulf between his campaign promises and worsening conditions on the ground. For several years after he came to office, Venezuela's president was busy repressing dissent at home; absent greater oil revenue he didn't have the clout to rankle international relations.

Until 2005 his only unequivocal ally in the region was Fidel Castro, whom Chávez credits as his mentor. Materially, the heart of their alliance is an oil-for-aid swap, whereby Chávez keeps the Castro regime afloat by sending the island 90,000–100,000 barrels per day (bpd) of oil, some of which the Cuban government is known to re-export for much needed foreign currency. Cuba, in turn, loans 20,000–40,000 doctors and other medical professionals to Chávez.

Newspaper reports suggest Cuba has perhaps five hundred military advisers in Venezuela. Tidbits like this lead some cold warriors in the United States to claim all sorts of Castro-inspired chicanery are at work undermining U.S. national security.[1] Yet Cuba is quite possibly the most benign ally that Chávez has, especially in light of the moderate tone that Cuba's foreign policy has adopted under Raúl Castro.[2] Cuba gave up trying to spread communist revolution long ago, and now its leaders have more pragmatic worries, like staying in power.

HUGO CHÁVEZ'S FARC SIDE

What is now apparent is that the Venezuelan president barely settled into office before he started reaching out to terrorist groups in neighboring Colombia, including the Revolutionary Armed Forces of Colombia (FARC), a Marxist insurgency that has been fighting a war against the Colombian government since 1964, and the National Liberation Army (ELN), a smaller but similarly nasty group. Since 1999, Venezuela's support for these groups has been ongoing, if not constant. To specific allegations of his government's links to Colombian terrorist groups, Chávez provides one of three broad responses:

1. Simple denial (rare).
2. Claiming that the charges are a part of an "imperialist plan" by the United States and Colombia to invade Venezuela (most common).
3. Cutting off, or threatening to cut off, diplomatic and economic relations with Colombia (most problematic, because Venezuelans rely on Colombia for much of their food).

Concurrently, Chávez vocally defends the FARC. For example, in 2008 Chávez said of the FARC and ELN: "They are in no way terrorist groups . . . .

They are insurgent forces with a political project that we here respect."[3] He regularly calls FARC members "brothers" and has lobbied for years to have the groups taken off Western governments' terrorist lists.

Brief Chronology of Hugo Chávez's Support for the FARC, 1999–2006

AUGUST 1999: Ramón Rodríguez Chacín, a Chávez aide, writes two letters to the FARC, offering the group money and fuel from the Venezuelan government.

Ignacio Arcaya, later to serve as Venezuela's ambassador to the United States, also gives cash to the FARC.

NOVEMBER 2000: Olga Lucía Marín (alias of Liliana López Palacio), a FARC leader, attended a Latin America Parliament meeting hosted in Venezuela's National Assembly. She praised Chávez and thanked the government for its "support."

Colombia reports the confiscation of four hundred rifles with the engravings of the Venezuelan army from a FARC camp.

FEBRUARY 2001: Interpol agents arrest ELN leader José María Ballestas in Caracas for hijacking a commercial airliner in 1999. Chávez orders Ballestas's release, then claims the arrest never occurred. Venezuela then states Ballestas was seeking political asylum, and he is finally rearrested and extradited to Colombia.

JANUARY 2002: Four female journalists release videotapes of FARC meetings with Venezuelan military officials in July 2000. Colombia intercepts a Venezuelan aircraft with ammunition that Colombian officials assert was intended for the FARC.

JANUARY–FEBRUARY 2002: Jesús Ernesto Urdaneta Hernández, Venezuela's intelligence chief, denounces Chávez for his support of the FARC. Urdaneta makes public letters detailing government collusion with the FARC. In the years that follow he will make additional allegations against Chávez.

JANUARY 2003: Venezuela's highest-ranking general, Gen. Marcos Ferreira, is sacked for dissent; in turn, he tells reporters that he knows of three Colombian guerilla camps in Venezuela.

DECEMBER 2004: Ricardo Granda, the FARC's "foreign secretary," is arrested at the Colombian border. He had been living in Venezuela with Venezuelan citizenship.

AUGUST 2006: The Federation of American Scientists notes arms transfers from Venezuela to the FARC "in lots of 50."

Thor Halvorssen, "Guerilla Nation," *Weekly Standard*, January 26, 2005.

"A Lack of Clarity on Terror," *Economist*, March 13, 2003, http://www.economist.com/node/1632905 (accessed April 26, 2010).

"Another Bump in a Rocky Road for Colombia and Venezuela," *New York Times*, November 30, 2000, http://www.nytimes.com/2000/11/30/world/another-bump-in-a-rocky-road-for-colombia-and-venezuela.html (accessed August 9, 2011).

"FARC-EP," U.S. Department of the Treasury, Office of Foreign Assets Control, http://www.treasury.gov/resource-center/sanctions/Terrorism-Proliferation-Narcotics/Documents/farc_chart_110107.pdf (accessed August 8, 2011).

Matt Schroeder, "Securing Venezuela's Arsenal," Federation of American Scientists, August 24, 2009, http://www.fas.org/blog/ssp/2009/08/securing-venezuela's-arsenals.php (accessed May 12, 2010).

In 2008 a handful of U.S. congressmen began calling for Venezuela to be declared a state sponsor of terrorism. While this may raise awareness, political realities prevent legislative action. The "state sponsor" label would necessitate trade sanctions, and Venezuela supplies the United States with around 10 percent of its oil.[4] Also, because of porous borders and a history of corruption among Venezuela's military, Venezuela harbored FARC terrorists even prior to 1999. Threatening to crack down on the FARC camps now risks giving the impression that the Chávez government is being targeted when previous administrations were not. If the United States labeled Venezuela a terrorism sponsor it would needlessly feed tensions between Venezuela and Colombia, a conflict which Chávez frequently cites as a potential staging ground for a U.S. invasion of Venezuela to seize the country's oil.

More importantly, though, Colombian president Álvaro Uribe Vélez (2002–2010) devastated the FARC, turning it from a terrorist group that killed upward of 100,000 people from 1964 to 2004 into a moribund nuisance. The FARC's territorial domain desiccated under Uribe's charge, and its ranks dwindled from an estimated 16,000 guerillas in 2001 to between 6,000 and 8,000 in 2008—a result of Colombian military raids, widespread defections, and government-sponsored rehabilitation programs for former rebels.[5] As Colombia made these gains, Washington disengaged from the region, leaving little diplomatic support for Uribe's attempts to flush the FARC out of Venezuela.

A Colombian raid on March 1, 2008, complicated the inconvenient truth surrounding Chávez and the FARC. Missile strikes on a FARC camp located 1.1 miles into Ecuadorean territory killed twenty-six, among them Raúl Reyes, the FARC's putative second-in-command.[6] More important, laptops belonging to Reyes were recovered, containing nearly 38,000 files detailing FARC meetings, operations, strategy, etc. The documents show that Chávez has backed the FARC with upward of $300 million in aid since 1999.[7] (Coincidentally, that's roughly the same amount Iran gives Hamas.) Predictably, Chávez called the raid a "war crime" and asserted the recovered files were fakes. But he didn't stop there. On his unscripted weekly TV show, *Aló, Presidente*, which Chávez uses to chastise critics and hold accountable cabinet ministers through public humiliation, Chávez praised Reyes as "a good revolutionary," called Uribe a criminal and terrorist, and ordered the commander of the armed forces to immediately deploy ten battalions to the Colombian border.

Undeterred by the posturing, the Colombian government handed over the files to Interpol, which analyzed the more than six hundred gigabytes of data—equal to 39.5 million pages of text—over the next three months.[8] On May 15, 2008, after more than five thousand hours of analysis by sixty-four researchers in fifteen different countries, Ronald Noble, Interpol's secretary general, declared at a press conference: "We are absolutely certain that the computer exhibits that our experts examined came from a FARC terrorist camp."[9] The Interpol probe, it must be pointed out, intentionally did not investigate the accuracy of any content; it only sought to establish if the files were counterfeit or tampered with after their recovery.

The March 1 cache was an intelligence coup for the Colombian government. Well before Interpol's assessment came down, intelligence agencies had lined up to gain access to the FARC files. A few weeks after the raid the intelligence helped the Colombian government seize $480,000 from a FARC safe house in Costa Rica. Politically, however, the results were mixed. At first Chávez appeared out of sorts, threatening war with Colombia, but then acting chastened at a regional conference of Latin American presidents. Uribe, for his part, refused to make the intelligence public, but his government gradually allowed bits and pieces of intelligence to leak out, making the region's leaders uneasy.

Fresh allegations continue to emerge. In March 2010, a Spanish judge accused the Chávez government of facilitating contact between the terrorist group Basque Homeland and Freedom (ETA) and the FARC.[10] According to the judge, operatives from ETA and the FARC repeatedly met in Venezuela for explosives training, especially with C4, a type of plastic explosive.[11] On at least one occasion Venezuelan soldiers met with FARC and ETA. On other occasions the Venezuelan government facilitated FARC-ETA meetings to plan the assassination of President Uribe.

These allegations coincided with an announcement by Spanish police of the arrest of three suspected ETA operatives in Normandy. One of the men taken into custody was José Ayastaran, known to be a senior ETA operative who not only lived in Venezuela for many years but was almost awarded citizenship in 2006 so he could avoid extradition.[12] Then, in mid-July 2010, just weeks before Uribe handed over the reins to his successor, Juan Manuel Santos Calderón, Colombia presented exact geographic coordinates of FARC camps in Venezuela to the Organization of American States (OAS), along with videotapes that showed activity in the camps.

But public perception had already grown wary, suspecting that President Uribe liked using the "FARC files" as a political cudgel, releasing intelligence about FARC positions in Venezuela in order to keep Chávez off balance.[13] Instead of diplomatic support in Latin America and from the United States, Uribe got blank stares and empty pleas for the FARC to lay down its arms.

SOCIAL POWER DIPLOMACY

Despite Chávez's efforts, Colombia is more secure from the FARC today than it was ten years ago. So instead of having a dogged insurgency to destabilize his regional foe, Chávez had to find some other means of fulfilling what he proclaimed to be a "Bolivarian vision" of a unified South American republic. Better fortune followed higher oil prices. Oil had begun its seemingly inexorable post-9/11 rise, and once he had complete control of Petróleos de Venezuela, S.A. (PDVSA) in 2003, Chávez could draw money out of the company within an hour to use as he saw fit.[14]

Chávez devised a shrewd, if not altogether sophisticated, strategy to fund like-minded leaders and parties throughout Latin America: social power diplomacy. Social power diplomacy is largely a blank check approach to international relations, writes Javier Corrales, a professor at Amherst College who fashioned the term: "Social power diplomacy attracts allies because it provides governments with far more latitude in domestic spending than is the case with any form of Western aid. This domestic freedom produces close international ties."[15] The International Monetary Fund (IMF) and World Bank are known for attaching "conditions" to loan and aid programs, mandating sound economic management, regular updates on poverty alleviation initiatives, and the like. Aid from Chávez, on the other hand, would come with no strings attached, an open-ended gift from "the people of Venezuela." Through this overt method of foreign aid, Chávez could present himself as a patron of democracy and development, rather than a crackpot sponsor of FARC terrorism.

Petrodollars in hand, Chávez set about reshaping the political landscape of Latin America. In 2005 Juan Evo Morales Ayma was elected president of Bolivia on a platform of indigenous socialism. (Chávez allegedly bankrolled the Morales campaign, but no proof has surfaced.) Chávez quickly gave Bolivia $1 billion in aid, a sum equal to 12 percent of the country's GDP. Checks from the Venezuelan embassy to the Morales government often went directly to mayors and citizens to spend as they saw fit.[16] The Bolivia experiment went off well, not just because Chávez succeeded in giving money away, but because he was able to co-opt Morales, superimposing his vision on the Bolivian president. Instead of a leader of an indigenous workers' movement meant to right the wrongs of centuries of foreign and ethnic exploitation through self-determination and nationalism, Chávez melded Morales into an agent of socialist internationalism. Conceptually, the latter is quite a departure from the former, which is the platform Morales initially promised.[17] While it was not Chávez's first attempt to play patron in Latin America—that honor went to Cuba, or possibly the FARC—it appeared to inspire in Chávez confidence that he could cultivate a clutch of elected proxies throughout the region.

Chávez went on to buy $5 billion in Argentine debt between 2005 and 2007 and established a barter agreement with Buenos Aires, oil for Argentine meat and dairy products.[18] He purchased Ecuador's debt, more than $300 million, obviating the country's need for IMF assistance.[19] He forgave Nicaragua's debt to Venezuela, and promised oil to mayors belonging to Nicaragua's Sandinista party, just one part of a wider "oil credit" incentive for Nicaraguans to elect the Sandinistas' presidential candidate, José Daniel Ortega Saavedra, in the 2007 elections.[20] And throughout the Americas, Venezuelan *misiones* were set up, including eye clinics, doctor offices, and food banks, all to serve the poor. Despite Chávez's shortcomings, the *misiones* prove that Venezuelan aid has nourished hundreds of thousands of people, providing medical care to those who would otherwise have to go without.

Part of Chávez's aid was wrapped in an institution named the Bolivarian Alternative for the Americas, or ALBA (*alba* is "dawn" in Spanish). Created in 2006 by Bolivia, Cuba and Venezuela, ALBA has grown to include Ecuador, Nicaragua, and a handful of Caribbean islands—Antigua and

Barbuda, Dominica, and Saint Vincent and the Grenadines—that enjoy fuel subsidies from Venezuela. Grenada, Haiti, Paraguay, Uruguay, Iran, and Syria have observer status in ALBA, the latter two obviously being the only states outside of Latin America affiliated with the organization.[21] Chávez intended ALBA to be an alternative integration platform that opposed the U.S.-backed Free Trade Area of the Americas. ("Alternative" originally made up the last part of the acronym, but in 2009 "Alliance" was officially substituted.) While Chávez has tried to flesh out ALBA with plans for a common currency, military academy, and other integration features, the real draw of membership is discounted Venezuelan oil. For many countries, barter arrangements were created: Venezuelan oil in exchange for foodstuffs.

By 2008 Chávez had committed to at least $43 billion in foreign aid across Latin America—some estimates placed the sum at $50 billion.[22] Not only did this far eclipse U.S. aid to the region over the same period,[23] it dwarfed that of most donor countries. For example, Petrocaribe, a Venezuelan program designed to ship oil to a few Caribbean and Central American countries, amounted to a foreign subsidy of $1.7 billion in 2008—roughly equal to the foreign aid budget of rich countries like Australia, Belgium, Denmark, Norway, Portugal, Spain, and Switzerland.[24]

Chávez seemed a stroke away from repainting the entire geopolitical canvas of Latin America to his liking. From roughly 2006 to 2008 his influence was so widespread that he appeared to offer Latin America a whole new path toward development. But the 2008 crash in oil prices quelled Chávez's reach, sifting his true allies from fair-weather friends and exposing the effects of his patronage.

THE HUGO SPHERE

In general, Chávez's aid proved most effective at gaining allies in countries where the political system could be most swiftly turned on its head. Where democratic institutions, such as courts, constitutions, functional legislatures, etc., were weak, Chávez could flush the country with aid, encouraging its president to use the money to tighten his control over the other branches of government and the economy. Chávez's aid didn't require accountability. He had developed a new export model—"the export of corruption." As Dr. Corrales points out:

Venezuelan aid is billed as investment in social services, but in fact it consists mostly of unaccountable financing of campaigns, unelected social movements, business deals, and even political patronage by state officials. In this era in which state elections are fiercely competitive almost everywhere in Latin America, Venezuelan-type aid is irresistible.[25]

In places where institutions are weak and populism has been on the rise, Chávez has carved out a Hugo sphere of influence. Beyond this precondition, two other features characterize the Hugo sphere:

1. Internalized anti-Western sentiment: countries where presidents practice anti-Americanism, not just use it as a rhetorical tactic.
2. Relatively untapped energy resources: countries known to possess energy resources, but exports are underwhelming because of a lack of infrastructure and past corruption.

The more of these characteristics a nation has, the more likely it is to end up under Chávez's thumb. Having all three can be a death sentence for democracy and sustainable economic development. Nations that share two or just one of these features are also susceptible to Chávez's designs, but in countries with stronger institutions personal relationships with Chávez are a more prominent factor. Consequently, Chávez's ties to these nations are less secure. Nations that exhibit none of these conditions—e.g., Uruguay—are politically and economically stable. This hasn't prevented Chávez from sending money their way; it just means he has little to show for it.

By meeting all three characteristics, Bolivia and Ecuador comprise the inner sanctum of the Hugo sphere, making them permanent minions of the Chávez agenda. In practice, Evo Morales and Rafael Correa Delgado (president of Ecuador) are more anti-American and anti-capitalist than Chávez himself. Nationalizations in Bolivia and Ecuador have been carried out twice as fast as in Venezuela; also, U.S. Drug Enforcement Agency officers have been kicked out in all three nations, and the U.S ambassador is regularly dismissed for a variety of unconvincing reasons.

Bolivia and Ecuador institute anti-Americanism by turning their backs on Western regulatory and oversight bodies. This began in 2007 when

Bolivia became the first country to ever withdraw from the International Center for the Settlement of Investment Disputes (ICSID), a World Bank convention signed onto by 155 countries for the settlement of contract disputes between multinational corporations and governments. The Morales administration claimed to do so because governments "never win" cases against corporations; however, in the year prior, El Salvador and Venezuela, among other nations, received favorable ICSID decisions.[26] Two years later, President Correa declared that Ecuador would also withdraw from the ICSID "atrocity" in order to liberate his country from "colonialism." Ecuador's withdrawal became official in early 2011, making it the second country to withdraw from the convention.[27]

More common than outright repudiation is willful noncompliance.[28] The Egmont Group, an anti–money laundering consortium made up of quasi-private banks, revoked Bolivia's membership in December 2008, making it and Ecuador the only two countries in the Americas not to have membership.[29] The informal collection of international agencies stated the suspension came because the Morales government did not criminalize the financing of terrorism.[30]

Similarly, Ecuador is considered lax in its commitment to block terrorist financing. In fact every year since Correa's election the Financial Action Task Force (FATF), an international organization created to combat money laundering, has reported Ecuador to be in noncompliance with more than half of its criteria. Although this still warrants an overall grade of "partly compliant," Ecuador is considered noncompliant on all nine of FATF's recommendations related to terrorist financing—this is noteworthy when it comes to Ecuador's recent relations with Iran.[31] By implication, this means Bolivia and Ecuador are also in violation of several other international conventions to which they are signatories.[32] The full implications of this tactical noncompliance will be explored in chapter 5, but suffice it to say that Bolivia and Ecuador's opposition to international regulatory regimes make them prime locales for illicit financing schemes.

Ecuador's decline into noncompliance is particularly stark, and worrying. A decade ago Ecuador was lauded for "positive steps to counter money laundering," including: a spate of laws defining and criminalizing money laundering; the creation of a financial watchdog group; and the arrest and conviction of Jorge Reyes Torres, one of Latin America's most infamous drug traffickers, in the 1990s.[33] However, Ecuador's 2008 constitution wiped the slate clean on previous anti–money laundering provisions, leaving the country to decline into a money laundering and counterfeiting hotbed.[34]

Anti-Americanism is the most obvious feature of the Hugo sphere, but in some ways it can be the least substantive aspect of foreign policy.[35] This is not the case with regard to Bolivia and Ecuador, where opposition against the West, and institutions regarded as tools of Western exploitation, feeds international isolation. Morales and Correa have not only adopted anti-Americanism as a rhetorical device, they have internalized it, de-linking their countries from Western oversight. As a consequence, Bolivia and Ecuador are so undesirable to major multinational companies that they must rely on Chávez's aid, as well as his connections with nations like Iran and Russia, to bring investment into their countries. The effects of this are likely to be more prolonged than other gestures of anti-Americanism. Cooperation with the DEA can recommence in short order and ambassadors can be easily brought back to the capital, but after years of nonmembership and/or noncompliance with international regulatory regimes, Ecuador and Bolivia will not be able to quickly bring their houses in order.

Bolivia and Ecuador were vulnerable to Chávez's influence from the get-go because they were extremely weak democracies. The actual voting process is generally the most functional democratic element in these countries, a disheartening sign.[36] Legislatures and courts are notoriously corrupt; in 2005, for example, Transparency International ranked Bolivia and Ecuador alongside Afghanistan in its annual Corruption Perceptions Index, the lowest ranking in Latin America except for Paraguay and Venezuela.[37] Other problems from the recent past include elitist and out of touch presidents, social and political exclusion of indigenous groups, and feckless economic management that has precipitated runaway inflation. In Bolivia, the wealthier states also liked to let the idea of secession linger in the air. These factors coupled with an unkind world economy from 1998 to 2005 to produce democratic dysfunction in Bolivia and Ecuador.

Under the surface, though, each country has a rotting political system. Parties rise and fall in rapid succession thanks to the shifting interests of elites. Grand proposals are made, presidents get elected without a clear mandate, crucial minority partners of the government grow fractious and withdraw their support, government is gridlocked, and disorder ensues. It's a familiar pattern in Latin American history, but, thankfully, it is becoming less common as democracy becomes the norm in the region and more presidents adhere to constitutional checks. Not so in Bolivia and Ecuador; both countries had six heads of state in the decade before Morales and Correa were elected.

Chávez's support has been integral to the rapid erosion of democracy in Bolivia and Ecuador. His quick outreach to Bolivia and Ecuador helped dismantle all checks to executive power. Chávez sent advisers to Bolivia to sponsor the constitution that Morales proposed, the seventeenth in the country's history.[38] The constitution espoused by Rafael Correa to "re-found" Ecuador—the twentieth constitution in its history, an average of one every nine years—is generally regarded as less radical than Bolivia or Venezuela's.[39] Still, it allows the president to serve two consecutive terms (previously the president was limited to a single term), and gives the president power to abolish the National Congress once each term (though doing so would trigger a new presidential election). Under their new governing documents Correa can serve until 2017, Morales until 2018.

Beyond the assurance of knowing his allies aren't going anywhere (coups notwithstanding), Chávez has chalked up an important strategic gain from the deterioration of democracy in Bolivia and Ecuador: indirect control over each country's oil and gas industries. Morales promulgated Supreme Decree 28701 on May 1, 2006, nationalizing Bolivia's hydrocarbons.[40] Three months later, Bolivia's Ministry of Hydrocarbons had to temporarily suspend the nationalization program because it lacked the funds and technical expertise to assume control of operations from foreign multinationals.[41] Similar, though less severe, problems threatened Ecuador's nationalization, outlined in the 444-article 2008 constitution. "Too statist" is how one Ecuadorean who voted against the constitution described it. But the voter's concern with Correa's constitution was not ideological; Ecuador's "lack of [technical] resources" in the energy sector, he said, made it hard to see how the government would be up to the task.[42]

Enter Chávez. PDVSA gained hundreds of millions in contracts in Ecuador and Bolivia, making the Venezuelan company the largest minority partner of Ecuador's state-owned Petroecuador. Although he hurried aid to Bolivia to shore up operations, gaining control over Bolivia's oil and gas proved more difficult. Brazil's Petrobras (Petróleo Brasileiro, S.A.), as well as Argentine and Spanish gas firms, had their operations taken over by the Bolivian government, making the nationalization a delicate diplomatic issue. Well-heeled opposition to Morale's proposed constitution caused another problem. Absent the new constitution, not only was Morales limited to one term, but the nationalization decree could be undone by 2011. In this environment gas exports declined for two years, until Morales managed to mollify the opposition, clearing the way for the new constitution to be passed. Investment pledges to Bolivia shadowed these events, increasing as Morales tightened his grip. Investment surged to an estimated $1.5 billion in 2008, most of it coming from two countries: Venezuela and Iran.[43]

All the while, Chávez worked to gain sway within OPEC. In the days before Chávez Venezuela had sown resentment within the oil cartel by regularly exceeding its production quotas. In 1998, just before Chávez took office, Saudi Arabia accused Venezuela of precipitating a worldwide collapse in oil prices by exceeding its quota by 30 percent.[44] Venezuela now had few allies in the cartel ready to brook Chávez's hopes of using the oil weapon by cutting production and hence driving up prices. Such a move would quickly fill PDVSA's coffers and might also hobble the American economy. But at the price floor he sought (more than $50 a barrel in 2006), recovery of oil from parts of the heavy and extra-heavy tar sands in the Orinoco Belt would become commercially viable, giving Venezuela potentially more oil reserves than Saudi Arabia.[45]

If he could find some OPEC allies, he could possibly gain the yes votes needed to outweigh the Saudis and Kuwaitis, who insisted on price stability. (The two gulf monarchies do so as part of an implicit understanding with America, and also because they fear that excessively high prices would lead to the development of new technologies that forever reduce demand for oil.) Chávez proposed that Bolivia be admitted to OPEC, to no avail. However, he did succeed in getting Ecuador reinstated as a member, after a fifteen-year leave of absence.[46]

Chavez's geopolitical energy plan offered several potential benefits. First, he could pack the cartel court, so to speak, giving him greater control over the price of world oil. Second, he could use his OPEC influence to ensure the nationalizations he was encouraging throughout Latin America would have a reasonable price floor, so that even if they were poorly managed they stood to make money.[47] Also, if oil and gas would be nationalized throughout the rest of Latin America, Chávez would then co-opt several other countries' energy resources by putting himself on good terms with those presidents.

UNDER THE INFLUENCE

Stepping out from the Andes, Chávez has cultivated strong alliances with President Ortega of Nicaragua and President Cristina Fernández de Kirchner of Argentina. Chávez spent millions to fund various projects in Nicaragua, helping to revive the atavistic Sandinista party that could share in the credit. After Ortega's election in 2007, Chávez committed yet more aid to Nicaragua.

Ortega, a Marxist revolutionary from the days when being one carried the risk of dismemberment in Latin America, at first played his role with gusto, also referring, as Chávez does, to the FARC as "brothers." In fact, the afterclap of the March 1 FARC raid also exposed Ortega's commitment to guerillas. Ortega sent a Nicaraguan air force plane to pick up two wounded guerillas and a Mexican "sympathizer" shortly after the raid. He then granted the three women[48] political asylum, even though authorities in Colombia and Ecuador wanted them.[49] To make appearances worse for Ortega, *La Prensa*, a major daily in the Nicaraguan capital of Managua, reported that several top members of the FARC flew there on a Venezuelan plane to meet with Ortega on July 19, 2008, the anniversary of his Sandinista party's seizure of power in 1979.[50]

Chávez's largesse also made its way to Argentina, where his support for the candidacy of anti-American populist Cristina Fernández de Kirchner brought some unwanted media attention when customs officials at the Buenos Aires airport stopped a Venezuelan man on a charter flight from Caracas to Buenos Aires. In his suitcase was $800,000 in cash, believed to be money from the Venezuelan government to fund Kirchner's campaign. Chávez immediately deemed the story a canard; candidate Kirchner called it "garbage." But in U.S. court testimony, Carlos Kauffman, one of five defendants in the money laundering case, claimed that Hugo Chávez not only had personal knowledge of the suitcase transfer, but that the Venezuelan president had tasked his intelligence chief with arranging the affair.[51]

Like Bolivia and Ecuador, Argentina has a weak democratic tradition, evidenced most vividly by the upheaval during the country's financial implosion in the years 2001–2002, which set off a series of six presidential resignations in two weeks. And the successive terms of the Kirchner family has witnessed a significant erosion of judicial independence, as well as the removal of central bank autonomy in 2008. Argentina's congress is supine, meeting infrequently. When it does meet, it mostly rubber-stamps legislation proposed by the president. Nicaragua, by contrast, has held regular elections since 1979 and has a relatively stable party system.

While these relationships are useful to Chávez's influence in the region, they are on the outer band of the Hugo sphere. Anti-Americanism is a staple of political rhetoric in Argentina and in Nicaragua, the latter deeply scarred from a U.S.-backed civil war in the 1980s. However, anti-Americanism rarely affects significant policy. The most that can be said about Argentina is that the country defaulted on scheduled IMF repayment under the administration of Nestor Kirchner, the current president's husband and predecessor, a decision that has been softened by Chávez's willingness to buy Argentine debt when no one else would. In an official letter to IMF in April 2010, Argentina claimed to "celebrate our well-gained economic independence," but Argentina nonetheless remains a member.[52] Ortega, meanwhile, announced that he would follow Bolivia in withdrawing from ICSID, but almost four years later Nicaragua has not taken any steps to do so. Neither Nicaragua nor Argentina has withdrawn membership from international regulatory bodies. In sum, anti-Americanism in these countries is traditional, but superficial. Kirchner and Ortega use attacks against the United States to score political points with their base and to weaken their opponents, but anti-Western fervor has not been internalized in the same way it has in Bolivia and Ecuador.

SEPARATE PATHS, SAME END

As the U.S. Director of National Intelligence recently reported to the Senate, Chavez's regional influence has "peaked."[53] Venezuela is too small to become a South American hegemon, or even exert lasting influence over more than a handful of countries in the region. However, Chávez has not only made Venezuela into a regional power over the past decade, but a lasting one. The economies of Bolivia and Ecuador have become more isolated as result of Chávez's influence and patronage, and each nation has distanced itself from both the West and international institutions in ways that increase their reliance on Chávez.

Iran utilized a bottom-up strategy for expanding its regional influence, by seeding insurgencies and then supporting them for years as they grew into significant political movements. Chávez has certainly tinkered with supporting insurgencies—the FARC and ELN—but this has failed to either weaken his regional competitor, Colombia, or increase Venezuela's influence in Latin America. Instead, Chávez has succeeded in carving out a Hugo sphere by taking a top-down approach of lavishing oil money on presidents in weakened democracies. "No strings attached" aid from Chávez has enabled allies to use the money to consolidate their grip on power. What the varied approaches of Iran and Venezuela share is the outcome they have produced—a regional sphere of influence—unlikely to be undone soon.

3

"Poisonous Fruit"

As Washington policy makers scramble to craft effective sanctions against Iran, they seem to have completely ignored Mahmoud Ahmadinejad's blossoming relationship with Venezuela's Hugo Chávez. This strategic alliance provides the Iranian regime with a clandestine source of uranium, helps it evade restrictions on trade and financing, and gives Middle Eastern terrorists access to weapons from Mr. Chávez's growing arsenal. So even if the West is able to implement a sanctions plan with bite, Tehran's partnership with Caracas might cancel it out.

—Roger Noriega, *Wall Street Journal* (April 9, 2010)

Manhattan's district attorney from 1974 to 2009 is an august figure. Nominated to be the U.S. attorney for the southern district of New York by President Kennedy in 1961, Robert M. Morgenthau served only briefly before being tapped as the Democratic nominee for governor of New York. Morgenthau lost to incumbent Nelson Rockefeller and was quickly re-appointed to his post as U.S. attorney. Over the next eight years Morgenthau not only established a reputation as a dogged prosecutor, but he also carved out a niche for his office by establishing a special investigations unit to try highly publicized fraud and bribery cases. He was pushed out by the Nixon administration in late 1969.

After winning a special election in 1974, Morgenthau became district attorney of the Manhattan borough, a post he would hold for thirty-five years. From 1985 to 2005 he stood unopposed before the voters, only encountering token opposition when he announced, in 2005 at age eighty-five, his bid for a ninth term, which he eventually won with 99 percent of the vote. It had been a good run by any standard. Morgenthau had tried some of the nation's most vexing and publicly charged cases, employed many of the country's most promising lawyers (including Sonia Sotomayor), and his reputation remained spotless.

Only such a long and distinguished career could overshadow Morgenthau's pedigree. His father, Henry Morgenthau Jr., was the most powerful secretary of the treasury in U.S. history, other than Alexander Hamilton, because of his role in financing the New Deal. Robert's grandfather had been U.S. ambassador to the Ottoman Empire. Involvement in international affairs ran deep in the Morgenthau family and popped up routinely in Robert's legal work, as shady financial deals with foreign entities routinely occurred in Manhattan. These sinews had fused well before September 2009, but they were rarely put on such public display. Just before his retirement, one of the world's most powerful prosecutors readied a final case, not to a jury but to a broader audience. For a man who generally avoided the media spotlight, this time he sought it.

Robert Morgenthau picked as his venues the op-ed pages of the *Wall Street Journal* and the Brookings Institution, a nonpartisan think tank in Washington. The message was clear and direct, as one would expect:

> Today Mr. Ahmadinejad and Venezuelan President Hugo Chávez have created a cozy financial, political and military partnership rooted in a shared anti-American animus. Now is the time to develop policies in this country to ensure this partnership produces no poisonous fruit.[1]

What followed was the most detailed account yet of a "Caracas-Tehran axis" threatening U.S. security, covering military, commercial, nuclear, and political ties.

Along similar lines, this chapter outlines the forms of cooperation between Venezuela and Iran, starting out with most apparent—political and economic—and then turning toward the illicit—nuclear, transportation, and asymmetrical military ties.

AN "AXIS OF UNITY"

While some trace Chávez's relationship with Iran back to his early days as president,[2] only in the twilight of the Khatami administration did a real political partnership emerge. Bilateral trade stood at around $1 million in 2004, and there had been only a handful of agreements signed between the nations, one of the most significant involving plans for a tractor plant in Venezuela. Truth be told, reluctance came from the Iranian side. Chávez happily casti- gated the United States, which Iran's ruling ayatollahs no doubt appreciated, but Iran's reform-oriented President Khatami (1997–2004) had a habit of parsing his criticism for George W. Bush so as not to deride America and everything it stood for.

Political alliance with Chávez had little draw at the time. The cast had not set on anti-Americanism as a unifying force *between* governments, street protests against the Iraq War in Western European cities notwithstanding. And there was even less willingness to countenance the anti-capitalism that Chávez bundled with his anti-American worldview. Only after Mahmoud Ahmadinejad became president in August 2005 did it become evident that "ties were taking on a new dimension," as the *New York Times* put it.[3]

Once the outline of a political partnership emerged, it did so with a fe- rocity rarely seen between nations not thrust together by war. Ahmadinejad restarted Iran's fallow nuclear program, and the West quickly responded with the threat of sanctions. Chávez became one of the first heads of state willing to publicly support Iran's "right to develop atomic energy for peace- ful purposes," and deed followed word.[4] In September 2005 Venezuela was the only nation to oppose resolution GOC/2005/77 of the International Atomic Energy Agency (IAEA), which accused Iran of violating its commit- ments under the 1978 Nuclear Non-Proliferation Treaty.[5] A few months later, in early 2006, the UN Atomic Energy Agency issued a separate rec- ommendation to the UN Security Council to sanction Iran for noncompli- ance with its charter on nuclear proliferation. The measure was opposed by three nations: Cuba, Syria, and Venezuela.

Chávez and Ahmadinejad began to frequently refer to each other as rev- olutionary "brothers," foreshadowing an alliance. In 2007 Chávez and Ahmadinejad declared an "axis of unity." "United" they vowed to "defeat the imperialism of North America."[6] As Ahmadinejad saw it, the alliance would eventually "untie" the Great Satan. At the Iranian port town of Asalouyeh, where the axis was proclaimed, posters showing Chávez and Ahmadinejad hug were plastered everywhere.[7] Public relations would be crucial; the "axis of unity" was not meant to be just an exclusive pact, it was also intended to be- come a full-fledged alternative to political and economic reliance on the West.

Beyond their fervor to bring about America's downfall, the political alliance between the countries was codified through a multitude of pledges. At least 340 memoranda of understanding (MOUs) were signed between them from 2005 to 2009, by one tedious count.[8] Presidential peregrinations became the norm; Chávez and Ahmadinejad have visited each other on at least a dozen occasions since 2005, not counting their "aside meetings" at international conventions, such as the UN General Assembly. Cabinet officers from the respective ministries of mining, defense, and foreign affairs are almost always in transit, so that scarcely two months pass without one high-ranking official being dispatched or hosted.

Other than antipathy for the United States, joint investments are the gel of political alliance. From $1 million in 2004, bilateral trade between Venezuela and Iran surpassed $50 million by the end of 2006 (Venezuela imported $37.4 million of Iranian goods, Iran imported $13.3 million worth of Venezuelan goods).[9] By 2008 bilateral trade stood at $57 million. While still heavily tilted toward the oil and gas industries in terms of capitalization, closer economic ties involve an array of sectors and industries. Car, cement, corn flour, milk processing, and alternative energy operations, such as methanol factories, were slated to begin operation between 2005 and 2008. Many of these projects were touted as beneficial for the poor.[10] For example, once operations got off the ground at the VenIran tractor plant located in the rural Venezuelan state of Bolívar, the tractors would be sold to farmers on heavily subsidized terms, ending demand for imported tractors. Of the fifty-seven industrial agreements signed between Venezuela and Iran from August 2005 to 2010, about three-quarters carried similar social development goals.[11]

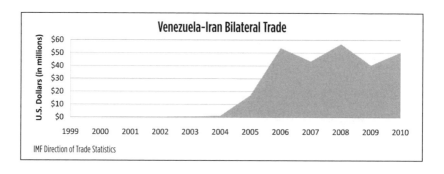

Venezuela-Iran Bilateral Trade

U.S. Dollars (in millions)

IMF Direction of Trade Statistics

Joint investments carried the explicit goal of reducing reliance on goods produced by the United States. The Venezuelans also yearned to break the country's dependence on Colombian food and manufactures.[12] "Now, no company will be able to stop food production or distribution," proclaimed Venezuela's minister of trade Ricardo Canán.[13] By implication, reducing economic reliance on the West would also make each government less exposed to economic coercion from the West, especially sanctions.

The Venezuela-Iran partnership also devised a platform for winning broad support in Latin America. A bilateral fund set up with $2 billion to finance the industrial collaborations already underway was expanded in scope to incorporate Latin American governments allied with Chávez. Chávez claimed the money "will permit us to underpin investments . . . above all in those countries whose governments are making efforts to liberate themselves from the imperialist yoke."[14] The success of this strategy is detailed in chapter 6, but it is worth noting here that this course toward "liberation" had two outcomes. First, Iranian support helped Chávez shore up a Bolivarian regional alliance, by giving Latin American governments allied with Chávez a second large investor/aid patron to pick up the slack for the decline in foreign investment they experienced as a result of nationalization and hostilities to foreign investment. Chávez also benefited because he stood as the gatekeeper through which Iranian investment flowed. Thus, Bolivia and Ecuador grew more dependent on Chávez because he co-directed Iranian investment into Latin America.[15] Second, Iran gained additional outlets where it could establish financial ties, which would become crucial as Western countries cracked down on Iranian banks known to finance the country's nuclear program.

While these political and economic ties grab headlines and serve as the public face of the anti-American alternative that Chávez and Ahmadinejad herald, they are also the least troublesome to international stability and Western security. As one Venezuela expert notes, the "anti-U.S. foreign policy stand is the best known but perhaps the least important aspect of Chávez's foreign policy"; much the same can be said of Ahmadinejad's foreign policy.[16] If the axis of unity were only a two-part mixture—a forum for vituperation against the United States and above-board bilateral investments—Western security would not be under significant threat. After all,

Latin America has a storied tradition of anti-American development models that advocated domestic production in order to sever ties with the West.[17] However, the Venezuela-Iran alliance uses these economic ties to mask illicit trade.

BAD SEEDS

The Manhattan DA's office probably first drew its attention to the Venezuela-Iran alliance when, in 2007, a subsidiary of the Export Development Bank of Iran (EDBI) opened in Venezuela under the name Banco Internacional de Desarrollo (Bank of International Development, or BID). Just as BID began operating, the U.S. Treasury Department sanctioned both banks for funneling, or attempting to funnel, money to Iranian military outfits in charge of Iran's nuclear program.

Morgenthau learned about Iran's illicit financial schemes a decade ago, when he brought a case against Lloyds TSB, a British bank, over its dealings with Iran. Lloyds eventually admitted to altering names on wire transfers to disguise the transfer of some $300 million through U.S. banks to Iran, in violation of sanctions.[18] The Manhattan DA also charged Limmt, a Chinese metals company, for operating a series of shell companies that deceived U.S. banks into processing payments ultimately intended to finance Iranian missile, nuclear, and dual-use technologies.

By 2008, Morgenthau charged that Iran was "exploiting" the Venezuelan financial system in order to "avoid economic sanctions."[19] Not only have such suspicions not stopped BID from operating, the bank has since expanded into Ecuador. Meanwhile, a jointly owned state bank—the Iran-Venezuela Joint Bank—opened in Tehran in 2009. With a start-up capitalization of $200 million, the bank is planning to grow to $1.2 billion in order to fund "development projects."[20] It, too, is a spin-off of the EDBI, though unlike its Latin-based brethren the activities of the Iran-Venezuela Joint Bank are directly overseen by the Islamic Republic's Central Bank.[21]

Interestingly, the EU waited until mid-2010 to sanction BID, apparently basing its decision on new evidence of illicit financing.[22] There is no ironclad proof of illicit financing by BID in the public domain; one has to either accept the judgments of U.S. Treasury and the EU or reject them as politically motivated. However, the business model should add to the suspicion that goes with operating under a charter from EDBI. According to an unnamed senior officer at BID, the entity "provides the public with banking services . . . in accordance with Venezuelan banking standards and regulations."[23] Yet an investigative report by the *Wall Street Journal* found day-to-day operations to be a bit of an anomaly. To the bank's credit, a representative from BID spoke on-site with a *Journal* reporter. During the interview, the reporter clearly observed bank tellers in the Caracas office, and even a security guard, twenty-one employees in all—but *no* customers.[24] As Banco's spokesman explained, because of U.S. sanctions the bank can't issue debit or credit cards to its two hundred customers—that would involve a relationship with Visa, American Express, etc. One might think this would restrict the bank's ability to service *the public*, yet BID has somehow found the business to also open in Ecuador.

MILITARY TIES

Another tendril coiling around this "poisonous fruit" is the military pact between Venezuela and Iran. In 2008 the nations pledged each other "full military support." The seriousness of this pact is a source of some debate. On the one hand, Chávez has claimed to be preparing for war against the United States should America attack Iran. On the other hand, Venezuela and Iran have not participated in any formal joint military exercises, and linguistic and cultural barriers are likely to impede widespread collaboration between regular combat units.

Instead of a regular military alliance—what one might associate with an "axis"—the threat stems from Iran's asymmetric forces. A month before Morgenthau's speech, United Press International (UPI) reported that Iranian military advisers had embedded with the Venezuelan military. Several weeks later, UPI noted that Iran's military, more sophisticated than Venezuela's, was "keen to lend its experienced personnel and offer their special knowledge" to Venezuela.[25] "Experienced personnel" plausibly means Quds Force operatives, giving credence to suspicions that the QF has been treading in Venezuela since around 2007. Reports of the Quds presence in Venezuela have increased dramatically since 2009, when secretary of defense Robert Gates, referring to the QF, accused Iran of "subversive activity" in Latin America.[26] Likewise, a Department of Defense report released in April 2010 notes that the QF is "increasing its presence in Latin America, particularly Venezuela."[27] Chávez deemed the charges "infamy and lies."[28]

Numerous security reports confirm that the QF operates in Venezuela. None give an estimate of force strength, but most draw on "fresh" intelligence, presumably compiled or reported since 2009. Several meaningful implications stem from the Quds presence. First, the Quds are widely believed to answer directly to the Supreme Leader of Iran,[29] not Mahmoud Ahmadinejad, suggesting that Iran's presence in Venezuela is not based on a whim of the mercurial president, but rather a more methodical attempt by Ayatollah Khamenei to establish an Iranian beachhead in Venezuela. Second, in addition to its functions as Iran's foremost asymmetric warfare unit, the Quds are known to be the primary suppliers and trainers of Hezbollah forces.[30] This begs two obvious questions: First, what are the Quds doing in Venezuela? Second, is Hezbollah in Venezuela, and if so, what are they doing there? The answers suggest a direct threat to Colombian and Israeli security, and an indirect threat to U.S. security.

According to STRATFOR, a global security analysis firm, Quds forces are in Venezuela to train Venezuelan troops and FARC guerillas in irregular warfare.[31] Chávez likely relies on the Quds to train the Venezuelan military in guerilla warfare in case of conflict with Colombia. Venezuela needs a potent guerilla warfare force because in any conventional-war scenario between Colombia and Venezuela, Colombia's U.S.-trained and equipped military would make short shrift of Chávez's forces. Also, by training the FARC, the QF may facilitate more lethal attacks against the Colombian military, if not civilians. This could provide a tactical benefit to Chávez: if Colombia increases military expenditures to keep up the heat on the FARC, Chávez can readily justify an arms build-up based on the strength of Colombia's military.

Hezbollah is a more nagging threat to regional security. Quds support for Hezbollah in Venezuela speaks more to the expanding scope of Hezbollah activities there than to the introduction of Hezbollah in South America: Hezbollah has been known to operate in the poorly monitored "tri-border" region of Argentina, Brazil, and Paraguay for over a decade. But beginning around 2006 intelligence experts started to report that Hezbollah was concentrating its presence in Venezuela.[32] Initially, this had to do with Argentina's crackdown on Hezbollah after a jury handed down indictments against Hezbollah members in 2006 for the Buenos Aires bombings in the 1990s.[33]

In October 2006 two self-proclaimed Islamic extremists were arrested for trying to plant pipe bombs outside the U.S. embassy in Caracas.[34] Several other Hezbollah reconnaissance missions have been observed. Intelligence officials have come to see these ham-fisted actions as a message. Hezbollah wants Western intelligence to know they're operating in Venezuela.

Venezuela may be a better base for Hezbollah than the tri-border region because it is closer to the United States and Western targets. After a car bomb killed Hezbollah leader Imad Mughniyeh in Damascus on February 18, 2008, Hezbollah and Iran vowed reprisals against the West, especially Israel, which is widely credited for the assassination.[35] From Venezuela, Hezbollah can nurse cells in Mexico, where there is a tradition of Lebanese immigration that offers a natural safe haven.[36] (Carlos Slim Helú, Mexico's richest man, is of Lebanese descent.) In June 2010, for example, a counterterrorism sting by the Mexican government led to the arrest of Jameel Nasr, who had been living in Tijuana. Nasr is accused of having traveled to Lebanon on a regular basis to get intelligence updates from Hezbollah leaders. He reportedly moved to Mexico in 2008 after a two-month stay in Venezuela.[37] Other sources report that Hezbollah is now moving into Mexico to involve itself in drug trafficking and human smuggling along the U.S. border.[38]

In June 2008 the U.S. Treasury Department froze the assets of a Venezuelan diplomat and a Caracas-based travel agent, both of Lebanese descent, for links to Hezbollah. Treasury accused Ghazi Nasr al-Din, the diplomat, of facilitating the travel of Hezbollah members to Venezuela and, on at least one occasion, of arranging for Hezbollah members in Venezuela to attend a "training course" in Iran.[39] Fawzi Kanan, the travel agent, is also charged with facilitating Hezbollah travel to and from Venezuela and Iran, as well as discussing "possible kidnappings and terrorist attacks" with senior Hezbollah officials in Lebanon.[40]

The 2006 attempts to blow up the U.S. embassy, followed by frequent indications of Hezbollah's activities in Venezuela, are Iranian deterrence at work. U.S. policymakers are aware of the threat, although they often refrain from acknowledging it because doing so would, in effect, be an admission that Iran has a lever to pull when it comes to U.S. foreign policy, and it may lead to public outcries to brand Venezuela a state sponsor of terrorism. As STRATFOR notes, "the threat is real" but it also "is not likely to be exercised."[41] Clear-cut evidence of Hezbollah's presence serves as a warning to the U.S. intelligence community. Hezbollah is active in America's backyard, and it is sending a message—Iran has global reach and an attack on Iran will bring retaliation not just in the Middle East.

A "VEN-IRAN" INFECTION

How exactly can Iran and Venezuela maintain such a high level of cooperation? Transit between the countries has been made easier by direct flights. In March 2007 Iran Airlines inaugurated the Caracas-Damascus-Tehran route under the name Conviasa. The number of Iranians living in Venezuela consequently increased from two hundred to more than two thousand in two years, largely thanks to the ease of direct travel, according to an Iranian businessman.[42] Sympathetic portrayals of this nexus see this as a collaborative effort to develop infrastructure in Venezuela.[43] But being the world's only commercial air route to link two countries on the U.S. "state sponsors of terrorism" list to a lone third locale brought some suspicion. Charges arose that the flights were meant to transfer unsavory "people and things," as one Western source put it.[44]

Apparently, unlike other air carriers that try to woo customers on the basis of price or luxury accommodation, Conviasa's key draw was being hassle-free. Very hassle-free, in fact. Security screening of passengers onboard Conviasa flights is lax or nonexistent. As the 2008 "Overview of Terrorist Activities in the Western Hemisphere" by the U.S. Department of Homeland Security (DHS) notes: "Passengers on these flights were not subject to immigration and customs controls at Simón Bolívar International Airport." Not only is there no reliable passenger screening, but according to DHS, "Venezuelan citizenship, identity, and travel documents remained easy to obtain, making Venezuela a potentially attractive way station for terrorists."[45] This makes the route a near perfect artery for the direct transmission of terrorists between Latin America and the Middle East.

Conviasa flights routinely raise eyebrows as new bits of intelligence trickle out. Reza Kahlili, a pseudonym of a member of the Revolutionary Guard who became a CIA informant, claimed that the Caracas-Damascus-Tehran "special flights" are integral to the creation of an Iranian terror network with global reach, bringing Iran's presence a pace from America's door.[46] Kahlili also believes that the Conviasa flights carried Imad Mughniyeh from Iran to Caracas before his assassination in 2008.[47] Others share the opinion of the former CIA director Michael Hayden, who insisted, "These concerns are not just in the abstract. We saw people traveling who made us wonder."[48] Most recently, in August 2010, the State Department bemoaned the route. Weeks later, Representative Eliot L. Engel (D-NY), chairman of the Western Hemisphere subcommittee, said he was "very troubled" about the flights because "Iran is the largest supporter of terrorism of any country on the face of this earth."[49]

CNN looked into the matter, first contacting the Venezuelan government for explanation. In a written response to CNN, Venezuela's ambassador to the United States, Bernardo Álvarez Herrera, replied: "There is absolutely nothing untoward about these flights—which take place between two countries that have shared relations for over 50 years."[50] Disregarding the Damascus leg of the route, he went on, "One can also fly to Tehran from Frankfurt, Germany, amongst other cities, so I still remain confused as to why this should be of any concern. Should you or your staff want to see for yourself, I greatly encourage you to take one of these flights."[51] Another Venezuelan official told the news outlet that passengers arriving from Iran and Syria are subject to regular screening and customs checks, and there "has never been any evidence that flights carried suspected militants."[52]

Taking up the ambassador's invitation, CNN tried to book a flight in late August 2010, but to no avail: "It was unclear whether seats were available to the general public—or whether the flight, which began in 2007, was even running at all."[53] In follow-up conversations with representatives from Conviasa, an agent said that round-trip fare was $1,450, and flights departed from Tehran on Thursdays and then back from Caracas on Tuesdays. The agent then disclosed that there were no seats available for the next four Thursdays, and after that the flight was not offered.[54] Yet another Conviasa representative told CNN that while the flight from Venezuela to Syria was still running, the leg from Syria to Iran had not been operating for some time, seemingly contradicting the Venezuelan statement made a few days before about passengers from Iran and Syria being subject to screenings.

Picking up the scent, Fox News reported that officials from the CIA and Israeli intelligence believed that purchasing tickets for the flights required the permission of the Iranian or Venezuelan government.[55] So Fox tried to buy up all the round-trip tickets linking Caracas, Damascus, and Tehran.[56] Fox also noted that booking flights involved calls being rerouted to a cell service in Argentina, "curious" given that all other Conviasa flight matters were handled at the company's offices in Caracas.[57]

The bit of stagecraft between CNN and Fox News worked. A month later Conviasa announced an end to the flights.

NUCLEAR COOPERATION

"How's the uranium for Iran? For the atomic bomb?" Chávez asked Venezuela's mining minister, Rodolfo Sanz, on state-run TV, a month after Morgenthau said that he believed Venezuela was helping Iran mine uranium for the Islamic Republic's nuclear program.[58] Morgenthau's charges were hardly new in the fall of 2009. Hubbub first spread in 2006 that Fanabi, the bicycle operation, was a front for uranium recovery and processing. At the time little evidence supported the claim.

Back in 2005, Chávez had ordered his policy hands to "follow seriously the project of manufacturing Iranian bicycles in Venezuela," a move that took place in the context of a recently restarted Iranian nuclear program; just months prior to that, Venezuela had announced that it would begin seeking a peaceful nuclear program. Vague charges surfaced in some right-wing Western media reports about the legitimacy of the plant, provoked by opposition newspapers near the bicycle factory that noted sarcastically, "We're making bombs." Flimsy evidence for these initial allegations gave Chávez the high ground when he countered in 2006 that talk of nuclear cooperation between Venezuela and Iran "shows they [the United States] have no limit in their capacity to invent lies."[59]

Chávez's nuclear gambit with Iran rankled Latin American affairs. Venezuela had plans set for the transfer of uranium technology from Brazil until the summer of 2005, when Brazil backed out. A statement from Brazil's Ministry of Science and Technology explained, "In view of possible Iranian participation, as President Chávez has suggested, such a partnership would be risky for Brazil." A Brazilian spokesman expounded, "Brazil is not interested in cooperating with countries that do not follow international treaties and whose programs are not monitored by competent authorities."[60] Argentina similarly turned a cold shoulder to Chávez's nuclear interest once Iran got involved.[61]

No matter. With a surge in oil prices and relations with Russia drawing nearer by the hour, Chávez had the money, and thus the influence, to gain some acquiescence for his nuclear ties with Iran. And over time, what began as snide retort became spiteful tomfoolery. Besides deadpanning to his mining minister on national TV, the president showed up at the Fanabi factory the day its first bikes rolled off the factory floor. Chávez deemed the product of Venezuelan-Iranian plant "atomic" bikes, so every bike made since— 4,860 in the first production run alone—subsequently bore an "Atomic" label. Given the spherical suspenders that keep the rider in orbit above the ground, to say nothing of the inspiration for vigorous pedaling that "atomic" conjures up, it's a very good name. Arguably more clever is the tactic. Chávez's mockery drowns out, and in some ways curtails, a reasonable suspicion: Venezuela is helping Iran mine uranium for the Islamic Republic's nuclear program.

The realm of contention is much smaller than one might think, because the Chávez government now professes cooperation with Iran's nuclear program. In his speech, Morgenthau cited a study by the Carnegie Endowment for International Peace, which disclosed that Venezuela might have fifty thousand tons of uranium. Morgenthau shared the view of the Carnegie Endowment that some of this was being sent to Iran. A few weeks later, Rodolfo Sanz made a fairly startling admission: "Iran is helping us with geophysical aerial probes and geochemical analysis" of uranium sites.[62] Chávez was more direct—he was planning for a "nuclear village" in Venezuela with the assistance of Iran.[63]

The only dispute is whether uranium is being exported from Venezuela to Iran, which would, of course, be a violation of UN sanctions against Iran. On this score, Chávez insists that Venezuela is not exporting its uranium to Iran. This is improbable, given:

1. The bevy of informed and specific allegations that point to Iran receiving uranium from Venezuela.

2. The extent of unmonitored means of transit, such as Conviasa flights, as well as a shipping line owned by the two governments.
3. The likelihood of illicit financial ties in support of Iran's nuclear program.

Setting all this aside, planning for a cooperative "nuclear village" violates international law. When Chávez first made mention of nuclear cooperation with Iran, in an interview published in the French magazine *Le Figaro*, French president Nicolas Sarkozy tartly reminded Chávez that any level of nuclear cooperation with Iran violated UN sanctions. In 2009 a French foreign ministry spokeswoman repeated the warning, adding that Venezuela was well "in its right" to have peaceful nuclear energy, but transfers to Iran were prohibited.[64]

Even presuming that Venezuela does not currently transfer uranium or nuclear-related materials to Iran, nuclear cooperation between the two is still a threat to Western security. Since 2009 Venezuela's nuclear program has started to take shape with Russia's assistance, and given the notion of a "nuclear village," it is likely that Iran could be using Venezuela as a nuclear surrogate. By advancing its own program, Venezuela could easily transfer its nuclear resources to Iran. In this way, Tehran can count on restarting its nuclear program from an advanced level by drawing on Venezuela's program. John Bolton, a hawkish ambassador to the UN under President George W. Bush, likens Venezuela's nascent nuclear program to Syria's clandestine program, which was bombed by Israel in 2007.[65]

WHERE THE POISONOUS FRUIT IS RIPEST

As a vehicle to advance Venezuela and Iran's designs, the "axis of unity" is an impressive pact. Political and economic ties have blunted Western countermeasures, which have mainly come in the form of UN sanctions against Iran. In the fall of 2009 Venezuela began shipping Iran 20,000 bpd of gasoline with the express intent of helping Islamic Republic bear UN sanctions, a symbolic gesture of defiance to the West. Nuclear cooperation is undeniably underway; the only question is whether Iran benefits from Venezuelan uranium or production of nuclear-related wares in Venezuela. These are all above-board advances, publicly acknowledged, that cloak signs of legerdemain. As the Manhattan DA said, evidence suggests that Venezuela is serving as "a perfect 'sanction-busting' method" for Iran to finance its nuclear program, indicated by the number of banks jointly operated in each country that have been sanctioned by both the U.S. Treasury and the EU.[66] These are vexing impediments to Western attempts to prevent Iran from developing nuclear weapons.

Even so, one can still argue that this level of cooperation does not amount to a direct or immediate threat to U.S. or European security. Iran with the bomb could not hope to reach the United States, and the ayatollahs surely know that any use of a nuclear device would result in their annihilation. Instead, Iran intends to use its nuclear program to make itself the dominant power in the Middle East. The closer it gets to that goal, the more of a direct threat it becomes not just to regional stability, but to the security of Israel.

Israel is directly threatened by the Venezuela-Iran alliance in two ways. First, as Iran's nuclear program advances, Israel's security is pared back. Not only is Venezuela complicit in Iran's nuclear advances, but the Quds Force and Hezbollah's growing foothold in the Americas means the United States is less likely to act militarily against Iran, as U.S. security officials recognize that these groups are poised to carry out retaliatory attacks against Western targets and perhaps even within the United States in the event of an American attack on Iran. Second, security experts believe Conviasa flights in particular could serve to transit Jews kidnapped in the Americas back to the Middle East. In this respect, the illicit aspects of the Venezuela-Iran alliance not only limit U.S. options when it comes to dealing with Iran, but to some degree may spook Israeli foreign policy.

Familial ties between Caracas and Tehran also present a direct security threat to Colombia. QF assistance to the FARC, as reported by STRATFOR, and accounts that Venezuelan forces are being trained in guerilla tactics by the QF are good reasons for Bogotá to worry. Also, reports that Hezbollah is helping the FARC traffic drugs from an operational base in Venezuela present a direct danger to Colombian security.

In conclusion, the "axis of unity" is less about the United States than it is about creating and preserving a sphere of influence for Chávez and the Islamic Republic. The Western allies that stand in the way of those designs are at knife's edge to the resources that Venezuela and Iran accrue as a result of their partnership. Given its creeping presence in Venezuela at the invitation of Chávez, Iran has become a transregional threat to security. As a result, not only is Colombia less secure, but Iran is using Venezuela as a base in the Western Hemisphere where Hezbollah and the Quds Force's known presence can act as deterrent to Western strikes on Iran.

Iran Infiltrates the Americas

When the Western countries were trying to isolate Iran, we went to the United States' backyard.
—Mahmoud Ahmadinejad (May 28, 2009)

Having solidified an alliance with Venezuela, Iran thrust its way further into Latin America, propagating alliances with Bolivia, Ecuador, and Nicaragua. Tehran even managed to boost trade ties with Argentina. Chávez accompanied Ahmadinejad at every turn, directing Iran's expansion into the region. These countries were complete strangers when Iran began to curry favor with them in early 2007. According to the former president of Bolivia Jorge Quiroga Ramírez in 2009, "We have no cultural, historical or commercial ties whatsoever. Bolivia knows nothing about Iran."[1] Nonetheless, Iran lured these countries into cozy ties with offerings of large aid packages. At first it appeared that public expressions of anti-Americanism among the newly elected presidents aroused Iran's interest, but Iran didn't keep all of its pledges of investment and aid. In explaining the inconsistency between promises made and promises kept, quid pro quo is at work. Where Iran can extract material benefit for its nuclear program, aid pledges are largely fulfilled. Where Iran has failed to lay down roots, its promises of foreign aid have not materialized.

FIRST ENCOUNTERS

If Iran's dealings with Venezuela had been infrequent prior to 2005, its experiences with smaller nations in the region were nonexistent. Iran only had a few embassies in the region, and no diplomatic presence in Bolivia, Ecuador, Nicaragua, or Uruguay.[2] Bolivia, meanwhile, had only one embassy in the Middle East at the time, in Egypt, but as a result of Iran's overtures it was moved to Tehran in 2008.

A look at economic ties is more startling. Iran's total bilateral trade (exports plus imports) with Argentina, Bolivia, Ecuador, and Nicaragua averaged well less than $100,000 a year from 2000 to 2006; in many years total trade was around $30,000.[3] In some cases total bilateral trade remained at zero dollars for a whole year, somewhat of an anomaly in the twenty-first century. More common, though, were zero exports from, say, Ecuador, and a few Iranian imports in the form of Persian rugs and dinnerware that made their way to the homes of the elite. For example, Ecuador exported nothing to Iran in 2000, 2006, and 2007, and $5,800 worth of goods in 2001, while importing between $25,000 and $280,000 worth of Iranian goods each year.[4]

The year 2007 brought rapid change. A quick tally shows that from 2007 to 2008 Iran's trade with Latin America tripled, to $2.9 billion.[5] More instructive is the mix of Iran's trade partners. For most of the last decade, Iran's leading trade partner in Latin America was Brazil, followed by Mexico and Peru, respectively: a sensible ordering given that Brazil and Mexico are the region's two largest economies. While Brazil continues to be Iran's largest bilateral trade partner in the region, Argentina supplanted Mexico to become Iran's second-largest trade partner under the presidency of Cristina Fernández de Kirchner, a remarkable feat given the tenor of Argentine-Iranian relations. And Iran's third-largest trade partner in Latin America became Ecuador. Although its economy is smaller than that of the state of Utah, bilateral trade surged from $16,000 in 2007 to over $185 million in 2008.[6] Most of the increase in Iran's trade with Latin America owes to the election of presidents closely allied with Hugo Chávez.

This represented the Islamic Republic's most concerted diplomatic offensive in its twenty-eight-year history. Even so, making inroads into the overwhelmingly Catholic region would have probably been impossible for the Shi'ite Muslim nation to muster alone, especially given the lingering suspicions of an Iranian hand in the Buenos Aires bombings in 1992 and 1994. A rough comparison exists: during this time Iran also attempted to build alliances in Africa, but these ties have yielded no discernable diplomatic, economic, or even illicit benefits for Iran. Yet, as the trade figures suggest, Iran's venture into Latin America is different. That is because Iran had a key middleman, Hugo Chávez. Acting as "godfather and relationship manager" to Iran's expansion, Chávez steered Iranian foreign policy toward his allies, which also helped solidify the Hugo sphere.[7]

In a flurry of diplomatic moves largely orchestrated by Chávez, Iran laid the groundwork for cozy relations in the region in January 2007.[8] On January 10, Daniel Ortega was inaugurated in Nicaragua. Five days later Rafael Correa officially became president of Ecuador at an inauguration ceremony attended by Mahmoud Ahmadinejad. In the interim, Ahmadinejad not only met with Bolivian president Evo Morales for the first time, he also became the first non–Latin American president to visit President Ortega in Nicaragua. Shortly thereafter, Iran announced a doubling of its embassies in Latin America, including new embassies in Bolivia, Ecuador, Nicaragua, and Uruguay. From a diplomatic point of view, the left-leaning governments allied with Chávez were worth the effort. These countries could impede Western efforts to pressure Iran in the UN by backing Venezuela in a bid for a rotating seat in the Security Council or by voting against preliminary statements to send a measure before the council. As Abbas Milani, Director of Iranian Studies at Stanford University, put it, Iran would have "more pawns to play in its dealings with the Europeans and United States."[9] On a more general level, an active Iranian mission in these countries could serve as reserve channels for Iran to avoid diplomatic and financial isolation in the event that the West successfully pressured the Islamic Republic's existing network of allies and financial outlets.

By the summer of 2007, diplomatic attention had been coupled with epic announcements of Iranian investment and aid. Ahmadinejad and Morales agreed to $1.2 billion in Iranian investment in Bolivia over five years. "It is such investment," reported *Time* magazine, that "along with massive amounts of aid from Venezuela . . . has put South America's poorest nation's economy on the upswing for the first time in years."[10] With an overall GDP of $9 billion, the allure of developmental aid was immense: investment pledges from Venezuela and Iran amounted to a quarter of Bolivia's economy.[11] Additional Iranian investment targeting Bolivia's underdeveloped energy sector soon followed.

Iran's aid pledges to Nicaragua were on par with those made to Bolivia, ringing up to around $1 billion, including funding for construction of hydroelectric power plants, milk-processing plants, hospitals, and ten thousand houses for the poor. The *Wall Street Journal* described it as a part of an Iranian campaign "to project power and greatness worldwide—including in America's own backyard."[12] The centerpiece of Iran's investment was a $350 million port complex at a remote area on Nicaragua's Caribbean coast, which would have greatly enhanced the country's woeful infrastructure.

By comparison, Iran did not publicly pledge any aid to Ecuador. This could have been because Chávez, acting as a "third vertex" between Quito and Tehran, preoccupied himself with finagling Ecuador's readmission to OPEC in order to bolster his (and Iran's) strategic position in the world oil market. Or it could have been because Ecuador is more integrated into the global economy than either Bolivia or Nicaragua. Hence Ecuador may have been deemed a better candidate for "trade, not aid" with Tehran, a view supported by the uptick in bilateral trade after 2007.

However, in the context of 2007, there is a more plausible explanation of Iran's aid pledges to Bolivia, Ecuador, and Nicaragua: within the Hugo sphere, Tehran initially embraced the more vocally anti-American presidents. This would have been a rational calculation: the leaders most critical of Washington would be the most beneficial partners of Tehran.

On this basis, at the outset of 2007 Ortega and Morales came across as most clearly in-step with the rabid anti-Americanism that Ahmadinejad and Chávez fancied. After coming to office, Ortega made no bones about the fact that he sought alignment with Tehran and Caracas.[13] Ortega met with Ahmadinejad three times in 2007, more often than either Correa or Morales, and even borrowed a plane from Muammar al-Gaddafi to make it to Tehran for the second rendezvous.[14] On that occasion, Ahmadinejad and Ortega declared, "The revolutions of Iran and Nicaragua are almost twin revolutions . . . since both revolutions are about justice, liberty, self-determination, and the struggle against imperialism."[15] A few months later Ortega met the Supreme Leader in Tehran, a rarity for a non-Muslim head of state. While there, Ortega repeated his earlier statement that "no one will choose who our friends are but us." He quickly made provisions for greater Iranian influence in the country by allowing Iranians to visit Nicaragua without a visa.[16]

Ortega had more credibility as an anti-Americanist than any leader in the region, save Fidel Castro. Nicaragua's inadvertent ties to Iran through the lurid Iran-Contra Affair in the 1980s notched a high watermark of U.S. neo-imperialism. And it was Ortega, as leader of the communist Sandinista party, whose election in Nicaragua touched off what became a U.S. proxy war against leftist groups all across Central America in the 1980s. So, in contrast to the tradition of listless ties between Iran and the countries in the Andes, a propinquity existed between Managua and Tehran that the other countries didn't share.

All of this fused in a way that made the Yankees "squeal," as Chávez might say. Some analysts saw it as a geographic advance, from Iran's long-known ties in the tri-border area, up to Venezuela, and now to Nicaragua. The U.S. State Department, which had seemingly refined a pitch-perfect dismissal of Chávez, began to openly worry about Iran's plans for a "mega embassy" in Nicaragua. Think tank reports, congressional testimony in 2008, and press releases all spoke of this hypothetical Iranian embassy.[17]

Evo Morales didn't shirk from criticism of the United States either. When running for president in 2005, he fashioned himself "Washington's worst nightmare." In office, he quickly embraced Chávez's anti-American vision by joining ALBA, booting the U.S. ambassador and DEA agents from Bolivia, and taking a defiant tone on coca eradication. "One might even say that Morales has gone further than Chávez and Ortega in his rejection of United States policy," noted one academic paper.[18] Morales became the first leader in the region to incur significant costs for his anti-Americanism: by ending cooperation with Washington on combating drug trafficking, Bolivia forfeited trade benefits afforded under the Andean Trade Promotion and Drug Eradication Act, later known as the Andean Trade Promotion Act (ATPA). As a result, fifteen thousand to thirty-five thousand jobs were lost in two of Bolivia's key export regions, El Alto and Cochabamba.[19]

During his first two years in office, Morales did a handsome job of isolating Bolivia within South America. His 2006 nationalization program included the seizure of Brazilian and Argentine businesses, and though Argentina quickly looked beyond the raw deal, Brazil remained wary of Bolivia for some time. Bolivia's relations with Peru ebbed to recent lows, and even after Correa's inauguration Bolivia's cooperation with Ecuador on bilateral issues was piecemeal, not automatic. Morales made Bolivia more reliant on Venezuela. By virtue of the president's anti-American policies and isolation in the region, by 2007 Bolivia was certainly amenable to Tehran's approach.

Rafael Correa cut a fine contrast. Instead of vituperations against the United States, Correa, ever the PhD-toting economist, pinpointed his criticisms, such as the gross damages done to Ecuador by foreign oil companies. A favorite whipping boy was the IMF and the rigid conditions it tied to loans. An interview in July 2007 gave a good indication of Correa's style: "The United States is no longer a Satan for America, but if we want to achieve an egalitarian world, it's impossible with the IMF or the World Bank."[20] If anything, Correa's statement could be taken as a rebuttal of Chávez, who ten months earlier had called George W. Bush "the devil" at the UN. Correa appeared a socialist, certainly, but not a firebrand looking to sow international revolution.

Ecuador's foreign policy initially reflected this nuance. Correa often complimented Chávez, but the two countries' foreign policies did not immediately cohere. For some time Correa remained autonomous enough "to agree or disagree on a case-by-case basis."[21] Correa took no time in pushing for a new constitution that expanded the powers of the president, which many saw as a key reason Chávez backed him. But the law of the land Correa proposed incorporated environmental provisions, a nonissue to Chávez.

Given this fine line, it shouldn't come as a surprise that the Correa administration downplayed ties to Iran. Initially, this wasn't a tall order. Unlike Bolivia, Nicaragua, or Venezuela, Ecuador did not receive any investment aid from Iran in 2007 or 2008.[22] After attending Correa's inauguration, Ahmadinejad tried over a period of months to coax Correa toward more regular trade ties, which engendered some response from Quito. To lay the groundwork, the first trade office opened by Correa would be in Tehran in early 2008.[23] Correa only gradually positioned Ecuador to take advantage of the opportunity for trade with Iran. As it did so, the Correa government tried to avoid getting caught up in "all geopolitical connotations" related to the Islamic Republic.[24] Ecuador's foreign minister keenly insisted that economic relations would not lead to "some other form of relationship that will have a political impact."[25] Despite a host of opportunities to collectively bash America, Correa gave

Chávez and Ahmadinejad little more than bland pronouncements that Iran had a right to peaceful nuclear energy.

PROMISES, PROMISES . . .

Three years later, Iran's pledges of aid to Bolivia, Nicaragua and Ecuador are partially realized. In general, development pledges to Bolivia have been kept, though projects have advanced on an irregular timeline. Iran built a hospital in Bolivia, and Iranian management, staff, and doctors continue to run it. Bolivia built a milk-processing factory in the town of Achacachi with Iranian cash in 2009. Iran is constructing a $230 million concrete factory too. Bolivians, especially the large indigenous community, have been broadly receptive to Iranian investment. While the milk plant was under construction the mayor of Achacachi said, "We don't ask why Iran is interested. . . . I've never met anyone from Iran. I know very little about that country. We just want the plant."[26] Conversely, there are no documented accounts of hostilities between Bolivians and Iranians.

Meanwhile, Iran's pledges to Nicaragua have come to naught. Felix Maradiaga, a political science professor at Nicaragua's American University, has tracked at least two dozen projects publicly announced by either Ortega or Iranian officials, including hydroelectric plants, the housing project, milk plants like the one in Bolivia, and the crown jewel—Iran's largest project in Latin America, the port complex.[27] As of September 2009, Maradiaga could find only one Iranian promise somewhat fulfilled—a hospital, estimated to cost $1.5 million—which broke ground that month.[28] Based on such poor follow-through, a nonpartisan study published by the Woodrow Wilson Center for International Scholars noted that assistance from "Iran is more theory than reality . . . the Iranian Government is taking advantage of the expectations it is generating among members of the Sandinista government, as Iran maneuvers to install a political and operational base in Nicaragua, while providing almost nothing in exchange."[29]

Between Ortega's officious diplomacy and Iran's initial interest in Nicaragua, at least one thing apparently went overlooked—demographics along Nicaragua's Caribbean coast. In fact, it seems Iran tried to make good on its $350 million promise. In early 2008 speedboats docked along the coast of Monkey Point, carrying an Iranian reconnaissance team to spec the port site. The Iranians reportedly believed the area was uninhabited jungle. Instead of finding empty tropical wilderness or impoverished Indians in need of work, when the Iranians landed at Monkey Point they found themselves in the midst of an autonomous region of Nicaragua inhabited by American expatriates. The expats videotaped the ensuing clash. "We said we would defend our homes with guns, knives, machetes, whatever," recalled William Claire Duncan. In follow-up interviews conducted by the *Wall Street Journal*, the expats at Monkey Point insisted they didn't harbor any animosity toward the Iranians; they just wanted to protect their property.[30] Regardless, the Iranians never returned to Monkey Point.

TEHRAN'S LASTING TIES

Iran's ties to Bolivia and Ecuador have accreted to greater consequence since 2008. Colombia's FARC raid into Ecuadorian territory provided the pretext for Quito to entertain closer ties to Iran. "Iran can supply us" with arms and credit, Correa said, because "we have a very serious problem on the northern border with Colombia, an irresponsible government that does not take care of its border."[31] Instead Russia would sell Correa the weapons. Bilateral trade between Ecuador and Iran burgeoned, as indicated earlier, well beyond the threshold of pistachios and a few rugs.

Iran quickly availed itself of the new allies, though the effects were not immediately apparent. To facilitate investments in Ecuador, Iran established ties with Ecuador's Central Bank, and BID opened an office in Quito in 2009.[32] Coincidentally or consequently, Ecuador's regulatory scrutiny of its financial system diminished. In February 2010, six months after the BID branch opened, the Financial Action Task Force reported that Ecuador was not "constructively engaged" and had "not committed" to international standards on money-laundering crimes. Thus, the FATF put Ecuador on a "black list" of other non-compliers—Angola, Ethiopia, Iran, North Korea, and Turkmenistan.[33] Occupants of this bottom rung are widely recognized to tacitly or actively allow use of their financial system for terrorist financing or illicit weapons programs.

Piqued, President Correa declared: "What arrogance! And why? Because we have relations with Iran. That's it!"[34] Correa then refused to undertake any measures to comply with FATF regulations. Ecuador's private bank association, incidentally, reached the same conclusion, but appeared less shocked as to why. It noted the relationship of Ecuador's Central Bank to Iran, as well as the fact that several Iranian financial institutions were operating in the country with no regulatory oversight as probable reason for the country's inclusion on the FATF blacklist.[35]

In Bolivia, a part of Iran's pledge of developmental assistance came in the form of mining, which has led to allegations that the two countries cooperate in uranium recovery. A secret three-page Israeli intelligence report leaked to the Associated Press in May of 2009 disclosed that Bolivia, in concert with Venezuela, was supplying Iran with uranium in defiance of UN sanctions.[36] Several Bolivian officials said that Bolivia had not even done the proper geological work to know where, and how much, uranium Bolivia had.[37]

THE CHÁVEZ BRIDGE

Iran's initial interest in Latin Amerca may have been an attempt to find "more pawns to play" against the West, but within the group of nations allied to Chávez Iran initially prioritized ties to the most anti-American governments. On this basis, Bolivia and Nicaragua stood out. While Evo Morales vowed to become "Washington's worst nightmare," it was Daniel Ortega who most unsettled U.S. policymakers. For this reason, Tehran likely viewed Nicaragua as particularly ripe for alliance. A footnote from Iran's 2009 presidential elections sheds some light on Iranian expectations. In the run up to the election, supporters of Ahmadinejad's opponent, Mir Hossein Mousavi, criticized the Iranian president for expending so much energy on Latin America. Ahmadinejad replied: "When the Western countries were trying to isolate Iran, we went to the United States' backyard, and I even delivered my strongest anti-U.S. speech in Nicaragua."[38]

Although Ortega offered his country as an Iranian beachhead, relations did not mature. Iran's promises to Nicaragua have been almost completely unfulfilled. But Iran has built financial ties with Ecuador and is allegedly helping Bolivia tap its uranium deposits. At least initially these countries benefitted from Iran's presence through expanded trade. In Bolivia's case, aid pledges have been fulfilled.

This process has yielded one clear winner—Hugo Chávez. His importance to both Iran and his allies in Latin America is buoyed by the way he brokers Iran's presence in the region. While it may appear as though Chávez is a benevolent patron bringing Bolivia and Ecuador a fresh source of investment and trade, he only compounds their reliance on him. In the 2009 annual threat report to the U.S. Senate, the U.S. Director of National Intelligence warned that Venezuela "is serving as a bridge to help Iran build relations with other Latin American countries."[39] Indeed, Venezuela looks to be the bridge from Iran to the countries of Latin America. It is a fairly sturdy bridge, built from a surge in authoritarianism and Iran's growing need to service its nuclear program. Chávez looks to be the troll.

A VIRUS of Instability

A number of states outside the post-Soviet region exploit deteriorating U.S.-Russia relations to improve their ties with Moscow and benefit from Russia's more assertive anti-American posture. The benefits have included diplomatic protection, favorable trade and investment, and arms sales, including sophisticated weaponry from Russian companies.

—Janusz Bugajski, *Dismantling the West: Russia's Atlantic Agenda* (2009)

In the 1970s and 1980s, Libyan dictator Col. Muammar al-Gaddafi did his best to court every anti-Western terrorist he could find. Credible evidence implicates him as a financier of the "Black September" operation that carried out the 1972 Munich massacre, as well as the mayhem of Carlos the Jackal, a Venezuelan convicted of murder in France. Gaddafi then refused to extradite two of the suspected bombers of Pan-Am 103, which blew up over Lockerbie, Scotland, on December 21, 1988. Economic sanctions and diplomatic isolation throughout the 1990s corroded Gaddafi's influence and appetite for international terrorism. In 2006 Gaddafi returned to the fold, apparently chastened, by agreeing to pay $2.7 billion for his role in the 1988 Pan Am 103 bombing, $10 million to each of the victim's families. In due course, he went from what President Reagan in 1986 called "the mad dog of the Middle East" to "an eccentric statesman with entirely benign relations with the West," as London's *Telegraph* put it in a 2006 profile.[1] Even in light of the 2011 revolt of the Libyan people against the dictator—including Gaddafi's brutal response, and the NATO air campaign that helped drive him from power—Gaddafi was clearly a threat to his people, not to the security of Western nations.

From 1994 to 2001 Kim Jung Il set about using his nation's poverty to blackmail the United States, and the Clinton administration resigned itself to offering the Kim regime millions in foreign aid in exchange for halting efforts to build a nuclear bomb. Only after the Bush administration stopped the payments and moved for deeper sanctions did North Korea test its first, then its second, nuclear bomb. Saddam Hussein, too, was contained after the First Gulf War. In effect, all of these "rogue states" were subdued through a combination of sanctions and, in the case of North Korea, economic aid. It wasn't an edifying solution, but it secured America's interests and resigned the bad apples to their respective bins.

What makes Iran and Venezuela, independently or even in league, any different from Libya, Iraq prior to 2003, or North Korea? In short, they enjoy the support of great powers, and diplomatic protection at the UN Security Council. This chapter considers Russia's role as the primary "great power" sponsor of each government. It describes how Venezuela, Iran, and Russia have formed a partnership, albeit a precarious one, for strategic and economic reasons, to help solidify one another's ambitions.

RUSSIA "LEAVES THE WEST"

Until recently, Russia was actively incorporated into the global power calculus, though perhaps with a bit of Western condescension. Beyond its permanent seat on the UN Security Council (SC), Russia routinely participated in multilateral initiatives to help resolve major international crises, such as "the Quartet" effort began in 2002 to broker a deal between Israel and the Palestinian leadership. Soon thereafter, Russia under President Vladimir Putin grew disaffected with the West. At least three factors caused Russia to "leave the West."[2]

First, and arguably of least import, Putin opposed the war in Iraq. Several traditional U.S. allies, especially France and Germany, shared this view. However, in Russia's case the opposition seemed more a product of the president's personal decision, rather than democratic pressures of the sort that caused European politicians to quail from backing the war. Analysts asserted that Russia's opposition resulted from the fact that the United States diluted its diplomatic power by giving up on the SC as the lone forum for authorizing war.

Second, Putin's Russia had had enough of NATO expansion. NATO enlargement in 1999 incorporated Poland, the Czech Republic, and Hungary, nations that Russia could not realistically hope to keep under its spell given the economic collapse it suffered in 1998. But in 2004 NATO grew to include Bulgaria, Estonia, Latvia, Lithuania, Romania, Slovakia, and Slovenia. These countries had a clear rationale for joining NATO: halting encroachment by Moscow. For Moscow the 2004 enlargement signified just the opposite, the "encircling" of Russia from the west and south.[3] Georgia and Ukraine were next in line for admission to NATO, each having just elected pro-West governments. To make matters worse for Moscow, the Bush administration announced plans to install a missile defense shield in Poland and the Czech Republic by 2012.

NATO's spread into what Russian leaders saw as their sphere of influence—termed the "near abroad"—also brought into focus the technological chasm between Europe and Russia. NATO military plans and operations consisted of highly mobile, quick-strike forces. Russia's military lacked modern equipment and professionalism.

By 2005, just a year after being reelected with more than 70 percent of the popular vote, negative perceptions of Putin were spreading throughout Russia and abroad. Protests erupted against the government. An analyst at the Carnegie Moscow Institute summarized the situation as follows: "Only two things have kept him going: Oil prices and lack of alternatives. If people are unhappy they start to look for alternatives."[4] Also, Putin's authoritarian instincts were becoming hard to ignore, opening a fissure with democratic governments in the West. Mikhail Khodorkovsky, Russia's richest man and one of the last major business people in Russia who refused to kowtow to Moscow, was arrested in 2003 and convicted on what are widely seen to be political grounds. A number of other critics were jailed on trumped up charges; others were less fortunate. In 2006 Anna Politkovskaya, a journalist critical of Putin, was murdered. Later that year Alexander Litvinenko, a former Russian intelligence officer granted asylum in Britain, was fatally poisoned. In February 2005, Sen. John McCain cautioned, "Sooner or later he has got to realize the path he is on will bring his government down. . . . You can't continue this kind of consolidation of power and not expect to be isolated, at least to some degree, in the world."[5]

For the first time since 1991 Russia's relations with the United States and Europe soured at the same time.[6] Though Russia was getting richer, it had sunk farther from the great power status Putin, and the cabal of former KGB *siloviki* ("men of power") surrounding him, expected. Instead of Russia being readmitted to the great power club coequal to the EU heavyweights and the United States, another rising power got the nod: China. The EU and China prioritized relations with Washington above all else. Russia would wend a different path.

THE VIRUS PARTNERSHIP

Although no longer a superpower, Russia still has an unassailable global relevance based not just on oil, but also the diplomatic power and military industrial complex inherited from the Soviet Union's collapse in 1991. When Vladimir Putin acceded to the Russian presidency in 2000, America's economy was twenty-seven times the size of Russia's.[7] Yet, when it came to getting things done in the Security Council Russia's say counted for just as much. And when it came to military hardware Russia had the largest stash on earth, by some metrics.[8] A basic realization took hold: hard-nosed diplomacy and arms, not economic dynamism or cultural allure, are Russia's competitive advantages in the world.

Putin's return to glory would require shrewdly marshalling Russia's assets to bolster a higher status on the world stage, and overtly backing Venezuela and Iran in an attempt to complicate U.S. support for its regional allies. Putin's Russia did so primarily through arms sales, which, beyond simply making money for Russia's arms industry, fuel "low boil" regional instability. Additionally, Putin would delay and dilute UN sanctions against the Islamic Republic. Venezuela and Iran, for their part, would serve as hubs for greater Russian geopolitical influence, and open up geostrategic outlets that might allow Russia to enjoy more leverage against the West, which is the focus of the next chapter. Finally, coordinating energy policies would allow each country to use its economic lifeblood as a political weapon. These ties formed the bonds of a concerted partnership that drew on each nation's comparative advantages in the international system in order to reinforce one another's regional ambitions. In so doing, they sowed conflict and tumult in the Andes, the Middle East, and Russia's "near abroad." In essence, Venezuela, Iran, and Russia had formed a partnership that is a VIRUS of instability.

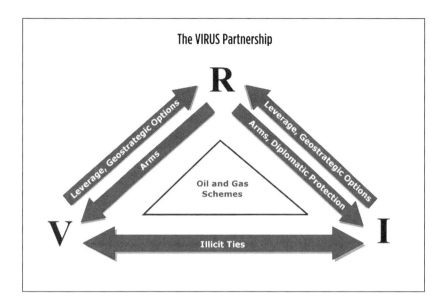

Russia began to cozy up to Venezuela in 2006, after the United States halted arms sales on account of lack of cooperation on counterterrorism. Chávez's initial response was indicative: he said he would sell some of Venezuela's old F-16s to Iran—a clear violation of the jet's end user certificates—because the United States refused to provide replacement parts for the aging aircraft.[9] Instead, Russia stepped in to make the sales. Within months of the U.S. embargo Russia sold Chávez 100,000 Kalashnikov rifles, raising a meek reproach from Washington, and contracted for two dozen Sukhoi fighter jets. A frenzy ensued as Venezuela bought Russian T-72 tanks, over a dozen anti-aircraft systems, thirty-three attack helicopters, and was even granted South America's first license to run a Kalashnikov factory.[10] By the end of 2009 Venezuela had spent $4.4 billion on Russian arms, making it the largest arms purchaser in Latin America. On per capita terms Venezuela far exceeds China and India, the countries with the fastest growing military expenditures. Russia, meanwhile, supplanted the United States to become the largest arms supplier to Latin America in 2010, a status that the UK-based International Institute for Strategic Studies attributed to Venezuelan purchases.[11]

Venezuela's procurements of Russian arms unsettled the regional security of South America. Brazil, typically the region's largest military spender—as well as Bolivia, Chile, Ecuador, Peru, and Chávez's regional nemesis, Colombia—all increased weapons purchases at an alarming rate over the course of 2007–2008. Given the improved economic growth in the region, one might argue this was a natural result of the "security dilemma"—one state begins to spend money on arms on account of its growing economic wealth, and this touches off a series of reactions by other states who feel increasingly insecure about their neighbor's intentions. Arms races are a common result. In such cases, international relations theorists often consider the personalities or political leanings of leaders to be irrelevant, because all states behave in a similar manner given the circumstances.[12] That's not how many leaders in this region saw it. Brazilian senator José Sarney spoke for many when he laid the blame clearly on Venezuela. After rattling off a laundry list of Russian-made weapons acquired by Caracas, he said: "It's very worrying. As Venezuela turns itself into a major military power, it obliges the other nations in South America to increase the power of their own forces. [An arms race] sadly seems to be getting under way."[13]

At the time of this writing an arms race in South America appears to have been averted, though the situation could easily change. Many of the countries involved, including Venezuela at the initial stages of Chávez's arms purchases, were simply replacing out-of-date military hardware. In Chile, historically the second-largest arms buyer in the region, a law on the books actually mandated a percentage of copper sales go toward the military; the legislature realized the law needed to be scrapped only after copper prices went through the roof. Most other countries—Bolivia, Brazil, Colombia, and Ecuador—bought defensive arms intended to monitor and interdict drug traffickers.

Russia's arms sales to Iran, coupled with technical nuclear support, are even more destabilizing. Russia has sold Iran weapons since 1992, but the total value of arms transferred accelerated greatly between 2002 and 2005 to $1.7 billion as Russia sought to use arms to expand its role in the Middle East and encourage greater cooperation with Iran over gas pipelines flowing from Central Asia.[14] Russia routinely peddled surface-to-air missiles, MiG fighter jets, battle tanks, and a long list of other armaments to help the Islamic Republic maintain its military posture. Until 2008, in fact, Iran was the third-largest importer of Russian weapons; its fall from the podium came thanks to Venezuela's inordinate arms purchases.[15]

Among Russia's arms transfers to Iran, one deal is particularly controversial. In 2005 Russia agreed to sell Iran S-300 anti-aircraft missiles.[16] An advanced weapons system capable of simultaneously tracking up to one hundred targets and engaging up to twelve, an S-300 can intercept incoming aircraft or missiles 90–180 miles away. Russian sources boast that it is technologically superior to American Patriot missiles.[17]

Russia regularly states that its arms deals with Venezuela and Iran are legal, intended for defensive use, and nothing more than smart business. To address these claims in order: Russian arms sales to Venezuela are legal, as there are no UN sanctions against Venezuela. In the case of Iran, Russia's arms sales were initially legal, but that is now more dubious. Take, for example, the potential sale of S-300 missiles. The fourth round of sanctions against the Islamic Republic, passed by the Security Council in June 2010, forbids arms transfers, but interestingly an exception was carved out for Russia, leaving open the possibility that Russia could complete the sale of the S-300s.

On the second point, related to defensive use, Russian claims are equivocations at best. Justifying a 2007 arms sale, Russian defense minister Sergei Ivanov stressed, "If Iran wants to buy defensive, I underline defensive, equipment for its armed forces, then why not?"[18] The particular arms to which Ivanov was referring, TOR-M1 anti-aircraft missiles, are highly advanced vehicle-mounted missiles, originally designed to protect tank and infantry formations in the event of a Soviet assault into NATO territory. Hence these anti-aircraft missiles have the design purpose of locking in gains, which could easily be applied to territorial conquest, or perhaps more likely, protection of nuclear sites. Pavel E. Felgenhauer, a leading defense analyst, considers the TOR-M1 missiles to be offensive weapons. Felgenhauer asserts that possessing these weapons gives Tehran reason to "believe that they can withstand, to some extent, American air supremacy in any kind of clash on the battlefield."[19] That belief will be even more warranted if Iran operates the S-300s, which would make Iranian nuclear sites "practically invulnerable" to air strikes and greatly complicate any American or Israeli effort to take out a nuclear facility.[20]

Chávez has also contracted for S-300s as a part of a $2.2 billion Russian arms loan in 2009. Although Venezuela is not believed to possess the S-300 yet, it stands to become the only nation in the Western Hemisphere with the systems.[21] This is only one of many items Russia has sold Venezuela that are hard to consider defensive. Col. Joe Nuñez at the U.S. Army War College classifies most of Chávez's fighter jets and helicopter purchases from Russia as having "a more offensive" purpose.[22] Ultimately, though, a weapon's purpose is a matter of intent. Scrutinizing Chávez's own words provides some insight. He repeatedly claims that Venezuela's new military wares are for defensive purposes, but when push comes to shove he changes tone. In the immediate aftermath of the March 2008 raid, which should have been a bilateral issue between Colombia and Ecuador, Chávez declared that "this could be the start of a war in South America," and then publicly threatened Uribe, telling him, "I'll send [over] some Sukhois."[23]

Third, Russia is adamant that its actions are simply driven by money. "It is not a secret that we are competing with the Americans and a number of European countries on the world's weapons market," said Russian foreign minister Sergei Lavrov in 2006. Referring to Venezuela, he noted, "Of course, if an opportunity to sell our weapons at a good price arises, we will do that."[24] Given that Russia's arms companies are all state-owned, and the fact that they provide a source of diversification for a hydrocarbon-reliant economy, the profit motive is obvious.

But Russia uses its sales to Venezuela and Iran to gain influence in Latin America and the Middle East, influence that accrues at the expense of U.S. influence. Larry Birns, the director of the Council on Hemispheric Affairs, considers the Russian-Venezuelan arms deals "an unprecedented and unanticipated undermining of the privileged status that the United States traditionally has occupied in Latin America."[25] This is more than a blow to U.S. influence—it also threatens regional stability. Analysts at the Stockholm International Peace Research Institute (SIPRI) deem the arms sales "disproportionate" to Venezuela's defense needs. Specifically, a SIPRI expert worries that the offense-oriented Sukhoi fighters have the ability to "destabilize the military balance" in the Andes.[26]

In the Middle East, Russia's conventional arms sales to Iran also contribute to a conventional arms race as regional rivals like Egypt, Israel, and Saudi

Arabia—which contracted for a whopping $60 billion in U.S. fighter jets and defense systems in the fall of 2010—move to check the growing influence of the Islamic Republic. Unfortunately, this is probably the least troubling aspect of Moscow's recent support for Iran. Russian arms are funneled to Hezbollah forces in large quantities, both through Iran and through Iran's ally Syria. The scale of Russian arms "leakage" wasn't a major diplomatic concern until it became clear that Russian small arms enhanced Hezbollah's dexterity during its 2006 war with Israel. Russian arms were so widespread that some media outlets, particularly the *Economist*, likened the situation to the Cold War: "a clash between proxy forces that tested armaments and tactics. While Israel's American-supplied gadgetry was far more lethal, Hezbollah's Russian weapons were effective too. Its anti-tank missiles knocked out scores of Israel's armored vehicles."[27] Shortly after the conflict, Israeli soldiers discovered Russian-made arms at abandoned Hezbollah posts.

Russian officials reportedly apologized to Israel. However, in the years since Russian leaders have more openly embraced their connections with Iran's terrorist allies. Syrian president Assad has publicly thanked Moscow for support "in defense of Golan" against Israel. Hezbollah reinvigorated and is once again preparing for war with Israel, strengthened by sophisticated Russian-made air defense systems that have sprung up in the eastern Bekaa Valley in order to shoot down Israeli jets.[28] Russia's arms sales to Venezuela and Iran are integral to the shifting balance of power in Latin America and the Middle East.

NUCLEAR PATRONAGE

Russia is a longtime sponsor of Iran's nuclear program, and today it is the only country verifiably supporting the Islamic Republic's nuclear efforts. Despite international pressure brought by Western and Middle Eastern governments over Iran's nuclear ambitions, Russia has constructed Iran's nuclear facility at Bushehr, which on August 21, 2010, became the first nuclear power plant to operate in the Middle East.[29] Bushehr is just one of four nuclear complexes that Iran is known to have—its uranium-enrichment facilities at Natanz and Qom and a heavy water reactor at Arak are all under construction—and Bushehr is generally regarded as the least threatening to international security because the IAEA routinely monitors Russian and Iranian activities.

Iran's nuclear program moved forward at a faster pace in the months following the June 2010 UN sanctions, which the Iranians attributed to the launch of the Bushehr facility, according to the *Tehran Times*.[30] On hand at the ribbon cutting ceremony at Bushehr, representatives from Iran and the head of Rusatom, Russia's Atomic Energy Association, stood together. And just prior to the facility's inauguration, Iran's ambassador to Russia said that the successful collaboration at Bushehr meant that Russia "will be given priority for future nuclear cooperation with Iran."[31]

Since 2007, both the Bush administration and now the Obama administration have acquiesced to Russia's development of Bushehr. Covering the story, the *Wall Street Journal* reported that "officials acknowledge the Bushehr project undercuts the U.S.'s efforts to present Tehran as isolated internationally," but they "consented" to Russia's involvement at Bushehr in order to get Russian cooperation on UN sanctions.[32] As a result, the United States, and perhaps more importantly Israel, face another constraint. While it is unlikely that any uranium will be weaponized at Bushehr, it going "hot" means that any military strike against the facility risks dispersing radiation over a civilian population on a scale akin to Chernobyl.[33] For this reason, Jamie Fly, in a "Shadow Government" blog post on *foreignpolicy.com*, conjectures that disabling Bushehr is impossible without "contaminating a large geographic area."[34]

Even if catastrophic civilian exposure to radiation could be averted—a big if—the most likely way to do this would be a special forces ground operation, which does not stand a high probability of success, as the Carter administration learned the last time a similar feat was attempted on Iranian soil. Leaving aside these immense hurdles, any strike, either bombing or special operations, would still risk casualties among the Russian scientists and technicians who are ever-present at Bushehr, creating quite a conundrum given that they "are working on a project that has been blessed by successive U.S. administrations of both political parties."[35] But should a military alternative exclude Bushehr and just focus on the more minatory facilities, it would plausibly drive the Iranians to concentrate their nuclear efforts at Bushehr. In short, by bringing Bushehr into operation Russia has greatly complicated military scenarios against Iran's nuclear facilities.

The status of Iran's nuclear program is shrouded in secrecy, and estimates vary—from 2012 to 2014—about how long it could take Tehran to reach the "breakout" point, when it could easily cross the boundary into having a nuclear bomb. In late August 2010 Iran proposed a "nuclear fuel production consortium" with Russia, whereby "some of the work will be done in Russia" and "some will be done in Iran," according to Ali Akbar Salehi, director of Iran's Atomic Energy Organization.[36] On the surface, this is a rather baffling proposition. Iran claims its program is advancing faster than ever before, yet it is asking for outside assistance. Moreover, the outline of the proposed Iranian nuclear consortium that has been made public is essentially the same as the proposal made by the international community earlier in 2010, namely that Iran cooperate with Russia and France to process its nuclear fuel. France, of course, is left out from Tehran's recent proposal, and the timing suggests that Iran is not progressing at its preferred pace and wants closer cooperation with Russia, which could entail less international oversight and enable more rapid nuclear development.

Russia's nuclear ties with Venezuela are less disconcerting, by comparison. Presidents Chávez and Putin spoke of cooperating on a nuclear facility in Venezuela, but only in November 2008, after years of scuttlebutt, did Russia sign an accord to help build a nuclear facility in Venezuela.[37] Venezuela announced specific plans for Russia to build a nuclear reactor in Venezuela only in October of 2010.

PETRO PLOTS

Crucial to the VIRUS pact is what its leaders don't prate about—oil and gas. During their presidencies, Chávez, Ahmadinejad, and Putin extended state control over not just energy-related industries, but all strategic industries within their countries. This has made state-owned energy companies— Gazprom (Russia), the largest energy company in the world; the National Iranian Oil Company; and Petróleos de Venezuela—appendages of political ambitions. Together these countries possess about a quarter of the world's known oil reserves. When other energy resources are considered—natural gas as well as the major servicing contracts these firms have in other countries—the centrality of these countries' energy assets rises.

Yet U.S. policymakers give little consideration to the energy weapon. Perhaps, as some suggest, this is because U.S. policymakers are generally incapable of tackling long-term problems. The more likely explanation is that any solo attempt to use oil as a political weapon just doesn't work; there are too many alternative sources. Should, say, Venezuela cut off all oil sales to the United States—1.3 million bpd—gas prices would rise at first, maybe by 10 percent, according to a U.S. Government Accountability Office (GAO) study commissioned by Sen. Dick Lugar, but the availability of oil from other producers would soften the blow. Not to mention that Saudi Arabia, which pumps 8 million bpd, has a tacit agreement with Washington to pump more oil if need be in order to offset a catastrophic interruption of U.S. supply. The Saudis could increase production to 10 million bpd if so inclined. This is to say nothing of the 700 million barrels of oil kept in the U.S. strategic petroleum reserve. Acting alone, Venezuela would be the one ultimately hurt from such a move. But cooperating with Iran within OPEC and partnering with Russia outside of OPEC, a concerted effort to manipulate energy markets for political gain could yield results.[38]

Venezuela, Iran, and Russia are coordinating their energy policy. Some of this comes by way of experimenting with new oil and gas cartel strategies. For example, in 2008 a Russian-Venezuelan energy consortium was established to pool each nation's fuel resources to sell oil and gas. A *New York Times* article on the deal, "Russia Flexes Muscles in Oil Deal with Chavez," quotes the Venezuelan president's assessment of the agreement as "a colossus being born."[39] Since then the consortium has expanded operations from Venezuela to Bolivia and Ecuador. Also, Venezuela, Iran, and Russia have initiated talks to form a "gas troika"—a natural gas cartel that would include more than 40 percent of the world's natural gas reserves—though plans have apparently been scuttled since 2009 because of the drop in gas prices and logistical barriers.

Here and now, coordinating with Russia on energy policy offers a tremendous boon to Venezuela and Iran. As the world's largest exporter of hydrocarbons (oil and gas combined), Russia could present a formidable challenge to the OPEC "price hawk" agenda. By not being a member of OPEC Russia can take advantage of supply restrictions to undercut the cartel, selling as much oil as it can pump and thus impairing OPEC's ability to maintain a price ceiling.[40] Historically, Russia has done just that. Yet Russia's opportunism subdued once its energy machinations with Venezuela and Iran began, despite the immense incentive to sell as much as possible as oil prices soared from 2005 to 2008. For its part, Moscow benefits by gaining privileged access to oil and gas projects in Venezuela and Iran. Much more important, though, Russia gains Venezuela and Iran's geostrategic support for its plan to dominate the flow of gas into Europe.

Venezuela, Iran, and Russia could move in unison to drastically limit energy exports and garrote the United States and Europe. Doing so would only be a tad more aggressive than actions they have flirted with on an individual basis. As noted in a 2006 report by the Council on Foreign Relations, "Major energy suppliers—from Russia to Iran to Venezuela—have been increasingly able and willing to use their energy resources to pursue their strategic and political objectives." The report goes on to spell out how the three nations are "increasing America and Europe's vulnerability while constraining an array of foreign policy and national security objectives."[41]

A dramatic push to move prices higher is unlikely in the near term, for three reasons. First, while the United States and Europe have alternative sources for energy imports, Venezuela and Russia do not have similar alternatives for their energy exports—China and India still consume just a fraction as much oil as the West. Second, when it comes to oil the House of Saud is an eight-hundred-pound gorilla that can't be ignored. Third, any drastic move by the VIRUS would be immediately recognized as an act of economic sabotage. The response of energy-importing nations might solidify as in 1990 when Saddam Hussein invaded Kuwait to gain control of its oil reserves. Right now any concerted move to choke off oil from the West will prove suicidal, not homicidal.

The story will change in the near future. China is estimated to have as many cars on its roads as the United States by 2030, and Venezuela is gradually diverting oil shipments from the United States to China. In a world where Asian demand equals that of the West, what would happen if a crisis kept Saudi Arabia from playing its crucial role? In 2006 a terrorist attack was foiled at the gates of the Abqaiq oil-processing plant in Saudi Arabia. Three-quarters of Saudi oil flows through the plant before being piped to a host of refineries and other outlets, making it the true "beating heart of the global economy."[42] In 2007 the Saudi government arrested 172 extremists linked to al Qaeda for scheming to fly planes into a host of Saudi Arabia's oil plants and refineries. A calamity, like a disruption in Saudi Arabia's oil exports, would set the stage for the VIRUS to delay oil shipments; the longer the VIRUS stalled, the higher prices would go. It is a frightfully realistic scenario. Thus, the threat to America stems not so much from its reliance on foreign energy, but rather any instability that affects supply from a crucial energy provider like Saudi Arabia.

Russia's Geostrategic Conundrum

I cannot forecast to you the actions of Russia. It is a riddle, wrapped in a mystery, inside an enigma.
—Winston Churchill, BBC Radio broadcast (October 1, 1939)

Though it covers about one-eighth of the world's landmass, spans eleven time zones, and has twice the amount of shoreline as the United States, Russia is becoming boxed into the middle swath of the Eurasian landmass. Its coasts are inaccessible ice sheets—hence the constant obsession throughout imperial Russian and Soviet history with warm-water ports. Its shrinking population becomes very sparse to the east of the Ural Mountains, and government control is weak over those territories. In the decades ahead, Chinese migration into the eastern third of the country could well result in de facto annexation of Russia's Far East, as the adjoining Chinese provinces have a population density sixty-two times that of the Russian territories.[1] Local Russians estimated in 2004 that ethnic Chinese controlled nearly half of the Siberian economy,[2] just one testament to "what looks like Russia on a map looks a lot more like China on people's faces."[3] Demography and geography portend an ill fate for Mother Russia.

Meanwhile, stewing Chinese rivalries, with India in the Indian Ocean and with Japan and potentially the United States in the Pacific, have led the People's Republic to invest heavily in its navy. Sometime after 2020 China's fleet will grow larger than America's—though it will remain less sophisticated—and is likely to include several nuclear-powered submarines and an aircraft carrier. This emphasis on naval over land power reflects a Chinese desire to secure several islands off its southern and eastern coasts and to protect vital trade routes, including the Straits of Malacca and Taiwan.

China's rise is butting Russia out of East Asia and the Pacific domain. Realizing these ineluctable trends, sometime last decade the Putin administration evidently made the decision to give ground to China, strategically if not literally, while also not standing in the way of Beijing's ravenous attempts to secure its energy needs.

Russia could find itself relegated among the world's large militaries with the classification of "continental land power." This in and of itself is a source of destabilization. Large armies, as opposed to large navies, are intended for sustained long-term occupation of vast lands, and given the crowding out underway in the Pacific and Far East, Russia's military will be left brooding over the land strips and bodies of water it shares with Europe and the Caucasus.

These areas are more likely to fall prey to fortified interpretations of Russia's "near abroad" because of the geopolitical shifts underway. War games between Russia and Belarus codenamed "Zapad" ("West"), as well as more recent military exercises that involved a hypothetical nuclear attack on Warsaw, serve as warning of John J. Mearsheimer's observation from his text on international relations, *The Tragedy of Great Power Politics*: "The most dangerous states in the international system are continental powers with large armies."[4]

Meanwhile, Russia's influence on world energy markets also risks being diluted. Millions of barrels of crude will be introduced onto world markets later this decade from huge discoveries of crude oil off the coast of Brazil, in Venezuela's Orinoco Belt region, and the reintroduction of Iraqi oil. These factors, along with smaller discoveries elsewhere and efficiency gains both in production and consumption in the West, will offset part of Asia's demand.[5] New Russian discoveries notwithstanding, natural gas, not oil, will be where Russia best stands a chance of marshalling enough market control to shape politics and maintain the country's position as an indispensable energy provider.

Accordingly, Russia must extend control over the remaining market where there are few alternatives to Russian energy—Europe. Today Europe relies on Russia's state-owned energy giant Gazprom for more than a quarter of its gas supplies, piped across various countries in Eastern and Central Europe, to keep the heat on. Seven of the twenty-seven EU nations are almost totally dependent on Russian gas; the Baltic nations of Latvia, Lithuania, and Estonia, for example, rely upon Russia for 90 to 100 percent of their energy.[6]

To bypass the transit countries, Gazprom is currently building Nord Stream, a "direct" pipeline that will snake from Russia under the Baltic Sea to Germany. Proponents claim this will facilitate more efficient and direct transportation of gas to Europe. "South Stream" is planned to go from southern Russia under the Black Sea, re-emerge in Bulgaria, and then go on to Italy, also skirting some Central and Eastern European transit states. Should both pipelines become operational, Russia's share of the European gas market would rise from 25 to 33 percent, according to Gazprom projections.[7]

Alas, here too plans are afoot that could reduce Russia's geostrategic and geopolitical influence. Gas companies from Austria, Hungary, Bulgaria, Romania, and Turkey are collectively working on a pipeline, known as Nabucco, to pump gas from Turkmenistan across the Caspian into Austria before splintering through Western Europe. It would never cross into Russian territory.

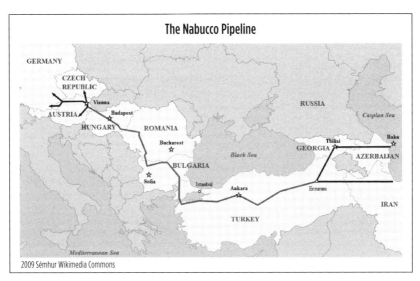

The Nabucco Pipeline

2009 Sémhur Wikimedia Commons

CONTROLLING THE CASPIAN

As former Soviet republics Kazakhstan, Kyrgyzstan, Uzbekistan, Tajikistan, and Turkmenistan formed independent Central Asian nations after the USSR's demise, surrounding regions watched to see how the sparsely populated but ethnically mixed states would congeal as a region. Smart analysis at the time proposed that Kazakhstan, due to its size and extensive border with Russia, would form "the shield" and Uzbekistan "the soul" of the region's independent awakening.[8] To the west, tiny Azerbaijan's development would likely be linked to its neighbor and the only other major power in the region: Iran.

Even before the dust settled on the Soviet Union's collapse Russia tried to (re)assert control over the gas-rich region. Central Asian leaders demurred, suspicious of Russian motives. Claims over the vast energy resources in the Caspian Sea—which is actually the world's largest lake, making the application of maritime law fuzzy—were also being made by Iran. Thus, for most of the 1990s friction between Russia and Iran over the Caspian, along with a wait-and-see approach by outsiders to finding out which nation would emerge as the dominant Central Asian power, delayed attempts to survey and begin extracting gas from the region. American and Argentine wildcatters tried to get at Central Asia's hydrocarbons by building pipelines through an alternative transit site, Afghanistan, but these ventures failed because of civil war and creeping Taliban control.[9] Only after years of impasse did Russia gain the upper hand by reducing its claim over the Caspian, gradually building rapport, and then brokering piecemeal energy agreements with several nations.

In 1998 a U.S.-backed pipeline initiative to transit crude from Azerbaijan to Turkey gained momentum, foiling Russia's plans. Relations between Iran and Russia ebbed, as Russia's "policy of working with Iran to keep the West out of the Caspian had clearly failed," and relations between Moscow and Tehran cratered further in 2001.[10] In July 2001 Iranian gunboats hustled prospector ships from British Petroleum out of an oil field in the Azeri sector of the Caspian, drawing rebukes from both Moscow and Washington. The incident reverberated widely, leading the Caspian states to align themselves with Russia.[11] Iran further isolated itself by insisting on an equal maritime and seabed division of the Caspian Sea at a regional summit held in April 2002. Putin responded, in turn, by calling for large-scale war games in the Caspian, which took place in the first two weeks of August; Iran was the only military player in the region excluded (though Iranian observers did attend). Russian defense minister Sergei Ivanov vaunted the exercises as unprecedented in either Russian or Soviet history.[12] The Iranians saw it as a desperate act of bravado. A commentary in *Iran Daily* charged, "Putin's Russia is aware that Iran's pivotal role in the region could be an obstacle to reviving its lost might in the region and therefore he resorted to military references."[13]

For its part, the Bush administration initially seemed content to share Russia's vision of the Caspian. A moderate degree of Russian control over the sea meant greater security from terrorist attacks on pipelines. It would also help isolate Iran, recently named into the "axis of evil."

Partitioning the Caspian Sea in a traditional maritime manner leaves Iran with the smallest share of any Caspian nation, just 13–14 percent. However, Iran has a powerful hand to sway Azerbaijan away from the Russian orbit. There are an estimated 14–16 million Iranian (or Persian) Azeris in Iran, 50 percent more people than the total population of Azerbaijan. Iranian Azeris hold tremendous clout in Iran, serving as key counselors to Iran's ruling Ayatollahs; they can sway politics in Azerbaijan, too. Iran also maintains strong ties to the government of Azerbaijan to ensure that no liberal impulses get carried over by Iranian Azeris.

Azerbaijan and Iran are inseparably linked, and Russia needs to secure Azerbaijan because the Nabucco pipeline flows through it. By dint of geography, Azerbaijan is "the cork in the Caspian bottle." In his seminal 1997 book, *The Grand Chessboard*, Zbigniew Brzezinski observed,

> An independent Azerbaijan can serve as a corridor for Western access to the energy-rich Caspian Sea basin and Central Asia. Conversely, a subdued Azerbaijan would mean that Central Asia can be sealed off from the outside world and thus rendered politically vulnerable to Russian pressures for reintegration.[14]

Russia can't "seal off" Azerbaijan without Iran because of the Islamic Republic's budding strategic presence in Azerbaijan. Azeri Hezbollah operates there, and though the group isn't a political force capable of toppling the government in Baku, it could be summoned to disrupt the flow of oil or gas through the country: "Iranians are confident that, given the need, a handful of proxies could disable Azerbaijan's Turkey-and-Georgia pipeline with a couple of pounds of explosives."[15] A hostile relationship between Russia and Iran could guarantee that a "non-Russian" alternative for European energy would be a truly independent competitor to Russia's pipelines.

Furthermore, while Russia came to control most of the gas flowing west out of Central Asia through bilateral contracts, it couldn't assume control over Turkmenistan. Turkmenistan can send its gas due south to Iran, skirting the Caspian Sea altogether. Under less hostile circumstances than those weighing on Tehran since 2002, Iran could become a key alternative transit point for Central Asian gas going to Europe. In such a case, Russia's hopes of being the necessary link between Central Asian gas and European consumers would be dashed.

Unlikely as it would have seemed in the mid-1990s, Turkmenistan is emerging as the pivotal producer of Central Asian gas in the twenty-first century; when it comes to plotting new oil and gas transit routes to Europe, Azerbaijan appears to be the key site. To keep the two from servicing the Nabucco project Putin sought rapprochement with Iran after Ahmadinejad's inauguration.

Iran and Russia didn't preclude the government of Azerbaijan from entertaining Western contracts, but they did help make the country a smorgasbord of corruption. Parag Khanna details the situation in his 2008 bestseller *The Second World*:

> The Aliyev regime's political and economic corruption makes it a liability for both Azerbaijan and the West. After all, it is the same regime favored by Russia and Iran precisely because it will play all sides. By cheating a Turkish company out of a contract to upgrade the country's electrical grid, it opened the door to Russia to complete a monopoly over the southern Caucasus power supply, and without a diversified economy, the second major source of income for Azerbaijan remains remittances from the two million Azeris in Russia. Drug smuggling is all but encouraged by politically connected gangs on the Russian and Iranian borders. As a result, Russia continues to hold strong leverage over Azerbaijan's foreign policy, and Iran continues its efforts to exert its sway over its Shi'a.[16]

By sowing mass corruption, Russia and Iran are able to spoil alternatives to their plans.

THE INNOCENTS ABROAD

Even as Russia scurried to corner Turkmenistan and Azerbaijan by forging an alliance with Iran, thereby shoring up control over the Nabucco route, new variables entered into the energy equation. Initially tolerant of Russian influence over the Caspian, the Bush administration began to reorder its preferences. Vice President Dick Cheney threw his weight behind the Nabucco alternative, telling a NATO summit in 2006, "No legitimate interest is served when oil and gas become tools of intimidation or blackmail, either by supply manipulation or attempts to monopolize transportation."[17] President Putin and Gazprom leaders bristled, emphasizing the need for more direct routes while archly enlisting the services of high-level European leaders, like former German Chancellor Gerhard Shröder, to advance Gazprom's interest in the EU.

In tandem, democratic "revolutions" against Russian influence brought pro-Western presidents to office, especially in Georgia and Ukraine. The "near abroad" was becoming less docile by turning toward Europe and the United States and away from Russia, forcing the Kremlin to assert its "privileged interests" and forcefully peel back the sovereignty of several of the Soviet Union's former satellites.

In August 2008 Russia invaded Georgia under the pretext of protecting human rights in two autonomous pro-Russia enclaves, Abkhazia and South Ossetia. Meanwhile, Ukraine was being subjected to a most extreme form of energy blackmail from 2007 to 2009. Russia cut off the flow of gas to Ukraine on several occasions. In so doing, "Moscow cared less about economic disagreements than about undermining Ukraine's pro-Western president . . . and building support in the West for Russia's plans to bypass Ukraine's gas pipeline system with a new network by emphasizing that Ukraine was an unreliable transit country."[18]

Given the limited possibilities for transporting gas from Central Asia to Europe, Georgia and Ukraine emerged in the last decade as "geopolitical pivots." They aren't individually powerful nations but they are crucial transit locales for any nation seeking to control the flow of gas to Europe. Ukraine is the most important link in Moscow's short-term designs—almost all of Russia's current pipelines run through Ukraine—but under the Nabucco scenario Georgia emerges as the most important link, as it, along with Azerbaijan and Iran, are the only Nabucco transit sites outside of Europe's orbit.

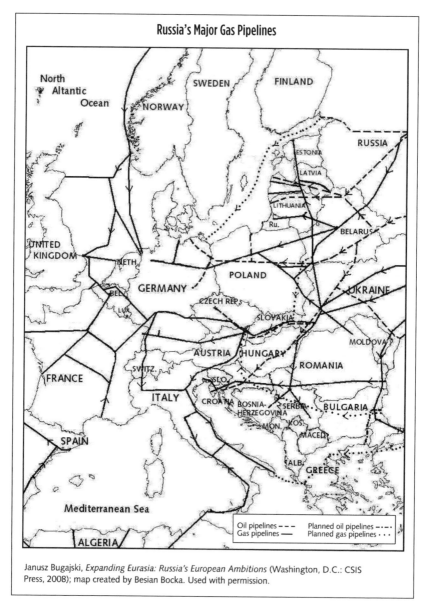

Russia's Major Gas Pipelines

Janusz Bugajski, *Expanding Eurasia: Russia's European Ambitions* (Washington, D.C.: CSIS Press, 2008); map created by Besian Bocka. Used with permission.

And unlike other former Soviet satellites, Georgia and Ukraine are still "in play." They have regularly scheduled elections, governing classes that share close ties with the West, and market-based economies that rely less and less on Russia. But unlike Bulgaria, Turkey, Estonia, or Poland, Georgia and Ukraine are not members of the EU or NATO. They are mid-stride,

Westernizing, but not yet fully part of the West, and so they are still susceptible to Russian pressure.

Still unresolved, claims of privileged interests over Ukraine and Georgia
are but the tip of a rapidly melting iceberg when it comes to Russia's
geostrategic moves.

THE ARCTIC PRIZE

Losing grip on traditional spheres of influence has led Russia to scamper
for a strategic toehold in an emerging sphere, the Arctic. In the past half-
decade several acts of bravado presaged the changing course of Russian
naval strategy. In 2007 two Russian subs and a nuclear-powered icebreaker
planted a Russian flag on the North Pole's seabed, raising eyebrows among
the other nations with territorial claims to the Arctic—Canada, Denmark,
Norway, and the United States. Two years later, in as much splendor as can
be mustered in Siberia, Vladimir Putin took a submarine ride to the bottom
of Lake Baikal, the world's deepest lake. These are scientifically legitimate,
arguably overdue, acts of exploration, but the real application of such ventures appears to be arctic navigation. Russia also recently resumed nuclear-
armed flights over the Arctic for the first time since the end of the Cold War.

No longer is the barren ice sheet at polar north just an outpost for scien-
tific research. "The great melt" is underway. Today the Arctic ice cap is less
than half the size it was fifty years ago. Perhaps 90 billion barrels of oil and
30 percent of the world's undiscovered natural gas lie at the bottom of the
Arctic, according to recent U.S. Geological Survey estimates.[19] Furthermore,
as Arctic sea-lanes open in the next decade, the cost of freight shipping
could drop by 20–25 percent in many cases. The Arctic is quite possibly
the world's greatest untapped resource, and yet no prevailing legal regimes
govern the rules of the road, and maritime claims are widely disputed.

In recent years Russia has posited varying claims over the Arctic.
According to one, Russia's control of the Arctic extends to the Lomonosov
Ridge, the drop-off that marks the end of the Eurasian landmass. By this
reading half of the Arctic Ocean would be Russian domain. A more general
measurement extends Arctic rights based on the slice of sovereign territory
closest to the North Pole. By this measure, Russia has rights to a 150° arc of
Arctic territory, or 40 percent of Arctic (150 ÷ 360 = .40). Of course, some

influential Russians, like the celebrated Soviet explorer Artur Chilingarov, who orchestrated the flag-planting feat, insist, "The Arctic is ours and we should manifest our presence."[20] A more realistic assessment is that Russia will enjoy legal claims to 40–50 percent of the territory.

Legal considerations aside, in practical terms Russia is likely to assume control of a vast Arctic seascape. Russia dominates Arctic navigation with eighteen icebreakers currently in operation, compared to the U.S. fleet of two icebreakers, giving Russia a huge military advantage. Furthermore, Russia is on the verge of christening the Arctic as an economic outlet, extracting gas from its Arctic territory in the Barents Sea. Shortly after Vladimir Putin became president, Gazprom solicited bids for development of the massive Shtokman gas field that is reported to contain 3.8 trillion cubic meters of natural gas— more than enough gas to power the world for more than a year.[21] In 2005 it narrowed the list of partner finalists down to Statoil, Norsk Hydro, Total, Chevron, and ConocoPhillips, only to dismiss them all in 2006, most likely because the project would have destined the gas to the United States, providing economic benefit to Russia but not furthering its strategic objectives.

In 2007 Gazprom contracted with France's Total and Statoil to begin work in Shtokman. If this partnership advances to recovery, the gas supplies will be split, half going to the United States and half going to Europe via Nord Stream.[22] To the extent that Gazprom can overcome the logistical challenges—operating in the dark for months at a time and devising platforms to deal with icebergs melting off from the polar icecap—it will be able to utilize its emerging Arctic primacy to tighten its hold on Europe's energy market.

These forays are unsurprising, given that Russia has long been unchallenged by global powers in these parts of the world. Furthermore, extending its dominance over tiny Georgia, larger Ukraine, and the promising but unproven Arctic are unlikely to offset the geostrategic headwinds of Asian development. Russia will need to gain sway elsewhere if it is to remain an energy superstate and a military power of global import.

Enter Venezuela.

A CARIBBEAN CONCOCTION

Russia's reach into the United States' "backyard," Latin America and the Caribbean, is astonishing. If America has ever had an imperial writ it is the

Monroe Doctrine (1823), which promulgated the idea that any foreign power's presence in Latin America would be considered a clear danger to U.S. national security. America first whet its imperial appetite in the Caribbean, instigating the Spanish-American War in 1898, which led to the liberation—or, annexation—of Cuba, the Dominican Republic, and Puerto Rico, giving the United States de facto control of 85 percent of Caribbean real estate. In the decades that followed U.S. presidents showed no qualms about intervening to keep the region under wraps. From 1900 to 1930, U.S. forces invaded a Latin American nation with a Caribbean coast almost twenty times. Since the end of World War II the United States has overthrown governments in the Dominican Republic (1965), Grenada (1983), and Panama (1989) in order to secure its interests in the region, to say nothing of U.S. involvement in Guatemala in 1954 and Cuba in 1961 and 1962.

While the Caribbean has long been regarded as the "American Mediterranean," the point of comparison being imperial Rome, the logic of intervention has always followed the Monroe Doctrine. Sending in the Marines had little to do with any Latin American government posing a threat to the United States. Rather, U.S. policy has been guided by a fear that European powers might establish a base in nearby Latin America to attack the United States.[23]

Yet after more than 150 years of a steadfast security policy, interspersed with bouts of imperial fever, American primacy over Latin America has ebbed. Primarily this owes to a strategic shift toward the Middle East. US military deployments now focus on Iraq and Afghanistan, as well as to a beefed up presence in tense sea-lanes like the Strait of Hormuz and off the Horn of Africa. This posture diverts troops from Latin America: in 2001, there were fourteen thousand U.S. military personnel in the region, most stationed at Guantánamo Bay, Cuba, and various other Caribbean posts. By 2004, the total number of troops in Latin America had dwindled to two thousand.[24]

A number of secondary factors also contribute to a de-emphasis of the Caribbean. Fewer Cubans and Haitians are attempting to float to Florida than in the past, easing the need for a deterrent presence in the area, so the U.S. Coast Guard now focuses more intently on drug interdiction. After 9/11, efforts were redoubled to seal off the south Atlantic coast from drugs, hastening a transition already under way. Instead of shipping cocaine from Colombia to the United States, the land route through Central America and Mexico has become the preferred manner for trafficking narcotics. Interdiction efforts have consequently shifted to the U.S.-Mexican border instead of the Caribbean. Finally, reinforcing these specific trends, U.S. naval strategy is shifting from a classical deterrent approach to security to a cooperative approach. Transnational threats such as piracy require many navies cooperating. As this strategy unfolds the United States is being less prickly about exclusive domains and more willing to allow other nations to play a part in patrolling the world's waters.

In the propeller wake of the U.S. Navy, Venezuela invited a Russian gambol. Joint Venezuelan-Russian naval exercises in late 2008 marked the opening salvo. Four Russian vessels, headed by the nuclear-powered warship *Peter the Great*, partook in exercises over four days with the Venezuelan forces. Chávez tried to play it up, telling the Associated Press that the Yankees could "go ahead and squeal." President Medvedev's explanation for the move was more telling: "With many of those states in the Soviet period we had rather powerful, serious relations. The time has now come to restore those relations."[25] Colombian leaders sounded an alarm; Washington shrugged.

Chávez then offered to host a Russian airbase in Venezuela. That too was dismissed as grandstanding, and for its part the Russian government downplayed the proposal as merely "theoretical."[26] But Maj. Gen. Anatoly Zhikharev, the Russian Air Force's chief of staff for long-range aviation, inspected facilities at La Orchila Island off Venezuela's coast, apparently sometime between November 2008 and March 2009. He told reporters in Moscow that the airstrip on the island was being extended to comport with the requirements of Russia's long-range bombers, after which it would be "ideal" for Russia's TU-160 "Blackjack" strategic bombers, an aircraft with a fuel range of 7,500 miles.[27] Most analysts insist that if Russia gained such a base in Venezuela (Cuba has been rumored as another site, but that is almost inconceivable), it would not pose a direct threat to the United States.[28]

This requires a truly naive interpretation of U.S. national security. An established Russian presence could possibly serve two strategic objectives. First, Russia could insure any military move made by Chávez in the Andes or Caribbean. Any bout of belligerence, any border skirmish, or creeping territorial claim would be quickly resolved in Venezuela's favor because Russian bombers would be ready to join the fray should tensions escalate. This is currently unlikely, but it isn't an inconceivable future scenario, especially if NATO were to intervene militarily in Moscow's near abroad.

Second, and of much more strategic import, Russia would gain a trump card over NATO policy. Any talk of full membership for Georgia or Ukraine would be moot, and any attempt to deploy strategic missiles on land or anywhere else in Central of Eastern Europe could be stymied because of a tit-for-tat escalation of Russia's military presence around Venezuela. The Kremlin stated in 2008 that its relations with Venezuela were a "counterweight to US influence."[29] True to order, a base off the coast of Venezuela would allow Russia a major bargaining chip over NATO policy.

ALL ROADS LEAD TO ROME

According to Zbigniew Brzezinski, "Russia's only real geostrategic option . . . is Europe."[30] Brzezinski, a former U.S. national security adviser, adumbrated that the rise of Asian powers would drive Russia to focus on Europe in order to avoid "geopolitical isolation." For all the changes that have transpired in the past fourteen years, Europe remains the real geostrategic prize for Russia. Its only hope for global power status comes from being an indispensable regional power. To achieve this Russia must dominate the energy corridor that sweeps from Central Asia to Europe. Failing to do so locks Russia into its current anomalous status—a second-rate power with an SC veto.

The reemergence of Russia's superpower ambitions first involved a concerted campaign to make Europe more dependent on Russian energy. Through energy cutoffs and invasion Russia managed to cow Ukraine and Georgia, the geopolitical pivots in Russia's energy corridor to Europe. But firmly exercising its "privileged interests" over these countries piqued business and political leaders in the Western world. The effects of Russia's energy cutoff to Ukraine in January 2009 spread throughout much of Europe. Talk of a "new cold war" became rampant. Russia's heavy-handedness renewed Western interest in finding an alternative to Russian-supplied energy for Europe. Short-term means were sacrificing the long-term end.

Moscow's tone has changed of late. Nicholas Patrushev, author of the Kremlin's official security strategy to 2020 and the former head of the

Russian Federal Security Service (FSB), says Russia will pursue a foreign policy to "exclude costly confrontation."[31] Over the past two years Russia has used more carrots and fewer sticks, offering concessions and helping to clarify territorial boundaries. On April 27, 2010, Norway and Russia signed an agreement to evenly divide a maritime boundary that had been contested for forty years. The Norwegian prime minister spoke of it as a historic day for the easing of relations between the two nations; President Medvedev said, "I believe this will open the way for many joint projects, especially in the area of energy."[32]

Ukraine also felt the Kremlin's softer side. In Ukraine's 2010 presidential election held in February, Moscow's preferred candidate, Viktor Yanukovich, defeated the more Western-oriented Yulia Timoshenko. Timoshenko is often criticized as a political opportunist, a charge with some merit, but when forced she ultimately sides with the West, favoring closer relations with Europe and the United States over Russia. Within three months of Yanukovich taking office Russia offered long-term discounts of 30 percent to Ukraine in exchange for Kiev agreeing to extend the lease on Russia's naval base at the Ukrainian port of Sevastopol to 2042. This agreement might save cash-strapped Ukraine $40 billion over the next decade. Russia also agreed to demarcate its land borders with Ukraine, a move that's been delayed since the collapse of the Soviet Union. So that boundaries don't hamper business, Prime Minister Putin now advocates "merging" Gazprom with Ukraine's state gas monopoly, Naftogaz.[33]

However, the seductive ploy of cheap gas irked some. On the day that the Ukrainian parliament voted on the lease extension, fistfights broke out on the floor of the Ukrainian parliament, Western-oriented opposition lawmakers pelted the speaker with eggs, and a smoke grenade went off. Minority parties claimed that Ukraine was "selling its sovereignty" to Russia.

In economic terms, Russia's subsea pipelines are three to four times more expensive than expanding overland routes via Poland or Ukraine.[34] The project costs of Nord Stream and South Stream are no longer economically viable if gas prices remain significantly below 2007 levels. And yet Russia previously agreed to generous terms with Turkmenistan. Given concessions to Ukraine and Turkmenistan, Russia can't hope to realize a profit within a decade of Nord Stream coming online, which will be in 2016 at the earliest.

Unless, of course, it acquires a virtual lock on the European gas market so that it can then resort to monopolistic pricing.

RUSSIA'S GEOSTRATEGIC IMPERATIVE

To the extent that the world is gaining a new ocean as a result of global warming, it will be one dominated by Russia. With the Caribbean added to the mix, Russia stands to gain an ocean *and* a sea, solid consolation for any perceived lost opportunities in the Pacific. But even in these temperately opposite waters Russia's ambitions are ultimately Eurocentric. When Russia begins to recover Arctic gas much of it will be fed into Nord Stream. In Latin America, Russia's strategic motive for bases has little to do with direct control of energy resources in the Americas or threatening Washington. Rather it is to gain a bargaining chip to halt NATO enlargement.

Meanwhile, partnership with Iran is corralling the only alternative sources of Russian gas to Europe. Over the past two to three years Iran and Russia have been able to piece together agreements with Turkmenistan and Azerbaijan that ensure very little gas will be transported from Central Asia to Europe without a Russian nod. The arrangement already helps Iran, allowing the Islamic Republic to draw in much needed foreign investment. Writes M. K. Bhadrakumar, a former Indian ambassador, "The Turkmen-Iranian pipeline mocks the US's Iran policy."[35] The benefit to Russia is the probable evisceration of the Nabucco project. From 2005 to 2009 Iran has been an unceasing energy partner. Invasion has compelled compliance in Georgia, where Russian troops remained for more than two years after the 2008 war ended. Turkmenistan has been given lavish price assurances so that Russia will be preferred over any other outlet. Europe's reliance on Russia as an energy provider has "gained irreversible momentum," though it may not be fully realized for several more years.[36] What appeared a foreboding geopolitical landscape a decade ago is being transformed.

A VIRUS Spawns

I want such buses to circulate in Venezuela.
—Hugo Chávez to Belarusian President Alexander Lukashenko (September 9, 2009)

During the talks it has been decided to launch assembly of buses from Belarusian spare parts in Syria. The sides have also signed an agreement on cooperation in the sphere of higher education, agriculture and even in the sphere of the Earth's remote sensing. However, observers believe that publication of the agreement is just an addition, and at the same time "a disguise," for the contracts that bring real money to Belarus . . . agreements on arms sales.
—*Kommersant* (Moscow), from an article titled "Belarus and Syria Hide Arms in Buses" (July 28, 2010)

The VIRUS quickly spread to incorporate Belarus and Syria, two states long known to be under the paws of Moscow and Tehran, respectively. Disentangling trade between these countries exposes how the VIRUS disguises illicit arms sales by using Belarus and Syria as go-betweens.

THE LAST DICTATOR OF EUROPE FINDS NEW FRIENDS

Belarus is rightly regarded as a vestige of Russian empire. In 1996 the two countries formed a "Union State"; as a result, the Belarusian economy is completely reliant upon Russia, and carries little weight on the world stage.[1] Belarus's president, Alexander Lukashenko, has systematically eliminated political opposition, and muzzled free speech since he came to power in 1994, earning him the moniker "the last dictator of Europe." Branded an "outpost of tyranny" by Secretary of State Condoleezza Rice in 2005, Belarus is so isolated today that Lukashenko can no longer obtain a travel visa to the United States or European Union. Because of these conditions, there isn't much reason for either politicians or businessmen to spend any time in Belarus; if a matter involves the small country it is usually best handled by landing in Moscow. Yet, since 2006 Belarus has developed cozy relations with two other nations—Venezuela and Iran.

From 2006 to 2008, Chávez and Lukashenko met five times. Their "strategic partnership" includes joint exploration of Venezuelan energy fields and Belarusian investment in construction and farming projects in Venezuela; and Chávez promised to provide Belarus with enough oil for the rest of the century. In March 2010 Chávez signed a deal with Lukashenko to provide Belarus with 80,000 barrels of crude oil a month.[2] This is an interesting wrinkle that apparently works against overarching VIRUS loyalties; by guaranteeing oil to Belarus, Venezuela enables Lukashenko to reduce his country's reliance on oil and gas flowing from Moscow.

Chávez wasted no time in shipping the oil. Lukashenko hurried to find the best way to take receipt of the 550,000 barrels of oil destined for his landlocked country.[3] All of Belarus's European neighbors with a Baltic coastline pitched in to help: Estonia, Latvia, and Lithuania. Lithuania appeared to be the best route, and was none too sad about the transit fee it stood to collect. But the Baltic states, all members of the EU, also saw the Venezuela deal as a positive sign for their atavist neighbor. By increasing trade with Belarus, especially trade related to gas, the Baltic nations could weaken Moscow's hold on Belarus and bring the country into the European fold.[4] This stood to have ripple effects for human rights and the prospects for real democracy in Belarus.

Surprisingly, Russia's ambassador to Belarus Alexander Surikov condoned Lukashenko's move to diversify energy partners, noting that Moscow sought greater diversification as well.[5] Ambassador Surikov then added two caveats. First, Russia expected increased usage of Russian parts in the processing of Belarus's oil imports. Second, and more telling, should there be "large oil supplies from Venezuela," i.e., enough to reduce Belarus's energy dependence on Moscow, then Moscow might "renegotiate" the duties attached to the oil it sold to Belarus, as laid out by the Belarus-Russia Protocol.[6]

Ninety days after Chávez and Lukashenko spread ink for oil, Gazprom started cutting gas supplies to Belarus, beginning with a 15 percent reduction. Gazprom chief executive Alexei Miller announced cuts would go up "day-by-day," eventually reaching 80 percent of total volume.[7] And all of a sudden Belarus had a debt, which Moscow said stood at $200 million. The debt would grow to $500–$600 million by the end of 2010, and Gazprom stood ready to collect.[8] Things got unusually tart. Belarus tried to barter the debt down, but Dmitry Medvedev ruled out repayment in "pies, butter, cheese or other forms of payment."[9] Within days Gazprom had cut gas supplies to Belarus by 60 percent.[10] Then, less than a week later, Moscow declared that Belarus had paid most of the debt. Gas service was restored. As with Moscow's energy cutoffs to Ukraine, once a wide swath of Europe started to feel the pinch Russia relented: 25 percent of Russia's gas to Europe flows through Belarus, and when Lukashenko ordered a halt of gas supplies to Europe, EU states started to complain.[11] EU energy commissioner Günther Oettinger described the debacle as "an attack" on the whole EU.[12]

Belarus' relations with Russia returned to normal by mid-September 2010. A chastened Lukashenko proclaimed his country a "reliable base and outpost" for Russia once again.[13]

BELARUS-IRANIAN RELATIONS

Putting the shoe on the other foot, in April 2006 Belarus and Iran signed a series of economic and trade accords, the first substantive agreements since they established formal relations in 1992. Later in 2006 Lukashenko visited Tehran, where he affirmed Iran's right to nuclear energy. The two leaders issued joint statements pledging to work against a unipolar world and to ensure one another's "stability and security."[14] By mid-2007 Iran and Belarus had also declared a "strategic partnership" aimed at joint economic development and opposition to American power. Among their publicly announced projects, the most significant is a $500 million deal to jointly develop the Jofair oil field near Iran's border with Iraq.[15] Iran also opened a bank in Belarus, purportedly to finance joint investment deals, but the U.S. Treasury sanctioned it, too, for money laundering.[16]

Venezuela and Iran's real interest in Belarus, the only reason why any nation that doesn't share a border with the former Soviet republic is interested in currying favor with Lukashenko, is arms. Belarus is a key locale for retrofitting Russian arms to make their origins untraceable. Lukashenko's government is highly corrupt, as one would imagine, and has a tradition of selling arms to terrorists. In 2001, for example, an investigation by the European branch of the *Wall Street Journal* implicated Belarus in the sale of $500 million in arms to Hamas, as well as sales to such state sponsors of terrorism as Iran, Syria, Saddam's Iraq, and Omar Hassan Ahmad al-Bashir's Sudan.[17] Moisés Naím in his 2005 bestselling book on the world's thriving black markets, *Illicit*, singled out Belarus as a "geopolitical black hole."[18] Tiny Belarus ranks as the world's eleventh-largest arms dealer, and off-the-books transactions certainly far surpass the stated figures. This concern led Congress to pass the Belarus Arms Transfers Accountability Act of 2009 in order to get the Secretary of State to undertake an annual study of just how much and what type of arms Belarus is selling. The text of H.R. 4436 cites Belarusian cooperation with two countries in particular, Iran and Venezuela, as a threat to U.S. national security.[19]

According to Michael Ledeen, a hawkish terrorism analyst in the United States, the Quds Force keeps a "considerable presence" in Belarus just to procure Russian arms.[20] In 2009 both Iranian and Russian media reported that Lukashenko was selling to Iran Russian-made Iskander-M short-range missiles—a "quasi-ballistic" missile system with a range of 310 miles.[21] More troubling still, since 2008 reports have regularly surfaced that Belarus was prepared to sell S-300 systems to Iran. In April 2010 Iran's semi-official Fars news agency reported that Iran had, in fact, acquired S-300s from Belarus; Belarus and Iran both deny it.[22]

The smoke-and-mirrors effect around the system benefits Tehran. If Tehran can cast doubt in the minds of Western military planners, especially Israeli planners, about Tehran's actual capability to defend a nuclear site from attack, air strike calculations become much more complex. Belarus, by serving as a legitimate alternative source through which Iran can acquire the S-300s, confers some of the deterrent effect of the S-300s.

If Iran gets the S-300s, Belarus's profuse arms trafficking will make it hard to pin the blame on Russia. In late October 2010, and just three weeks after President Medvedev categorically denied that Russia would deliver S-300s to Iran, reports began to circulate that Russia would send them to Venezuela. This, in turn, led to speculation that Venezuela would serve as a back channel for transporting S-300s from Russia to Iran. Such a handover has been made more feasible because Chávez, having visited Moscow in mid-October

2010 and then Tehran a few days later, announced that Venezuela and Iran planned to create an exclusive new shipping company to send oil and possibly other goods to Iran.

Similarly, Syria provides an extra layer of subterfuge when it comes to VIRUS international relations. Long viewed as an extension of Iranian power to the Levant, the Mediterranean side of the Middle East, Syria has historically trafficked arms from Iran to Hezbollah and Hamas. Syria is also a training ground and refuge for insurgents. However, its relations with Russia and Venezuela are a recent phenomenon.

Chávez became the first Venezuelan president to visit Syria in 2006, laying the groundwork for an "anti-imperialist" union.[23] As with the other bilateral ties between VIRUS members and minions, fulsome praise is mixed with grand vision. When Syrian president Bashar al-Assad visited Caracas on June 24–25, 2010, Chávez proclaimed, "Arab civilization and our civilization, the Latin American one, are being summoned in this new century to play the fundamental role of liberating the world . . . from the imperialism and capitalist hegemony that threaten the human species. Syria and Venezuela are at the vanguard of this struggle." In response, Assad hailed Chávez as an "Arab leader" and said the two nations, as well as Iran, had the right to develop nuclear energy.[24]

In advancing their union, Syria and Venezuela have pledged full military cooperation and signed more than a dozen economic initiatives, including, for example, a plan for Syria to begin distributing olive oil to Latin America, using Venezuela as its regional base.[25] Most important to their economic agenda is a plan to boost Syria's petroleum output: Syria's oil production has dropped steadily, from 590,000 bpd in 1996 to around 340,000 bpd in 2010.[26] Venezuela agreed to build an oil refinery in Syria, and Iran agreed to provide the financing, which would lift Syrian oil production, but so far the plan has yet to be put into action.

Although Venezuela's relationship with Syria suggests a broad political and economic union, here, too, relations center on illicit ties. Problem is, Syria and Iran's murky relations are so interwoven it can be impossible to tease out all the necessary distinctions. Much of the illicit trade, be it in people or things, between Syria and Venezuela went aboard the Caracas-Damascus-Tehran flights. Álvaro Vargas Llosa, a Peruvian commentator on

Latin America and world affairs, has coined the Venezuela-Iran-Syria grouping an "axis shrugged," unified by their ambition to spread terrorism, but collectively disregarded by the West.[27]

By comparison, Russia's relationship with Damascus more narrowly focuses on arms and nuclear energy; Israel is the primary victim of these ties. President Bashar al-Assad of Syria expressed his gratitude for the arms provided by Russia during the 2006 war between Israel and Hezbollah, vowing to "never forget how Russia stood by us during the battle for the Golan [Heights]" against Israel.[28] In the years since, Israel has urged Russia to cease arms deals with Syria, calling into question Syria's ability to pay. Said one Israeli diplomat, "Syria at the present time cannot afford to pay for this sophisticated weaponry, indeed, it has hardly enough money to buy food for its citizens. One can only wonder what is the real reason behind this dubious deal."[29]

Russian officials almost certainly make arms deals with the Assad government knowing the weapons will end up in the hands of Hamas or Hezbollah. Of course, no Russian president would openly boast of sending arms to Hezbollah or Hamas, but President Medvedev's visit to Syria in 2010 included a meeting with exiled Hamas leader Khaled Mashaal, which raised the hackles of the Israeli government.[30] In fact, Russia does not list either Hamas or Hezbollah as a terrorist organization and has even invited the group's leaders to Moscow.[31]

Beyond the economic rationale, many analysts see Russia's moves as an attempt to dampen any possible rapprochement between Syria and the United States. Certainly Russia's arms sales have precipitated Syrian cooperation on energy matters. In fact, Syria and Russia's most recent arms deals were announced in tandem with Syria's declaration that Gazprom would take a leading role in Syria's oil and gas industry. In a further turn of the screw, Medvedev assured Assad that "cooperation on atomic energy could get a second wind" after Syria's lone nuclear reactor was bombed by Israel in 2007.[32]

A SHORT HISTORY OF TRACTORS

Perusing the various "strategic partnerships" between Venezuela and Iran, or Belarus and Venezuela, or Iran and Belarus, turns up a bit of an anomaly. Though most of these partnerships start out quite vague, heralding only an increase in trade so that each country "does not need the United States to survive," when specific agreements emerge the second most frequently cited industry targeted for cooperation, after oil and gas, is tractors and tractor parts. Why tractors?

In his excellent study on Venezuela's development entitled *The Magical State: Nature, Money, and Modernity in Venezuela*, City University of New York (CUNY) anthropologist Fernando Coronil describes the factors complicating Venezuelan agriculture. He cites feasibility studies from the mid-1990s that indicate Venezuela's demand for tractors was on the order of four thousand units annually, large enough to support only one domestic tractor plant. Even then, Coronil posits that the plant would require generous state support to stay operational.[33] An additional complication involves maintenance: when tractors break down they can't be taken to a local mechanic's shop; they must be serviced on site. This created a precarious milieu: "Foreign tractor producers had been obliged to submit bids for the production of tractors. For some of them the local market was not large enough to justify industrial investment but was sufficiently lucrative to entice them to invest in productive facilities in order to preserve their commercial presence."[34] While the firm that wins the contract would have a captive market, this scenario means the government must close off the tractor market to all other manufacturers, either by imposing quotas or tariffs. The government would be granting a monopoly to a foreign firm. Otherwise, the investment required for selling and servicing tractors in Venezuela simply wouldn't be worth the cost.

Assessing this situation, a pragmatic policymaker might overlook capitalist mantra and argue the best way to solve the problem would be to solicit competitive bids for a foreign tractor producer to have a monopoly contract over Venezuela's market for a designated period of time. A socialist, by contrast, could argue that a state-owned tractor manufacturer offered the best solution. "Venetractor," as it might be called, might become a reliable provider of tractors and tractor parts, employ hundreds if not thousands of workers, and even eventually become a badge of national pride. Although it may not turn a profit in the short-term, it would be a social enterprise with tangible benefits for Venezuelan society, similar to the national champion firms in Europe.

One might expect the Chávez government to adopt the latter track, seizing the opportunity to further realize "Bolivarian socialism" in an industry the government is clearly preoccupied with. After all, not only has Chávez aggressively nationalized all industries deemed "strategic" to the welfare of the Bolivarian Republic of Venezuela, but Article 305 of Venezuela's constitution, a product of Mr. Chávez's first year in office, espouses "sustainable" food security and pledges state financial and commercial resources to "achieve strategic levels of self-sufficiency" in food production.[35]

However, this hasn't been the case at all. From 1999 to 2004, the last year data is available, the total stock of operational tractors in Venezuela held more or less constant, ranging from an estimated forty-eight to forty-nine thousand units.[36] In March 2006 VenIran, a joint Venezuela-Iran tractor company, began producing forty tractors a week. But the thousands of tractors meant to form a "nucleus of endogenous development" soon sputtered; rifts between Venezuelan workers and Iranian management emerged and resulted in a workers strike. Meanwhile, farmers, at first grateful for the subsidized loans and reasonable price of the bright red VenIrans, soon grew tired of the "crappy" Iranian tractors.[37] (Empirical evidence supports this last normative claim. According to a research paper by a group of agricultural engineers at Tehran University, the life expectancy of an Iranian tractor is thirteen years. Life expectancy for similar models of American and Japanese tractors is estimated to be thirty years.[38]) At the outset, VenIran production aimed, over time, to use 100 percent Venezuelan parts. However, the latest report on the VenIran tractors, in September 2008, noted that 18 percent of the tractor's parts were made in Venezuela, according to *Iran Daily*, an English-language trade publication put out by the Iranian government.[39]

In lieu of "endogenous development," since 2008 Venezuela has opted to simply buy foreign tractors. It can be difficult to ascertain exactly what goods—and how many—are flowing into Venezuela because the government now controls all ports and discloses information as it sees fit, but statistics from export countries give some sense of recent tractor imports.[40] In 2009 Venezuela imported 400 tractors from Argentina; in 2010 Venezuela agreed to import 1,000 tractors from Belarus, as well as 500–750 from China. All the while, Iranian tractor imports continued. When the final numbers are tallied they fall well short of the four thousand–plus figure one would expect the annual demand for tractors to be in Venezuela. Yet since 2007 Venezuela has actually exported dozens of tractors through the Hugo sphere and also to Sudan, then opened a VenIran plant in Bolivia, a country not known for its fertile terrain.

This arrangement doesn't dovetail with the economic edicts of capitalism, socialism, or common sense. It's a loser no matter how one looks at it. Importing tractors from Belarus and Iran, two countries not reputed as tractor manufacturers, only ensures shoddy equipment, almost guaranteeing replacement parts will be needed on an ongoing basis. But because farm equipment parts are not generally interchangeable, replacements will be required from several different countries. Or else Venezuela will just have to ask for a refund, as it did in 2006 when farmer cooperatives in Bailadores, in the southwestern state of Mérida, reported widespread defects in the engines, gearboxes, and transmissions of Chinese tractors.[41] (The president of the local cattleman association noted that the eighty-horsepower tractors weren't suited for work in hilly terrain.)

Perhaps some sense can be made of Venezuela's tractor-importing tactics in light of events on December 30, 2008. On that day, Turkish authorities at the port of Mersin detained an Islamic Republic of Iran Shipping Lines (IRISL) vessel headed from the Islamic Republic to Venezuela. Upon inspection, twenty-two containers marked "tractor parts" instead contained lab equipment suitable for producing high-grade bombs and explosives.[42] To cast more doubt on the tractor trade, Dr. Norman Bailey, president of the Institute for Global Economic Growth, in his testimony before various House subcommittees on October 27, 2009, claimed that Iran "produces weapons in the [VenIran] 'tractor' plant in Bolivia."[43]

The Iranians may be the world's savviest illicit traders. One time U.S. inspectors interdicted an Iranian shipment of "olives" only to discover they contained C-4 explosives shaped into oblong balls and painted like olives, and sealed in cans.[44] And the ongoing need for tractor replacement parts means large cargo shipments of bulky crates. "Tractor parts" headed to Venezuela may turn out to be lab equipment for bomb making. Or, what's just as likely, "tractor parts" could be industrial products that have a dual use.

COMPLEX DEPENDENCE

Globalization's scaffolding is what social scientists term "complex interdependence": lots of governments, banks and other businesses, and civic organizations, all trying to get what they need from some other party.[45] It's a complex web of pledges, agreements, and semi-formal understandings. And each player is more or less dependent upon its partners in order to meet its goals. The outcome is a web of far-flung actors trying to make the best deal for themselves while recognizing that they will have to enter into similar arrangements in the future, so they try to keep a good reputation.

Complex interdependence has been on tepid display in countries like Belarus, Bolivia, Ecuador, and Syria. In previous decades relatively few multinationals operated in these countries, and foreign relations have been rather simple because diplomacy only involved a handful of governments. In recent years, though, the VIRUS has exploited this isolation to manufacture a system of *complex dependence*—a dizzying ball of trade ties that masks the movement of arms, oil, and equipment that can be used for civilian or military purposes. Unlike the basic dependence of, say, Belarus on the Russian economy, complex dependence has many of the trappings of complex interdependence: pledges of foreign investment from state-owned energy companies, fawning diplomacy, and developmental aid coming in from not one but two or three nations, all of which give the impression of integration and development. Belarus can imagine itself the next Estonia and Ecuador the next Panama, all without the hassle of uncomfortable economic and political reforms, or transparency. Unfortunately, it's a canard.

Rather than becoming more integrated and developed, Belarus and Syria are becoming more suspect. These countries are ceding a slice of their sovereignty to the VIRUS partnership in exchange for pledges of economic support. Head of state visits give the impression of political and economic substance, even if it doesn't exist.

Belarus and Syria add elbows to the distribution of arms sales, not only from Russia to Iran in violation of UN sanctions, but also from Russia *and* Iran to terrorist groups, including Hamas and Hezbollah. Without these channels Russia and Iran would be directly accountable for arming terrorists. Instead, Moscow and Tehran are able to siphon deals through an array of outlets in order to retain deniability. So when Hezbollah rockets are discovered by Israel it is generally easy to ascertain if they were manufactured in Russia, as is often the case. But it isn't at all clear whether Hezbollah acquired them from Belarus, Iran, or Syria. The extraordinary corruption among the military brass and bureaucratic brokers in Iran, Belarus, Russia, Syria, and Venezuela makes a crackdown nearly impossible.[46] The West should call the Belarusian and Syrian links what they are—B.S.—and act accordingly.

"Going Out" with China

China's dependence on resources from abroad increasingly affects the way in which Beijing interacts with the international system. In favorable circumstances the pursuit of natural resources has led to increased contacts and interdependence with the international community, although Chinese strategy has at times seemed to be neo-mercantilist and almost always devoid of human rights or humanitarian considerations. Of future concern is that in some crisis or discord, the drive to acquire stable supplies of resources could put strains on the international system, perhaps even of a similar nature to those that contributed to the violent rise of Germany and Japan.

—Richard Ellings, president of the National Bureau of Asian Research (September 2006)

Accelerating development in many parts of Asia, especially in China and India, has been the primary driver of global economic growth so far in the twenty-first century. The re-centering of world growth toward Asia and away from the North Atlantic economies encourages the ambitions of many developing countries in other regions that export the commodities needed in China and India. Venezuela and Iran are significant beneficiaries of this trend, and their governments are strengthened because of China's energy needs. Sizable oil investments notwithstanding, in important ways China's motives and methods for dealing with Iran and Venezuela are less problematic than Russia's.

SINO-IRANIAN TIES

Through the 1980s and into the 1990s, China sold a significant amount of arms to the Islamic Republic, though it never came close to rivaling the Soviet Union or the arms trafficking free-for-all that marred Boris Yeltsin's Russia. In part, this owed to the fact that the Soviet Union was far and away

the better manufacturer of military hardware; Chinese and Pakistani armaments were often just inferior knockoffs of Soviet arms. But in the struggle
for communist primacy that characterized the Sino-Soviet split, China's leaders viewed Iran as a geostrategic bulwark to expanded Soviet influence, leading them to sell air-to-air missiles, surface-to-air missiles, small arms and
artillery, and armored personnel carriers to Iran.[1] Chinese arms sales to Iran
probably peaked in the 1980s, when China badly needed foreign currency
and Iran was looking for an edge in the Iran-Iraq War.

China peddled nuclear technology too. In 1989, a year after the Iran-
Iraq War ended, Iran began buying electromagnetic isotope separators from
China. Iran also procured a three-axis turntable from the Chinese Precision
Machining Import/Export Company, a technology that could be converted
for grinding explosive lenses for a nuclear triggering device.[2] Recent evidence has also surfaced indicating that China supported Iranian nuclear aspirations by training some Iranian nuclear engineers from 1988 to 1992
and by selling dual-use technologies such as chemical precursors to the
Islamic Republic.

Chinese arms sales fell dramatically after 1997. At first, China declared a
halt to nuclear cooperation with Iran, then in January 1998 it quietly pledged
to the U.S. government to stop transfers of certain cruise missile technologies
to Iran, or otherwise aid in Iran's domestic ballistic missile program.[3] In 2002
China enacted export controls related to sensitive WMD components, which
most analysts agree has significantly curtailed transfers of WMD-related wares
from China.[4] China still sells some arms to Iran, and from 2003 to 2006 more
than a dozen Chinese companies were issued sanctions by the U.S. State
Department, probably for sketchy ties to Iran. But there is plenty of reason to
believe Chinese officials' insistence that they have "scaled way back" sales of
conventional arms to Iran.[5] More important, no credible evidence has surfaced
that the Chinese government actively supports the Islamic Republic's nuclear
program or the development of Iran's advanced missile systems.[6]

Meanwhile, China has amped up its stake in Iran's oil industry over the
last decade. An oil exporter until 1993, China's oil is now reserved for domestic use, and its reserves are likely to be exhausted by 2018, if not before.
In 2003 China supplanted Japan as the second-largest consumer of energy
in the world. A year later China began investing heavily in Iranian energy

projects to slake future demand: the nations signed one of the world's largest oil contracts for China to develop Iran's Yadavaran field, located near the Iraqi border, in a deal estimated to be worth $70–$100 billion over the coming decades.[7] Also in 2004 the Chinese agreed to buy $20 billion worth of liquefied natural gas from Iran at a graduated rate until 2030.[8] These deals, pledged before Ahmadinejad's election and the restart of Iran's nuclear program, are indicative of the Chinese leadership's expectations for future fuel consumption, and give some insight into Beijing's energy security strategy.

By investing in Iran, China's energy security is met in several ways. First, as indicated by Russia's motive for co-opting Iran into the VIRUS partnership, Iran has tremendous geostrategic importance because it occupies a rich swath of land between the Persian Gulf and the Caspian Sea that is crucial to accessing the flow of oil and gas from Central Asia and the Caucuses. The Chinese often call it the "energy silk road," an important land route for transferring oil and gas to China that, in time, will nimbly mitigate what Beijing considers its "Malacca dilemma."

Deemed one of seven "energy chokepoints" by the U.S. Energy Information Association, the Strait of Malacca is the primary oil artery linking the Indian Ocean and the South China Sea. Through Malacca, 15 million bpd of oil are shipped, about 20 percent of worldwide oil consumption.[9] More to the point, in 2005, 80 percent of China's oil imports transited through Malacca.[10] At Malacca's narrowest point, the Phillips Channel, the strait is just 1.7 miles across. Not only are piracy and terrorism mounting problems in Malacca, but the congestion of tankers and other ships sailing the route make it perhaps the world's most treacherous bottleneck; poor visibility due to chronic haze makes navigation even harder.[11] As a land route, Iran is an integral part of the solution to the energy conundrum that Beijing faces.

Second, Iran may offer better return on investment for China. Because of poor infrastructure investment by the government, Iran's oil facilities are outdated or decrepit. Consequently, Iran's oil production has dropped 50 percent since 1977. Not only will Chinese investment allow it access to enormous untapped oil fields, but Chinese investment in existing Iranian capacity can lead to significant gains in Iranian oil production. This logic also applies to Iran's natural gas. From 2000 to 2008 Iran accounted for about 16 percent of the world's known natural gas reserves, yet it stood for just 0.5 percent of world gas exports annually, again primarily because of lack of capacity.[12] Over time China can mend the Islamic Republic's chronic mismanagement of its energy sector.

Third, and related to the second reason, Beijing believes it is cheaper to invest in foreign energy ventures rather than simply buying oil off the world market ad infinitum, as the Japanese do. In 2007 a Chinese report concluded that it would be $5 per ton cheaper to drill abroad for oil rather than import it.[13]

Finally, Iran represents a counterweight to what China perceives as American hegemony over the Persian Gulf. Chinese policymakers can well imagine a great power rivalry akin to the many precedents laid out by Paul Kennedy. In his classic text on the history of international relations, *The Rise and Fall of Great Powers*, the declining and ascendant powers fall into major conflict as the declining power tries to maintain its status before it is overtaken. If even a mild rendition of this scenario plays out, the Chinese worry that the United States could delay oil shipments from the Persian Gulf. Iran has the potential to greatly reduce China's reliance on Arab oil exporters, denying America a potential lever of power against China.

To summarize Sino-Iranian relations over the past generation, the People's Republic of China has gone from a cash-strapped, third-world nation willing to trade "arms for oil" to a calculating, rising power mindful of the problems it will inherit in the coming years. Based on a series of economic and tactical calculations, Chinese policymakers have pursued a strategy of direct investment into Iran's oil and gas fields in order to help meet its energy security needs. Acting on behalf of its gargantuan investments in Iran's energy sector, the Chinese government has used its Security Council veto to help shield Iran from sanctions that could hamper the Islamic Republic's ability to export oil and gas to China. But China has become more selective in its ties to Iran, focusing narrowly on securing access to Iranian oil and gas, while decreasing arms sales. And as far as any outsider can tell, China has stopped working with Iran's nuclear program.

CHINA'S TIES TO VENEZUELA

Chinese investment in Venezuela's energy sectors has also surged. As recently as a decade ago, Venezuelan trade with China totaled less than $200 million.

After 2003 Sino-Venezuelan trade grew swiftly, reaching almost $7.2 billion in 2009, according to Chinese government statistics.[14] Focusing on oil exports, Venezuela exported 39,000 bpd to China in 2005. A quick three years later Venezuela was exporting 120,000 bpd to China, according to U.S. Energy Information Administration statistics.[15] While on the surface this may suggest Chinese interests in Venezuela and Iran are similar, there are certain differences.

After his brief ouster in a 2002 coup, Chávez became increasingly vocal about diverting oil away from the United States, pinpointing China as the best option for ending "100 years of U.S. domination" over Venezuela's oil industry. His advisers keenly recast this as nothing more than Venezuela's natural desire to diversify its oil exports. Their suggestion points to a gross problem facing Venezuela, one that Chávez has exacerbated. Venezuela suffers from a "dual dependency": it depends on one product, oil, for most of its revenue, and it is also dependent on selling that oil to one place, the United States.[16] (By contrast, Iran's largest export markets are outside the West.)

Still, U.S. officials took Chávez's bait, feeding the Venezuelan president's bluster. Senator Richard Lugar, chairman of the Senate Foreign Relations Committee, enjoined a GAO analysis of the impacts of a potential curtailment of Venezuelan oil exports to the United States.[17] Lugar's paranoia about Chávez quickly morphed into a broader worry based on America's reliance on foreign oil. Subsequent U.S. actions carried a whiff of Washington's old hegemonic ways. Other countries in the region started to receive veiled threats not to facilitate Venezuelan exports to China. For example, one U.S. official warned, "The U.S. will not look favorably on Panama aiding Venezuela to sell its oil to a competitor of the U.S."[18]

At the time Washington had little reason to fear a Venezuelan cutoff. If anything, Chávez's takeover of Venezuela's oil industry actually stabilized the country's oil exports: the only time that Venezuelan oil shipments to the United States have been interrupted under Chávez occurred in 2002 and 2003, when Chávez temporarily lost control over PDVSA operations because of a ten-week workers' strike.

More generally, a wholesale redirection of Venezuelan oil to China would require both countries to place political interests well above economic self-interest. Because of the difficulties posed by its location, China is not a natural market for Venezuelan oil. Transit from Venezuela to Asia takes forty days, compared to just five days to transit it to the southern United States.[19] This also means the overall costs of shipping oil from Venezuela to China are much higher than shipping to the United States. Given that the Panama Canal can no longer accommodate most oil tankers,[20] getting Venezuelan crude oil to China requires transport across the Straits of Magellan at the southern tip of South America and across the Pacific, or around Cape Horn and through the Indian Ocean. Though both routes have been tested, for the Chinese the Indian Ocean route is less desirable because it requires the oil to be tanked through the Straits of Malacca.

Furthermore, China lacks the refineries to process Venezuela's heavy crude, which contains high amounts of sulfur and metals. In fact, most of the refineries in the world set up to process Venezuelan-type crude are in the United States, many created by PDVSA's American subsidiary CITGO decades ago. Adjusting to Venezuela's crude oil will take Chinese refineries an estimated two to five years. For these reasons, when the fracas about oil being diverted to China arose, Venezuelan crude exports to China made up less than 2 percent of the amount Venezuela sent to the United States.

But for Chávez, political motives trump economic realities, at least to some degree. For the Chinese, energy needs have outstripped even robust predictions made in 2000. "Going out" to Iran was a handy boost to China's energy security dilemma, but rising U.S. pressure on Iran over its restarted nuclear program made investment there more uncertain. Parts of Africa are promising alternative sources of gas because many countries there are not members of OPEC, and therefore are not subject to the cartel's production quotas. But ongoing civil conflict and a lack of infrastructure, even by developing country standards, retard long-term investments. In 2005 and 2006 Venezuela weighed in as OPEC's third- or fourth-largest producer, but unlike Kuwait or Saudi Arabia it certainly wasn't betrothed to the United States. Also, unlike the Arab OPEC states, Venezuela did not have to transit its oil and gas out of the Persian Gulf and was thus able to avoid the chokepoint of Hormuz en route to China.

For Hugo Chávez, Chinese interest in Venezuela promises two benefits: foreign investment to help build infrastructure and a potential market for diversifying oil exports. On a more basic political level, the Venezuelan president's rhetoric was diverging more and more from reality. Venezuela was actually selling *more* crude oil to the United States, not less. Some months Venezuela's oil exports to the United States even surpassed Saudi Arabia's. Susan Purcell, director of the Center for Hemispheric Policy, said of Chávez's problem: "He rants and raves against the U.S., but he is dependent on the U.S. market. Trade is increasing between the two countries, and that opens him up to charges of hypocrisy."[21]

The sustained spike in oil prices mid-decade accentuated Sino-Venezuelan trade. Venezuela's oil exports to China, averaging 14,000 bpd in 2004, grew to 39,000 bpd the following year. By 2008, amid Chávez's cries that his country would provide China all the oil it needed to rival the United States as a global superpower, exports rose to 120,000 bpd. The rapid acceleration of world oil prices helped spur the trend, not because the Chinese thought oil prices would always go higher but because Chávez offered to subsidize the additional cost of shipping oil to China.

Venezuela's oil exports to China have increased of late, but the uptick is not as pronounced as Chávez might like the world to believe. He regularly promises to export 1 million bpd to China by 2012, up from 360,000 bpd in 2009. Not only do U.S. Energy Information Administration statistics place Venezuelan oil exports to China at one-third of the amount Chávez claims, but Chinese figures also report a much lower range of Venezuelan crude imports, slightly below 120,000 bpd.[22] The discrepancy has gone almost unnoted, except for a lone article in the *New York Times* on April 18, 2010, which quipped it "something of a mystery" that Chávez claimed to send 460,000 bpd to China yet Chinese statistics reported Venezuelan oil imports of 132,000 bpd.[23] The most probable explanation seems to be that Chávez is playing up Venezuela's importance to China as a way of sending a message to both Washington and Beijing: Venezuela is a major oil producer and as goes its oil exports, so goes world primacy.

To indemnify its future access to Venezuelan oil, China offers generous developmental aid to Venezuela. From 2004 to 2008 Beijing committed over $4 billion in social development projects in Venezuela, primarily earmarked for basic infrastructure—railroads, housing, roads, and schools.[24] Perhaps more telling, since 2008 the two countries have announced a joint development fund of $12 billion ($8 billion coming from China), to go toward infrastructure projects in Venezuela. These pledges show that China intends to draw on Venezuelan oil for years to come.

China won the right to develop the Boyaca 3 site in the Orinoco Belt region in 2009. In 2010 China National Petroleum Corporation (CNPC) loaned Venezuela $20 billion to help PDVSA develop its ultra-heavy oil reserves, China's biggest loan to a foreign country to date. Over the next twenty-five years, repayment will come in the form of more than 2.5 billion barrels of crude oil. In a side agreement, China promised to build three thermal power plants, with a combined output of nine hundred megawatts, designed to run on petroleum coke, a form of power generation on par with coal-fired power plants in terms of environmental impact.[25]

All tallied, China has pledged more than $30 billion in developmental aid to Venezuela since 2008. Critics insist that many Chinese-backed projects will never come to fruition, but the Chinese government has already provided billions in "soft loans" since 2008, a lifeline to Chávez, who is reeling from the most inhospitable global environment of his presidency.

Arms are another tool of ingratiation. Unlike China's pattern of relations with Iran—arms sales for a time, then a gradual reduction as investment in the energy sector grew—in the case of the Chávez government China's arms sales were interspersed with oil investments. The first major arms deal between the two governments, in 2005, involved China selling Venezuela three truck-mounted surveillance radars at a total cost of $150 million. The only other major deal between the two nations, contracted in 2008, provided for China to sell eighteen K-8 military training aircraft to Venezuela (Venezuela originally wanted twenty-four, but the two sides eventually agreed on eighteen), intended to help Venezuela train military pilots and intercept drug traffickers.[26] This particular deal is noteworthy because it is actually a replacement order; China did not propose the contract. Venezuela originally tried to buy the aircraft from Brazil, but the deal was nixed because U.S. hardware on the Brazilian planes forbade their sale to Venezuela under the 2006 U.S. arms embargo against Venezuela.[27] China also assembled and launched Venezuela's first satellite, and while Chávez claims its purpose is to help break America's "media control" over Venezuela, the orbital could conceivably become a military technology.

Beijing isn't squeaky clean; it does occasionally sell arms to Venezuela, though certainly less than Russia. (In fact, Chinese arms sales to Venezuela are smaller than those of the United States to Venezuela before the 2006 arms embargo.) However, three reasons should allay concern over China's relationship with Venezuela. First, according to the U.S. government, there are no significant military-to-military ties between Beijing and Caracas.[28] Second, Beijing's arms deals appear intended toward defensive and counternarcotics systems, as opposed to advanced missile systems, tanks, etc., that have an offensive purpose.[29] Third, China has not made any large arms deals with Chávez's allies, so at least the prospect of an arms race in South America isn't broadened.

Another trend may also be at work, one that qualifies the general notion that Beijing simply showers every oil-rich nation in the world with cash in order to gain a stake in the country's energy reserves. To recap, after China's massive investment in Iran's energy sector in 2004, the People's Republic only slowly began work at the sites. Chinese investment then slowed from 2005 to 2008, probably in response to the growing likelihood of conflict between the United States and Iran. As Western pressure on Iran mounted in recent years, Beijing's investment in Venezuela increased. Although this is a tentative conclusion, Chinese interests in Venezuela may derive from the need to use Venezuelan oil as a hedge against any disruption in supply from Iran.[30] This would also explain why China is reaching out to Venezuela despite the delivery problems associated with Venezuelan oil.

DEALING IN SHADES OF GRAY

China's ravenous consumption of oil and gas drives the global price up and creates other side effects for the United States. Beijing's foreign investment in Iran and Venezuela has provided enough cash to buoy the regimes in Tehran and Caracas against the headwinds they face. In this sense, Chinese investment serves as an insurance policy.

Yet from another angle Chinese interests in these two countries indirectly work to America's advantage. China is, like the United States and unlike Russia, an oil-importing country. The point is obvious, but the implication is often overlooked: China shares the United States' desire to keep the oil flowing and prices moderate. As long as China and America get what they want, the VIRUS is weakened because it is denied use of the oil weapon. However, this shared interest could be foiled by an event that dramatically pushes prices up, like an attack on Iran. One analysis posits: "If a confrontation between Iran and the United States were to occur, leading to a disruption in Iranian oil to China, the tacit alliance between the United States and China will become strained. At the very least, China will want to find new suppliers, making Venezuela a more attractive option."[31] China and the United States are passive partners in energy consumption, but their common interest could quickly shatter, leading to a mad dash for energy resources if war with Iran enters into the equation.[32] If, however, pressures on Iran abate, China would probably grow more comfortable in the security of its oil investments in the Islamic Republic, which could lead to a more tepid relationship between Beijing and Caracas.[33]

Stability appears to be the overriding concern of Beijing in its dealings with both Caracas and Tehran. Beijing defines its strategic interest in each nation as the long-term procurement of hydrocarbons. All indications are that China has both greatly reduced its overall arms sales to Iran and almost surely stopped cooperation with Iran in nuclear, biological, and chemical technologies. When it comes to Venezuela, and the Hugo sphere in general, China sells relatively small amounts of military equipment, and only those that Beijing reasonably claims are intended to aid in the crackdown on drug traffickers. Beyond limited arms sales, the Chinese risk unsettling regional security in the Middle East and Latin America, possibly jeopardizing its providential oil access strategy.[34]

In the past seven years China has pledged more than $140 billion to explore and extract hydrocarbons in Iran and Venezuela by 2030. This investment, combined with Western-backed sanctions against Iran, has clearly hastened Iran's turn toward China as its key export market. It has also made Iran and Venezuela the second- and third-largest sources of oil imports for China.

Given the extent of Chinese investment and energy needs, China is likely to veto any sanctions proposed before the UN Security Council. Undoubtedly, Chávez and Ahmadinejad are emboldened by Chinese support. They can lambast at will. For the belligerent petrodrunks in Caracas and Tehran, China is serving up courage in a barrel.

Yet while Chinese interest may keep each government from quaking, the People's Republic generally plays a stabilizing role. The level of economic investment far outstrips military aid. A quick back-of-the-envelope calculation using the mean amounts of energy investment and arms deals reveals the following disparity between China and Russia's role. Since 2004 China has contracted for at least twenty-five times more oil and gas than it has delivered in security assistance to Iran, with the Yadavaran deal alone accounting for at least a 10:1 ratio. The approximate ratio of China's energy sector investment and developmental aid versus sales of military equipment to Venezuela is even more lopsided, over 60:1 since 2005. Even when considering all contracts for the delivery of Chinese aircraft to Venezuela, aircraft that could conceivably serve a military rather than civilian use, the ratio changes only slightly. By contrast, the ratios are in the opposite direction when it comes to Russia's arms and investment deals with Iran and Venezuela. All of these ratios are best-guess approximations because while both contracting parties disclose the size of their oil deals, the Chinese are often tight-lipped when it comes to discussing arms deals. Hence, these estimates rely on arms analysts' projections and the delivery of military hardware reported in the public domain.

NECESSARY DISTINCTIONS

Rising world powers are often placed in the same lot. Much of this has to do with an operational assumption of realism, the theoretical approach to international relations that dominates considerations of how power is accumulated and exercised in world affairs. Two large groups in the realist camp, generally dubbed "offensive" realism and "defensive" realism, contend that particular state characteristics—democratic or autocratic, political values of society, etc.—are of little ultimate importance to state behavior because all states behave similarly in situ. Given that there is no prevailing power beyond the level of the nation-state to mediate conflict and ensure just behavior, each state is forced to compete with the others for power, because only by accumulating power can a state guarantee its survival. The structure of the international system breeds this condition, and while this may be unsettling to high-minded optimists hoping for an end to war and conflict, it at least provides the solace of predictability.

Even if one wants to quibble with the notion that all powers act the same under similar circumstances, the coldly calculating logic of realism seems overwhelmingly pertinent in the present-day international system where there is one "superpower," the United States, and several prominent "rising powers," chiefly China and Russia, that do not share the same political values. In contrast to the United States, both states are de facto, if not de jure, autocracies.

Russia is not the lone supporter of Iran and Venezuela. Indeed, both "Russia and China are promoting an international order that . . . can protect autocratic governments from foreign interference," as Robert Kagan duly noted in his 2008 book, *The Return of History and the End of Dreams*.[35] But Russia and China's strategic interests are different, and consequently their forms of support for Chávez and the Islamic Republic are different. Beijing hopes to provision its own energy security in the decades ahead, in large part by drawing on the rich hydrocarbon deposits in Iran and Venezuela. Its willingness to extend diplomatic protection to these governments stems from the sizable investments it has made in each country that will take decades to recoup.

However, Russia's relations with Caracas and Tehran are more problematic to Western security. Because Russian support is far less oriented around economic investment and trade and more heavily focused on arms sales—often of an offensive nature—and technical nuclear assistance, the Kremlin's role is more destabilizing than Beijing's. Russian arms are integral to the military build-ups in both the Middle East and Latin America. Also, a nuclear afterclap may be in the offing. Iran's nuclear ambitions, made possible by Russian technology, are on the verge of triggering a nuclear arms race in the Middle East. Since Iran publicly revived its nuclear aspirations in 2006, ten nations in the Middle East have announced plans to build nuclear power plants. While many of these nations couch their actions as a quest for peaceful civilian energy, Saudi Arabia is planning a "nuclear response"—i.e., nuclear weapons programs of its own—should Iran get the bomb.[36]

In conclusion, China's "going out" to Iran and Venezuela is problematic for Western policymakers because it undermines Western attempts to pressure the Islamic Republic. When Western firms leave Iran because of sanctions, Chinese entities "backfill" abandoned projects, as one frustrated U.S. official recently told a House panel, and the Chinese simply "are not changing their behavior" toward the Islamic Republic, despite sanctions.[37] China is also helping Venezuela to diversify its oil exports away from the U.S. market, giving at least some credence to Chávez's rhetoric. For strategic reasons,

Russia, too, offers Iran significant diplomatic cover, and the same will be true should Chávez ever need it. This diplomatic coincidence obscures Chinese and Russian motivations for preventing the economic isolation in Iran. China and Russia engage Iran and Venezuela seeking different outcomes. Ultimately, it is Russia's influence, through its arms and nuclear know-how, which is more unsettling.

Cracks in the Facade

Buoyed by petrodollars, Russia, Iran and Venezuela hectored the West as they extended their reach abroad, backing separatists in Georgia, Islamists in the Middle East and Leftists around the world.
Now those oil-producing powers may be forced to draw in their horns as crude prices tumble. They face austerity budgets that could force them to scale back their military spending and foreign assistance even as falling oil prices fuel domestic dissent.
—*London Sunday Times* (October 18, 2008)

The year 2008 may have marked the apex of VIRUS cooperation. There wasn't a concerted effort to counteract the cooperation between all three of the powerful petroleum exporters, but longstanding Western allies responded to its different manifestations. For example, the Saudis fretted about their eventual loss of status as the world's "swing" oil producer because of Iran and Venezuela's newfound strength in OPEC. But the possibility of Iran with a nuclear bomb worried Riyadh even more.[1] The House of Saud deemed this prospect a direct threat to its security, and a source of instability to the wider Middle East. Russia's involvement also shifted into focus. Hence, one analysis summarized Saudi Arabia's foreign policy during this time as simply "doing anything they can to undercut [the] Russian-Iran alliance."[2] In fact, the Saudi foreign minister flew to Moscow in February 2008 to offer a $50 billion package to President Putin, whereby Saudi Arabia and Russia would cooperate to control Middle East crude oil and Riyadh would step in as a major Russian arms buyer, dwarfing Russian sales to Tehran and giving Russia the pleasure of turning a customer of American arms toward the Kremlin.[3] In 2009, after years of "no comment" about

Chávez's foreign policies, a spokesman for Secretary of State Clinton finally took the bait, calling Chávez's ongoing purchases of Russian arms a "serious challenge to stability."

Diagnosis of the VIRUS came amid this flare up of symptoms. Perhaps the most authoritative synopsis came from *The Economist*. The October 25 edition of the magazine acknowledged Russia, Iran, and Venezuela to be a "trio, bound together by dislike for America, and confidence based on surging energy revenues."[4] Yet the wonkish British publication then laid into the pairing, as if forced to dine on halibut with Cabernet:

> Each of the trio has different aims. Venezuela wants to create an anti-American block in Latin America. Russia likes the idea of challenging the United States in its backyard: a suitable response to what it sees as American meddling in Russia's own neighbourhood, where its president, Dmitry Medvedev, claims "privileged interests." But Russia's backing for Venezuela is constrained by its ties to other countries in the region, such as Brazil.
>
> Similarly, Russia likes to play the "Iran card," signaling to Mr. Bush that he may have to give ground in, say, Georgia if he wants help in the Middle East. But as far as any outsider can say, the Kremlin does not want Iran to have the bomb.[5]

Based on this rationale, the magazine resolved that the partnership was "mostly tactical, not strategic" and that the drop in oil prices, already well under way, would rupture the fair-weather ties between them.[6]

On July 11, 2008, oil prices peaked at $147.27 a barrel in response to Iranian missile tests and speculation that the Islamic Republic might try and block oil shipments through the Strait of Hormuz.[7] Although the various VIRUS schemes did not abate, oil prices quickly dropped from their summer highs. Barely four months later crude contracts sold for less than $34 a barrel, foreshadowing the world's worst economic contraction since the 1930s.

For Iran, Russia, and Venezuela, this pitted the loss of revenue—for how long and at what price remained anybody's guess—against the strategic opportunity of an economically weakened West. *New York Times* correspondent Simon Romero noted as much in late 2008, "Mr. Chávez has continued his overtures to Russia. He, Prime Minister Vladimir V. Putin of Russia and President Mahmoud Ahmadinejad of Iran may now see the United States, hobbled by financial crisis, as even more vulnerable."[8] Indeed, leaked Venezuelan government documents suggested that Chávez, in an alliance with Iran and stocked with Russian weapons, planned to stir up trouble for the United States on many fronts at once in order to eventually bring about the collapse of "the empire."[9] Chávez had taken to repeating the phrase "war is in the air" on his weekly television show and in other forums, a not-so-subtle threat to Colombia. Beyond financial meltdown, the fall of 2008 became hairy precisely because of the rising tension between Western-leaning governments and the VIRUS.

Russia's August 2008 invasion of Georgia led many analysts, from Harvard to major think tanks to NATO, to conclude that Moscow was doing its best to use the recession's onset to start a "proxy war against the West."[10] As pointed out in chapter 5, Georgian president Mikheil Saakashvili aligned with the West and pursued NATO membership. Furthermore, his country stands as a main transit route for the Nabucco project, the most serious contender to Russia's gas lines. Moscow quickly overwhelmed Georgia and "liberated" the pro-Moscow enclaves of Abkhazia and South Ossetia. Moscow then declared the regions to be independent countries, though the international response to the move was less than enthusiastic. So far, the only countries to follow Russia in recognizing the independence of Abkhazia and South Ossetia are Nicaragua, Venezuela, and the tiny South Pacific island of Nauru.

In the last days of 2008 Israel invaded Gaza in an attempt to destroy Hamas after the group ended a six-month truce by firing rockets into southern Israel. Somehow Hamas avoided disarticulation at the hands of the Israeli military, a minor miracle of guerilla warfare. Soon after the conflict, which lasted until the end of January 2009, the credit for Hamas's staying power, if not their will, went to Iran and Syria for smuggling the group Russian-made arms, most likely funneled through Syria. Many believed Hezbollah was also arming for war with Israel. "The price of oil may be low," wrote terrorism analyst and former CIA officer Reuel Marc Gerecht in the *Wall Street Journal* on January 7, 2009, "but the mullahs have seen worse economic times." However, he noted, "In 30 years, they have not seen a better constellation of forces."[11]

PAINFUL ADJUSTMENTS

As the months passed, oil prices settled in at a price range of roughly $70 to $80 a barrel, half their peak levels in 2008. Domestic problems mounted in Venezuela, Iran, and Russia. Late that year, Chávez's party lost mid-term elections for the first time since he came to power, largely because his global ambitions ignored domestic realities. "We're supporting something like eight countries," said one voter, a former Chavista. "How is it that he spends so much money everywhere, when the problems are here?"[12] Given that Chávez needs crude to sell for around $95 a barrel to make ends meet, the global reach of Bolivarian revolution duly went from lavish foreign gas subsidies to less expensive projects, like encouraging rice cultivation in Haiti.[13]

For Russia the loss in oil revenues led to an economic contraction of 8 percent in 2009, amid a series of failures—the ruble's value plunged and the stock market lost 72 percent of its value in the fourth quarter of 2008 alone.[14] President Medvedev, in a moment of national criticism rarely offered by a sitting world leader, said that the recession showed "our current state of affairs leaves much to be desired." In an essay he penned entitled "Go Russia!" Medvedev asked:

Should we continue sticking to the primitive economy based on natural resources, to the deep-rooted corruption, to an outdated habit to rely only on the state, on foreign countries, on any kind of a cure-all, on anyone but on ourselves? Does Russia, overloaded with such burdens, have a future?[15]

Medvedev traveled to Silicon Valley for inspiration and pledged that Russia would reclaim its greatness on the basis of innovation and manufactures, not just raw materials.[16]

Compared to Venezuela and Iran, Medvedev faced fewer domestic constraints as a result of the financial crisis. But Russia's strategic objectives were acutely hobbled. Just before the recession hit Gazprom entered into long-term gas contracts with Azerbaijan, Georgia, Turkmenistan, and Ukraine. In many cases Gazprom started pipeline construction and agreed to buy hydrocarbons at close to peak levels, all with an eye toward eliminating competing pipelines. As one article in *Foreign Affairs* put it, "Moscow . . . is left with plenty of sunk costs but without any new ideas."[17]

While Russia searched for new direction, Venezuela convulsed. The economy contracted by 3.3 percent in 2009, and more than 6 percent in 2010 (the only negative growth rate in Latin America). Chávez had to move his international agenda to the back burner for the first time since 2003. Try as he might, he could find no way to blame the United States for many of Venezuela's problems, such as violent crime, rolling energy blackouts and worsening water shortages. In a country that claims perhaps the world's third-largest oil reserves and one of the world's mightiest rivers, the Orinoco, the president was reduced to chiding Venezuelans: "Some people sing in the bath for half an hour. . . . What kind of communism is that? Three minutes is more than enough!"[18]

Iran's economic fortunes, unlike those of its partners, actually improved. The Iranian economy experienced growth of 2.6 percent in 2009. Paradoxically, the successive rounds of sanctions against the country insulated it from the slowdown in global trade.[19] Dozens of multinational firms invested in Iran's energy sector from 2005 to 2009 despite Western sanctions, allowing Iran all-important access to refined gasoline.[20] Iran averted the whims of the global financial crisis while nonetheless benefitting from foreign investment.

Of course, there were serious political challenges. The Islamic Republic endured massive protests in the summer of 2009 as millions took to the streets to oppose Ahmadinejad's reelection. Meanwhile, Western powers threatened "biting sanctions" against the Islamic Republic. But instead of squawking about excessive showers or the pitfalls of a petroleum-based economy, Iran's president strutted about the world stage gloating that Iran was the "world's most important nation."[21] Recession's gale somehow doused the Russian captain and the Venezuelan navigator, but left the Iranian mate almost unscathed.

THE WEAKEST STRAND OF THE VIRUS

Of all the strands that weave into the VIRUS, the relations between Iran and Russia require the most commitment, as each government must set aside ingrained animosities and suspicions. Iran's economic fortunes made apparent

Russia's lax construction of the Bushehr nuclear reactor, originally slated for completion in 1999. To Iran it seemed like Moscow temporized just to preserve leverage with Tehran and Washington, which is surely true. President Medvedev began to rethink the level of support previously afforded to the Islamic Republic when the international community discovered in the fall of 2009 that Iran was operating a huge, previously unknown nuclear complex at the holy city of Qom.

When President Medvedev countenanced further sanctions in spring 2010, Ahmadinejad lashed out at his tenuous ally and diplomatic protector. Ahmadinejad cautioned Medvedev that joining the "U.S. plot" was against Russia's interests.[22] Public statements between Moscow and Tehran became heated for the first time since the Caspian dispute. "Iran and Russia clash in worst row for years," Reuters reported.[23] A headline from the BBC read, "The 'Unraveling Relationship' Between Russia and Iran."[24] Rumors spread that Iran's parliamentary national security committee was considering a symbolic downgrade of ties with Moscow.[25] However, once UNSCR 1929 passed, Iran's tone became one of regret. "At least Russia could have abstained," a senior Iranian official told the *Tehran Times*.[26]

Russia's turn away from Iran had a short life. Five weeks after the fourth round of sanctions *Time* noted, "Russia is changing its tone on Iran, the Kremlin appears once again to be playing both sides."[27] Ministers from each government agreed to restart shipments of nuclear fuel rods to Bushehr. Russia's energy minister Sergei Shmatko declared, "The sanctions cannot stop us," a statement interpreted by the *New York Times* and other media outlets as a renewed Russian "defiance" of the West.[28] Bushehr became operational two months after UNSCR 1929 came into force, to be hailed by both countries as a new high-water mark of Russo-Iranian relations.

On another, arguably more consequential matter, Russia made a similar quick pivot away from the West and back toward Tehran. Shortly after passage of the sanctions, the wording had been interpreted to mean that highly advanced weapons systems, particularly the S-300, could not be sold to Iran. Indeed, Russian deputy foreign minister Sergey Denisov conceded, "Moscow believes that the sanctions resolution clearly forbids the sale of the S-300 system to Iran." Russia's Federal Service for Military and Technical Cooperation concurred.[29] Weeks later, after President Medvedev returned from a friendly trip to Washington during which President Obama declared the two countries' relations "better than ever," the Russian government struck a different tone.[30] Officials reversed course, declaring that the sale of the S-300s could go ahead because the sanctions resolution pertained to the UN Register of Conventional Arms, which does not list the S-300 system.[31] The S-300 contract remained in limbo until September 22, 2010, when Medvedev, just before traveling to New York for his annual speech before the UN General Assembly, announced that Russia would not deliver the missiles.[32]

As of this writing, Iran and Russia appear to have mended their 2010 spat over the UN sanctions. However, the argument highlights a larger tension in Russo-Iranian relations. Iran and Russia are natural competitors when it comes to control of the Caspian and Caucasus. For years Iran has been cultivating a network of alliances in the Caucasus and Central Asia, primarily as a means to check the influence of Turkey and Pakistan, considered stalwart U.S. allies. An inchoate alliance of Farsi-speaking states sometimes called the "Persian crescent" is emerging between Iran, Tajikistan, and the Karzai government in Afghanistan.[33] Turkey, for its part, has shown inklings of "moving eastward" of late, toward Iran and Syria, owing to its frustration with the EU's refusal to seriously consider Turkey as a full member of the European club. In July 2010 Iran and a private firm in Turkey agreed to a $1.3 billion deal to build a gas pipeline across Turkey and into Europe.[34] American and EU officials were predictably frustrated, but the move may be of more strategic significance because in three years' time it would be operational, exporting gas outside Russia's control, and to the detriment of Russia's strategic interest.

Two can play at that game. Moscow's relations with Israel cratered in recent years, in inverse relation to Russia's partnership with Iran. But as the Russo-Iranian strand of the VIRUS is put in doubt, Russia and the Zionist regime may be testing the waters of rapprochement. In the spring of 2010 Russia announced its first-ever military purchase from Israel, a multi-year deal for twelve drone aircraft.[35] Angered, Israel's former defense minister Moshe Arens argued in an op-ed—which unsettled many in Washington and Tehran alike—that if the United States wasn't willing to let Israel make its own adjustments to the U.S.-made F-35, then Israel should consider buying its fighters from France or Russia.[36] Overlooking the recent unpleasantness between them, Russia's defense minister explained that the two countries are "close or identical" when it comes to "terrorism and non-proliferation of weapons of mass destruction."[37] Ehud Barak, Israel's current defense minister, played up historical ties in his country's diplomatic response: "We know the truth: the state of Israel would not exist if the Red Army had not defeated fascist Germany."[38]

It's not clear how long Russia and Iran will remain "strategic" allies. Russia's willingness to operationalize Bushehr so soon after the fourth round of UN sanctions quickly mended the wound, and Iran's leadership celebrated the active reactor as a high point in cooperation. Yet Iran and Russia's geostrategic interests do not coincide in the long-term. Though both governments are anti-American, Moscow needs a quiescent Iran to achieve its ambitions, while Tehran needs constant, if not rapid, changes in the geopolitical landscape in order to avoid being steamrolled by sanctions. Sensing the other's schemes, each nation is now exploring a new battery of partnerships. These are tentative steps at finding new allies, and they don't add up to a wholesale divorce between Tehran and Moscow. But at some point reality must set in. There are two major players when it comes to orchestrating the flow of gas out of Central Asia and into Europe: Russia and Iran. Ultimately, their interests are likely to conflict.

RUSSIA-VENEZUELA TIES

Just as Russia's relations with Iran became stressed in 2010, similar forecasts were made about the souring of Russia's relationship with Venezuela. Analysts posited that Russia's backing for Venezuela would be constrained by the growing importance of Brazil to Russia.[39] Witty pundits opined that Chávez's appetite for Russian arms would be "shop 'til you drop"—he would keep buying the Sukhois and S-300s until the price of oil dropped, at which point Russia would lose all interest in Venezuela.

However, neither pronouncement has proven accurate. For starters, Russia and Brazil are not major trade partners. And while Brazil is generally considered to be the biggest arms buyer in South America, since 2008 Venezuela has been the largest buyer of Russian arms in Latin America. Theoretically Brazil's rise should check Chávez's influence in Latin America because foreign governments and companies would fear fallout with Brazil, South America's most powerful country and largest trade market, and thus be chary of Chávez. But this hasn't been the case at all because Brazilian president Luiz Inácio Lula da Silva took a hands-off approach to Chávez's regional wrangling. Realist theory about power dictating influence got up-ended; Chávez influenced Lula, not the other way around.[40]

And recession hasn't kept Chávez from affording Russian arms. In September of 2009 Chávez and Putin agreed to a $2.2 billion loan for Venezuela to buy ninety-two T-72S tanks, Smerch missiles, an S-300 air defense system, and possibly submarines.[41] Only after further arms agreements were announced in April 2010 did U.S. officials express concern that Venezuela's Russian weapons might "migrate into other parts of the hemisphere," a veiled reference to Chávez's support for the FARC.[42]

Continued arms deals are but one indication of closer Russian-Venezuelan relations since recession hit both countries. Russian accords to help Venezuela with nuclear energy, major contracts for Russian companies to drill in Venezuela's Orinoco Belt, and Russia's attempt to bring PDVSA into an exploratory group at the Arctic Shtokman site all point to the consolidation of a major alliance between the two nations.

Odd as it may seem for two recession-addled countries on opposite sides of the world, their symbiosis continues to yield mutual benefit. Venezuela's ongoing "need" for arms can only be sated by Russia because of the U.S. arms embargo and China's preference for weapons transfers that are truly defensive in nature. Also, Russia is the only country (other than Iran) proffering nuclear cooperation to help Chávez realize his plans for a "nuclear village." And Venezuela now appears more promising as a geostrategic outlet for Russia. If Russia's chances of dominating its near abroad and Europe's energy corridor decrease, Venezuela is worth more as a strategic partner and asset.

Underpinning Venezuela's elevated importance is Russia's declining influence in Europe. A 2008 article in the *New York Times* suggested that Russia is losing its capacity for energy blackmail: "Europeans may no longer be as intimidated, knowing that Russia is less able to pressure its customers."[43] This is because natural gas, the backbone of Russia's energy strategy, is now beset by new discoveries and projections for lower long-term demand. When combined, these factors are likely to "turn the geopolitics of energy on its head."[44] U.S. natural gas output surpassed Russia's for the first time in 2009, as new shale gas deposits made it to market.[45] Since 2008, Norway and the Netherlands have become major gas exporters to Europe,[46] and promising exploration is underway in Austria, Germany, Hungary, and Poland. Mandated efficiency standards also play a role. Based on EU efforts, some analysts believe that the bloc might import a third less gas in 2030 than forecast in 2005.[47] To make matters worse for Moscow, just before the recession Gazprom made many investments that assumed prices would roughly triple in the mid-term from 2007 levels; instead 2009 gas prices stood at about one-fifth of the 2007 levels.[48]

IMPACT ON THE VENEZUELA-IRAN ALLIANCE

Recession should have rattled the Iran and Venezuela alliance. As the U.S. director of national intelligence wrote in his 2009 annual report, declining oil revenues were "likely to put the squeeze on the adventurism of producers like Iran and Venezuela."[49] Undoubtedly the foreign aid model used to create the Hugo sphere is gone. Venezuela ended its heating oil subsidy to two hundred thousand poor families in New England, and Chávez had to insist on new terms to Petrocaribe, getting more cash upfront from the Central American and Caribbean beneficiaries.[50] Other slated projects, such as a transcontinental gas line and at least eight refineries proposed across South America and the Caribbean, were halted, and with them Chávez's plan to shore up Venezuela's regional influence.[51] Less influence for Chávez also means less room for Iran in Latin America. Hence, as pointed out in chapter 4, Iran's pledges of developmental aid to some countries—Nicaragua being the most obvious example—never materialized. As one key adviser to Ortega pointed out, the Sandinista government hasn't even been able to get Iran to forgive Nicaragua's bilateral debt; "they say the Koran doesn't permit them to."[52]

Still, Iranian commitments to Bolivia and Ecuador continued in spite of the global recession and UN sanctions. In August 2010 Iran offered Bolivia a developmental aid package of $250 million, a considerable sum given the South American country's size.[53] Ecuador received a similar pledge of $200 million the following month in a deal that President Correa said was, in part, a hedge against Chinese investment that has been slow to materialize.[54]

AN ALLIANCE UNMASKED

The VIRUS has been in flux since 2008. Because the partnership relies on high oil prices to finance its regional and global ambitions, the fall of crude oil and gas threatened to dash VIRUS cooperation. As one source put it, "Friendship won't last if oil prices stay low."[55] However, declaring the menace subdued is an overstatement; a series of direct conflicts between the VIRUS, including Iran's proxies, and Western allies have shadowed the onset of global recession.

Direct conflicts ended by early 2009 as the weight of recession compelled each member of the VIRUS partnership to turn its attention to domestic problems. Russia's foreign policy shifted away from strident backing of Venezuela and Iran under President Putin to more subtle, but persistent, support under Prime Minister Putin. Rhetoric and pomp may have subsided, but Russia's ties to Venezuela have only accelerated since oil prices dropped. Examples include joint naval exercises in the Caribbean, an increase in Venezuelan purchases of Russian arms—thanks to Russian loans since 2009—and expanding nuclear ties.

Certainly tension has arisen between Iran and Russia. Diplomatic conflict during the first part of 2010 likely arose from differing views on the timeline for the development of Iran's nuclear program. But more generally, this tension points toward the competing geostrategic aims of Moscow and Tehran: Moscow needs Tehran in order to control gas lines flowing to Europe. Not only can Tehran spoil Moscow's energy strategy, it can also incite radical Islamic elements in Central Asia and parts of Russia that will roil Moscow's plans. Hence, as Michael Eisenstadt of the Washington Institute of Near East Policy noted, Russia's objective "is to strike a balance . . . supporting Iran that can tie the U.S. down while not creating a Frankenstein that can threaten their own interest."[56]

This leg of the VIRUS is the most tenuous, and it remains to be seen if cooperation will continue. Even if Russia and Iran prove incompatible, the remaining bilateral ties that make up the VIRUS are likely to continue. There is no reason to think that Russian-Venezuelan relations, or Venezuelan-Iranian relations for that matter, will be impaired if Russia and Iran discontinue collaboration.

Cooperation has only intensified between Venezuela and Iran. Though bilateral trade decreased in 2009, it rebounded in 2010. As a result of harder economic times, outreach efforts by Caracas and Tehran across a broad swath of the Americas ebbed. Infrastructure investment and other forms of aid to Nicaragua and Argentina have fallen short of what Chávez and Ahmadinejad pledged prior to the global recession. It is reasonable to expect the Ortega government in Nicaragua and the Kirchner government in Argentina to rethink their reliance on Venezuela and Iran as a result.

Weighing the loss of Chávez's allure in Latin America against the intensification of ties with Iran suggests two conclusions. First, Venezuela and Iran can no longer afford to offer a full-fledged anti-American alternative project. For a time this was the case; joint aid pledges from Venezuela and Iran, assistance in building infrastructure, and the opening up of new trade outlets offered left-leaning governments in Latin America an opportunity to reduce their reliance on the American market. Second, recession has wiped away the veneer of economic ties upon which Venezuela and Iran disguised their illicit cooperation. The Venezuela-Iran alliance has not weakened as a result of recession; it has intensified, focusing more narrowly on the aspects that allow Iran to blunt the impact of sanctions while helping Venezuela threaten the stability of the Andes. Instead of being cowed by the drop in oil prices, Venezuela and Iran have become emboldened in their illicit cooperation.

Inoculation

The ultimate objective of American policy should be benign and visionary: to shape a truly cooperative global community, in keeping with long-range trends and with the fundamental interests of humankind.
—Zbigniew Brzezinski, *The Grand Chessboard* (1997)

To focus on the global war on terror, American policymakers in the last decade have shifted their attention and resources to the Middle East and away from other parts of the world, particularly Latin America. U.S. policy toward Latin America subsequently foundered into a period of "benign neglect" from which it has yet to reemerge.[1] As Fernando Henrique Cardoso, president of Brazil (1995–2002) noted in his memoirs, "I understand that America's foreign policy focus changed forever after 9/11, but that didn't give America carte blanche to turn its back on the rest of the world."[2] Similar opinions continue to resound throughout many of the region's capitals, even if public support of U.S. policies remains tepid.

Cardoso has a point. America's military presence in the region is a shell of what it was just ten years ago. Perhaps more telling, America's last effort at widespread engagement with Latin America, the Free Trade Area of the Americas (FTAA), was a halfhearted attempt at a free trade bloc spanning the Americas that died without dirge in 2005.

As the United States has withdrawn from Latin America, U.S. policymakers have haphazardly responded to changes in the region, with mixed results. The Bush administration's quick recognition of the coup-installed government after Chávez's brief ouster in 2002 is one glaring example. Chávez was a democratically elected first-term president. By endorsing the coup the Bush administration unwittingly gave a seed of credence to the "Mr. Danger" moniker that Chávez came to favor for President George W. Bush. Public missteps are certainly not the exclusive domain of Republican administrations. The highest-profile acknowledgment of Iran's growing influence in Latin America came from Secretary of State Clinton, in May of 2009. She said, "The Iranians are building a huge embassy in Managua, and you can only imagine what that's for."[3] She was misinformed; there is no large Iranian embassy in Nicaragua. As one senior Nicaraguan official said (and U.S. officials have privately conceded), "We don't have an Iranian mega-embassy. We have an ambassador in a rented house with his wife."[4]

Herein lies one of the big problems for global powers when they seek to disengage from a large part of the world—when engagement does occur, there is little room for error. If the president makes a gaffe visiting the Prime Minister in Britain, for example, it shows up on the BBC one evening, is gone the next, and doesn't affect popular opinion in a way that can stir policy. Ongoing diplomacy quickly drowns out rhetorical foibles, and regular interactions between diplomats and other professional bureaucrats prevent a gross misunderstanding from having a snowball effect. That hasn't been the case with regard to U.S. policy toward Latin America during the era of disengagement of the last decade. The U.S. government has trod a treacherously narrow path that allows for few missteps, yet obtuse American statements have allowed the weeds of Hugo Chávez and Iran to sprout between the cracks.

This chapter provides an outline for countering the Venezuela-Iran alliance. The tone is this: between fatuous hopes for regional engagement and grim indifference, there is a middle path for the United States, which will turn back Venezuela and Iran's influence in Latin America, where the alliance has nested. Beyond this strategy, a series of issues should be taken up by U.S. policymakers in order to directly combat the most pressing threats to the security of the United States and its allies.

BROAD STROKES

If the United States recommitted to a regionwide engagement of Latin America, it could foster regional solidarity on core issues such as trade and drug trafficking. Doing so would help isolate Chávez within a region of his peers. Crucially, this effort would bear the mark of consensus and avoid a heavy U.S. fingerprint. Both intellectuals and policymakers in the United States and Latin America generally share this perspective. Shortly after his inauguration President Obama urged "equal partnership" between Washington and Latin America at the Summit of the Americas in April 2009.[5] For many the starting point for this process involves offering Latin America what its nations have collectively sought since at least 1948: a free trade agreement spanning the Americas.

Leaders in Washington and many Latin American nations put FTAA on ice in 2005 for different reasons. To seriously restart talks, the White House will need to expend some political capital to remove lavish trade protections that Congress gives to U.S. farmers. Maintaining these subsidies and tariffs is an anachronism, and it's hypocritical coming from the world's most prominent champion of free trade. More pragmatically, the two largest nations in the region—Brazil and Mexico—feel the brunt of U.S. agricultural protections. If America wants the full weight of their support to address regional problems, it will have to be more sensitive to their interests.

From Latin America's perspective, indifference or downright hostility to FTAA had a lot to do with ebbing support for free trade a decade ago. Between 1997 and 2002, a series of global economic shocks—the financial crisis in Asia, Russia's economic collapse, a currency devaluation in Brazil, and the implosion of Argentina—gave plenty of reason to be wary of economic integration, as several of these economic crises started in other parts of the world. Furthermore, much of South America's Southern Cone had a ready alternative to a free trade deal with the United States in the form of Mercosur, a free trade agreement between Argentina, Brazil, Paraguay, and Uruguay. And several countries, including Chile, Mexico, and most of the Caribbean and Central America, already had working trade deals with the United States. Colombia and Panama also had preferential trade treaties pending before the U.S. Congress. So the number of countries that faced clear benefits as a result of a regional trade deal was fairly limited.

By mid-decade, another factor weighed in. Chávez's oil-endowed alternative model to economic cooperation in Latin America featured barter-style exchanges and avoided the hassle of potentially painful trade reform. Though the fundamentals of Chávez's economic integration scheme were shoddy, by 2006 all those interested in Chávez's "anti-neoliberal" bloc understood that any glitches would quickly be smoothed over by Chávez's willingness to spend Venezuela's oil revenues with little expectation of economic reform, just continued loyalty to "Hugo Boss."

Now there is reason to believe Latin American views on trade with the United States have changed. In 2006 Venezuela was invited into Mercosur, but rather than working to incorporate his country into the union of Southern Cone states, Chávez quickly tried to impose his ideology on the group. A "reformatting of Mercosur" to focus on anti-imperialism, Chávez said, offered the best route to "decontaminating the contamination of neo-liberalism."[6] The organization quickly became defunct after Chavez's "anti-imperial" assault subverted the pragmatic purpose of reducing tariffs between its members.

Recognizing the damage, Uruguay's president Tabaré Ramón Vázquez Rosas, a socialist, approached the United States about the possibility of a bilateral free trade treaty. Uruguay has not been alone in seeking closer trade relations with the United States. In the years since, there has been a slow drip of presidents in Latin America that have sought to test the waters of free trade with the United States.

In New York for the annual UN General Assembly meeting in 2010, Chile's president Miguel Juan Sebastián Piñera Echenique told talk show host Charlie Rose that now "the U.S. is missing opportunities" because of its failure to form free trade agreements with Latin America. He advised:

There are many, many Latin American countries that would like to reach a free trade agreement with the U.S.—which is beneficial to both parties. . . . The U.S. could do a better job vis-à-vis Latin America. And I'm not talking about aid. I'm talking about partnership, facing together the challenges of poverty and the future. Where is the will?[7]

However, taking such a step requires time—roughly a decade, by any reasonable estimate—and would entail a serious political commitment by the U.S. government.

The United States should also robustly support regional security agreements. Most working U.S. security arrangements are bilateral in essence, if not in letter, including cooperation with Colombia and Mexico. The working bilateral agreement with Colombia is Chávez's favorite excuse for increasing Venezuela's arms expenditures and aggressive military posturing. The nascent Caribbean Basin Security Initiative (CBSI), which involves cooperation between the United States and a host of Caribbean island states, is a promising forum that cannot easily incur the same response from Chávez. President Obama announced the CBSI in 2009, and it came to life in May 2010 with a congressional appropriation of $37 million. In 2011 funding is likely to be on the order of $79 million.[8] CBSI has three main goals:

1. Combating drug trafficking and organized crime.
2. Strengthening the rule of law.
3. Promoting social justice.

Unlike many previous drug trafficking initiatives, CBSI is heavily tilted toward social justice efforts, building up effective police forces and judiciaries that can eventually stand up to the corruption associated with drug trafficking.

Of course, the designated purpose of the CBSI is to stymie the flow of drugs leaving Colombia and Venezuela en route to the United States and Europe. Beyond this the CBSI could indirectly serve to contain Chávez's influence. Chávez has long relied on the Caribbean to support his Bolivarian revolution—a recent book by Michael Penfold and Javier Corrales deems him a "dragon in the tropics" (and uses the phrase as its title)—and he has doled out significant subsidies, through Petrocaribe and other programs, for these countries' nominal backing. U.S. funding through CBSI is currently too small to compete with Petrocaribe, but the institution-building component of the program, and the working relationships between American and Caribbean officials it stands to foster, provide hope for inuring these ministates against Chávez's sway. Importantly, because the mass of manpower in the CBSI is drawn from its Caribbean members, the organization doesn't appear to be a U.S. imposition.

Another broad approach recommends ending the power of Venezuela, Iran, and other anti-American energy exports: "energy independence" is heralded as the cure-all to reliance on these regimes. However, as suggested in chapter 5, talk of energy independence is simply unrealistic. America has limited leverage over its primary oil providers, including Venezuela, as long as it draws on its traditional foreign policy toolbox.[9] For the United States the most realistic objective over the next twenty years is modest reductions in reliance on hostile producers like Venezuela through the introduction of increased fuel economy standards. Also, greater reliance on biofuels, such as Brazilian ethanol, would offset some price volatility in oil markets.

FRIENDS WITH BENEFITS

Between an idealistic approach that advocates broad, regional partnership and the power politics involved in the United States dealing directly with Venezuela and Ecuador, there is a middle path that can limit the influence of Chávez and Iran, and, not incidentally, serve the interests of the United States' allies in Latin America. The United States should foster bilateral relationships that stand to offer multiplier effects: as these U.S. allies benefit from improved ties with the United States they can serve as beacons of Western values, crowding out the appeal of anti-Americanism. In the 1990s, Argentina president Carlos Saúl Menem called such intense bilateral ties with the United States "carnal relations." Now U.S. policymakers should seek "carnal relations" with Colombia, Peru, and Brazil. These three countries can whittle away the influence of Chávez and Iran, and stifle the emergence of dangerous forms of anti-Americanism in the region in the future. As it does so, the United States should welcome contact with all states that want to foster closer relations, especially leaders from the Hugo sphere.

A starting point for this approach is simply U.S. support for its current friends. Colombia is the U.S. ally in most obvious need of help. On the surface, the United States has shown its willingness to help Colombia wage its war on narcotraffickers by offering support via Plan Colombia. Since the 1990s this effort has succeeded in dismantling Colombia's powerful drug cartels and in restoring stability to vast parts of the country. Without a doubt, the Colombian government's ability to quell the FARC has been made possible by U.S. funding.

But simply spending money to fight traffickers is insufficient. Colombia requires political and economic support that the United States affords to its other strategic allies. Unfortunately, when President Uribe made allegations relating to the FARC's hideouts in Venezuela and Ecuador, his government received almost no political support from the United States. This was certainly the case in the wake of the March 1, 2008, Colombian raid into Ecuador. The United States clearly acknowledges the threat posed by the FARC by classifying the group a terrorist organization and offering a $5 million reward on information leading to the arrest or capture of its leaders, like Raúl Reyes. Yet the State Department routinely refrains from diplomatic support for Colombia. To cite one example, in the summer of 2009 Colombia released a slew of evidence from captured FARC camps that pointed to Venezuelan support for the group. But when asked about the situation in August of 2009, a State Department spokesman would only say, "We do not comment on intelligence matters."[10]

Jorge Castañeda, a former foreign minister of Mexico and a leading voice on Latin American affairs, argues that more diplomatic and political support are crucial: "Only with active US backing can Colombia take its case to the Organization of American States (where it would currently lose), to the United Nations (where it might win), and to friends and allies in Europe and Asia (where it would undoubtedly have the upper hand)."[11] Indeed, a concert of American, Brazilian, and European backing should exist when the Colombian government lodges specific, credible allegations of FARC-Venezuela ties. The international drug flow threatens all three parties, as both the United States and European Union have had their citizens kidnapped—or killed—by the FARC.

On the economic front, the U.S. Congress needs to pass the free trade agreement with Colombia that has been stalled in its chambers since 2007. This will boost Colombia's growth prospects and further consolidate democracy in Colombia. Critics of the trade deal cite concern over Colombia's human rights record, one reason why it has remained pending for so long. Why reward a Colombian government that allegedly has ties to right-wing paramilitaries who violate human rights? If one concedes that human rights abuses occur in Colombia because of the government, concern over U.S. policy should be directed toward Plan Colombia, which helps arm the Colombian government, and not a free trade deal. Closer economic ties with the United States would only enhance respect for human rights in Colombia.

As Colombia grows richer and more stable, doubts will grow within Venezuela about the merit of Chávez's rule. A growing developmental gap between the liberal Colombian state and Venezuela's broken economic system will become more apparent and should put bottom-up pressure on the Chávez government for change. Furthermore, America needs to show that it still supports its friends in the region.[12] A free trade agreement with Colombia will be a message to others in Latin America that working with the United States still entails benefits, which is probably the reason why Chávez has lobbied against the bilateral deal.

While Colombia is most deserving of U.S. support, Peru is also a crucial ally because it can have ripple effects throughout the Andes. Since 2007 Peru has had a free trade arrangement with the United States that promises to boost exports of Peruvian textiles and commodities to the United States. It has been a foil for leftist criticism because in several respects—child labor and environmental considerations chief among them—the United States has left the door open for exploitation of Peruvian law by companies that aim to export their goods from the country. For the United States to make the most out of these partnerships it needs to ensure that social considerations, such as improvements in labor conditions, take place. In a policy booklet published by the Inter-American Dialogue, Michael Shifter said that to counteract Chávez's appeal "Andean countries, such as Colombia and Peru, already allies, should be treated with greater generosity and far-sightedness on critical questions concerning trade and development assistance."[13] Doing so will diminish the appeal of radical leftist movements not only in a country like Peru, but in other parts of the region as well. Peru can also serve as a model should Ecuador or Bolivia decide to change paths, as its trade preferences began with the 1991 Andean Trade Promotion Act (ATPA), which grants preferential access to the U.S. market in return for cooperation with Washington on drug trafficking. By being fair if not beneficent to its allies, the United States will build rapport among countries watching nearby, to the detriment of Chávez and Iran.

Building a closer bilateral relationship between the United States and Brazil is another linchpin in shrinking Chávez's influence. Bizarrely, the United States has not regarded Brazil as a strategic asset since WWII when it was the only South American nation to send troops to fight against the Axis. Brazil became "the forgotten Ally" for its efforts, portending a streak of almost continuous indifference by Washington. Brazil and the United States did not sign a military agreement from 1952 to 2010, an astonishing interval that is only partly excused by the fact that Brazil fell under military dictatorship from 1964 to 1985. Moreover, Brazil and the United States have never come close to a major free trade agreement, mainly because America refuses to end tariffs and subsidies to agribusiness.

A Brazilian patriarch is needed in South America. This isn't because South Americans, or Latinos more generally, are intellectually backward, as some have suggested, nor are they constitutionally incapable of governing themselves. Rather, the nations that spoon Brazil are, with a few exceptions, geographically small in size and have low population densities. Average income is low, and yet these nations are replete with coveted natural resources. History attests to the result: foreign powers give money to governing elites and then proceed to extract the natural resources with little regard for the fact that the masses do not benefit. Today, China is moving into the role of principal investor and extractor, but other countries such as the United States, India, Brazil, Spain, France, and, yes, Venezuela and Iran, are all a part of this process. Brazil as patriarch is best situated to prevent further pillaging of the continent through its foreign aid programs by selectively serving as an interlocutor between China and smaller countries, and by preventing regional squabbles (like the ones that Chávez is known to instigate) from turning into regional wars.

Brazil's strategic interests coincide remarkably well with the United States', and Brazil's rise on the world stage make it a very suitable—in many ways more suitable than the United States itself—hegemon in South America. Brazil is America's most kindred ally in the looming BRIC (Brazil, Russia, India, and China) world. Unlike China and Russia, Brazil is a vibrant democracy. And unlike India, Brazil's path to regional dominance is not contested by rival great powers. While it might not seem like America and Brazil are close partners now, given Brazil's close relations with Iran and insistence that Washington end barriers to agricultural trade, Brazil's willingness to tackle the tricky issues of international relations bodes well for the United States in the long run.

As a strategic ally in Latin America, Brazil is unrivalled. It shares a border with ten other countries in South America, every country in the continent except for Chile and Ecuador. Thus, every security issue in South America—immigration, drug trafficking, contested borders, the presence of major foreign powers, natural disasters, etc.—is of concern to Brazil.

Brazil is also a rising energy power. Brazil's Petrobras discovered oil deposits off the nation's coast in 2006 that are believed to be the largest deposits found in the last thirty years. Long self-sufficient in energy because of its cane-based ethanol industry, Brazil is poised to become an oil superpower in the coming years. This is a boon to the United States but a hindrance for Venezuela and Iran, because it will further dilute OPEC's ability to set prices.

Furthermore, Brazil's foreign aid programs have the potential to roll back some of the insidious aspects of Chávez's own foreign aid. Brazil's foreign aid spending is ramping up dramatically as its position in the world seems more assured, making it one of the world's biggest providers of assistance to poor countries.[14] Brazil's aid model, like Chávez's, doesn't come with IMF-style conditions. And unlike, say, China's foreign aid programs, which focus heavily on building infrastructure in order to best extract commodities from recipient countries, Brazil's aid focuses largely on social programs and agriculture.[15] Including foreign loans from Brazil's development bank, Brazil's commitments to institutions like the UN Development Program and direct bilateral aid programs, such as those to Haiti, Brazil spends around $4 billion a year on foreign aid.[16] Maybe Chávez spent more on aid throughout Latin America in 2007, but Brazil has quietly stepped into that role since.

Developing nations like Brazil understand the plight of poverty alleviation and inequality. This, of course, affords Brazil an empathetic image in the region, but it also gives Brazil unique standing to counter the arguments advanced by the likes of China that rich countries were allowed to develop without environmental or human rights considerations. To the rest of South America, Brazil is only half-foreign, unlike the United States, and traditional resentments of falling under the influence of another nation are subdued. Carlos Escudé, an Argentine foreign policy analyst, notes, "We would rather not be anyone's satellite, but there is far less opposition to our being a star on the Brazilian flag than our being a star on the American flag."[17]

Finally, Brazil is the standard-bearer of a responsible leftist government. Accepting governance from the political left is necessary for U.S. policymakers, be they Democrat or Republican. Vast historical inequalities, the return to democracy on the heels of mass human rights abuses by right-wing military governments, and widespread poverty throughout the region all contribute to the emergence of leftist governments in Latin America.[18]

Although Brazil is generally accommodating to Chávez, he tends to guard his tongue in meetings with Brazil's president Lula (as he is popularly known). Carlos Mauricio Funes Cartagena, elected president of El Salvador in March 2009 as an avowed leftist, was hailed by Chávez as proof of a "historical current that has been rising in Latin America in this first decade of the 21st century."[19] But Funes politely rebuffed Chávez's overtures in favor of Brazil, making his first foreign trip there and frankly stating, "I identify more with the Brazilian model than with Venezuela's."[20]

While Brazil is, in many ways, America's most promising ally in South America, relations between the two have been fraught since 2002. Under the presidency of Lula (2003–2010) Brazil asserted itself as an interlocutor between developing nations and the developed world. Lula called for Western countries, and especially the United States, to "stop your hypocrisy" over free trade by getting rid of farm subsidies.[21] Deed followed word, and Brazil started using the WTO as a conduit for challenging U.S. trade policy. In the spring of 2010 the WTO ruled in Brazil's favor regarding U.S. cotton subsidies, which amount to $3 billion annually. At this point, if not before, most developing nations cave, either because of U.S. pressure or the recognition that their legal victory, if turned into action, would only cause more economic damage. Instead Brazil announced hundreds of tariffs across a wide range of industries to retaliate against Washington's illegal subsidies. Rather than fulfill its commitment in essence, the Obama administration spent money in order to paper over the problem, agreeing to pay Brazil $147 million a year in order to keep its cotton subsidies.[22] Still, the United States has a host of other trade barriers that prevent Brazilian goods from being competitive in the U.S. market, and Brazil is threatening to settle other matters before the WTO. Eventually this could cost U.S. taxpayers much more than $3.147 billion a year.

Given Brazil's immense strategic potential to U.S. policy, the United States should devote diplomatic energy and expend political capital in Congress to make Brasilia a reliable partner. To improve relations with Brazil the United States should work to boost trade between the countries. Removing a $.53 a gallon tariff on Brazilian ethanol is a good first step. In return the United States can reasonably expect Brazil to end threats, voiced often over the last decade, to reverse-engineer patented drugs. On the diplomatic front, Brazil has frequently worked against U.S. interests in Latin America. Brazil mounted a robust, arguably priggish, campaign to restore José Manuel Zelaya Rosales to office after a bloodless coup toppled the Honduran president in 2009. Yet on other matters, notably the rise of authoritarianism among governments allied with Hugo Chávez and Chávez's attempt to start an arms race in South America, Brazil has looked the other way (while leading the region in military spending).

Brazil's wrangling is constructive. Under Lula, the country has lobbied for adherence to the norms of free trade as laid out by the WTO. It is also pushing for a permanent seat on an expanded Security Council. There are both idealistic and practical reasons for acquiescing to Brazil's agenda. In an idealistic sense, Brazil, like Colombia, should be embraced because both *are* Western. Of course, they are culturally distinct from North America and Western Europe. But, more important, they represent "the triumph of the Western idea" that Francis Fukuyama feted two decades ago—clear, if imperfect, democracies with vibrant market economies. Now Brazil wants "to be among the nations who make the rules."[23] Emulation warrants accommodation. Brazil is the most natural check to the influence of Chávez and Iran in the Americas. Fostering an alliance with the country will aid U.S. security and economic interest in a splendid fashion.

SELECTIVE ENGAGEMENT

Chávez's rhetoric is not going to change, and while what he says is often more important than the public image of a buffoon that he cuts, his words are also typically misleading. Instead of directly responding to his outlandish rhetoric, U.S. policymakers should carefully target their criticisms of Chávez. Responding to Chávez's broadsides only feeds his message that Venezuela is a major preoccupation of Washington, and that malicious U.S. interests—policymakers and the CIA, in general—do little else but plot against him. Thomas Shannon, the highest-ranking diplomat over Latin America during the Bush administration, followed a careful approach that should serve as a standard. After 2006, public criticisms by the United States declined, a concerted product of Shannon's efforts to avoid rhetorical squabbles with Chávez.[24] In fact, a chart in Corrales and Penfold's book ventures to track the decline in public criticism by the United States of Venezuela in recent years.[25] When Shannon did speak on the topic of Chávez he did so in measured tone and with credible intelligence reports to back him up. "In Latin America, Iran sees a way to demonstrate that they can exert themselves on an international level. . . . It's a way to push back on us," Shannon said in May of 2008. "And we remind them about the continuing relationships that exist in the region between groups in Latin America and groups that we consider to be terrorist in the Middle East, especially Hezbollah and Hamas."[26] Shannon then went on to state that Venezuela, as a member of the UN, should weigh its commitments to the international community when dealing with Iran. Contrast this with Hillary Clinton's comment about Iran's embassy in Nicaragua.

Moving beyond rhetoric, the United States needs to engage Venezuela on the issue of arms purchases. Given Chávez's appetite for arms and the likelihood that small arms may end up in the hands of the FARC, many experts believe the United States should expand the 2006 arms embargo against Venezuela.[27] Take this passage from Douglas Schoen and Michael Rowan's 2009 book *The Threat Closer to Home*:

> We can strengthen the strategic arms embargo of Venezuela that was imposed in 2005 [*sic*] when Venezuela was upgrading its U.S.-made jet fighters and making disproportionately large arms purchases that alarmed the United States and Colombia, among other nations. That embargo has been costly and inconvenient for Chávez; but he circumvented it by spending approximately $5 billion for arms purchased from Russia, Belarus, China, Iran, and elsewhere.[28]

The major flaw in this argument is evident in the second sentence, yet the authors do not engage the fact that the embargo correlates to a surge in arms purchases, mainly from Russia.

Rather, it would probably work to the United States' advantage to end its arms embargo of Venezuela. This might be viewed as rewarding Chávez for bad behavior, and it could also be seen as adding to a potential arms race in South America. These criticisms are fair, but larger geopolitical issues make it necessary, a viewed shared by at least some at the U.S. Army War College's Strategic Studies Institute.[29] The direct benefit of this approach would be that U.S. firms could begin to shift the balance of Venezuela's arsenal to include more defensive and less offensive systems. No doubt this will not impact Chávez's anti-American streak. But at the same time Chávez proves every day that he is not willing to let ideology get in the way of doing business with the United States.

America's big benefit would come from the loosening of Venezuela's ties to Russia. Should Chávez slow his country's acquisition of Russian purchases, Putin is likely to downgrade Venezuela on Moscow's list of client states. What would follow? Fewer joint oil and gas deals, a lethargic approach to Venezuela's nuclear program, and slower delivery of arms to Venezuela are all possible. Venezuela would be a blocked pawn in Moscow's attempt to check NATO expansion. For Moscow, engaging Latin America would have to take on a more natural approach, prioritizing Brazil amid relations with several individual governments. Chávez would no longer be a hot node for transmitting Russia's influence through the region. The best starting point for achieving this outcome is to reduce the flow of Russian arms to Venezuela by permitting U.S. arms sales to Caracas.

While selectively engaging Venezuela, the United States should exert firm pressure on the government of Rafael Correa in Ecuador. Unlike Bolivia, whose few trading partners are mainly other South American countries, Ecuador relies on trade in nonstaple goods for its economic well-being. Roses account for 2 percent of the country's GDP, and approximately 100,000 people in the country owe their living to the flower.[30] Furthermore, the cut flower industry and the fruit industry owe their prosperity to the ATPA.[31] The United States is under no obligation to keep renewing the ATPA. Also, Equador is extremely vulnerable to pressure from the U.S. Treasury because of the nation's banks and official currency, the greenback. The purpose of hard economic diplomacy should be narrowly targeted to focus on Ecuador's poor enforcement of international financial standards, which threatens to make the country a haven for Iranian money laundering as well as black market operations in general. By eliminating Iranian outposts, such as those in Ecuador, the illicit activities of Iran and Venezuela are concentrated, making denial harder and monitoring easier. Representatives from the Obama administration should make it clear to Correa that the U.S. Treasury and Congress will rethink trade concessions and financial ties to the country if Quito doesn't work harder to stop money laundering.

AN AXIS OF IMPUNITY?

Dealing with the Venezuela-Iran alliance in the context of Latin American dynamics is necessary but insufficient to halt the threat. China and Russia are patrons of the Venezuelan and Iranian governments, and their support threatens to cast the "axis of unity" into an axis of impunity. Not only do they play to Tehran's interest by delaying and diluting UN sanctions over the Islamic Republic's nuclear program, but China and Russia both have economic ties with Iran and Venezuela that assume, above all, that Chávez and the Islamic Republic stay in power in order to protect Chinese and Russian interests. A passive approach to this sort of sponsorship would be to let international economics run their course and hope China or Russia calculate that their interests are best served by downgrading ties with Chávez and Iran. Essentially, this is the course U.S. policy currently favors. In one respect, this book is a recounting of how that strategy has failed.

At the other end of the spectrum stands the prospect of a Western confrontation with both China and Russia because of their support for such avowedly anti-American regimes. One view is that the United States and EU should implement sanctions against Chinese and Russian oil businesses with ties to Iran, including banning Chinese subsidiaries from having assets in the States and barring Gazprom from selling natural gas in the country.[32] Tough measures like these entail risks to U.S. relations with China and Russia, but security experts Reuel Marc Gerecht and Mark Dubowitz believe that conflict at some point is inevitable:

> We were always going to have a test of wills with Russia and China over Iran. That day has arrived. Connoisseurs of power politics— Vladimir Putin, Hu Jintao, and Ali Khamenei—are watching. So is Israeli Prime Minister Benjamin Netanyahu, who will decide one of these days whether a nuclear-armed Iran is acceptable, or not.[33]

That final line references a widespread belief that Israel will launch attacks against Iran's nuclear sites if Prime Minister Netanyahu decides that UN sanctions are not scuttling Iran's nuclear program.

Still, China and Russia are dealing in shades of gray when it comes to Iran and Venezuela. As chapter 8 made clear, China's interests in Iran and

Venezuela are more narrowly defined to focus on procuring oil and gas supplies. Another factor to be considered is the depth of economic interdependence between China and the United States. One implication of "Chimerica" is the United States lacks clear diplomatic leverage over the Chinese. Breaking China away from Iran means severing China from over $100 billion in investment, which is likely to be a futile task. Regarding Venezuela, it is more likely that the relationship will wane if oil prices stay low because Chávez will eventually lose his ability to subsidize the shipping cost required to get Venezuela's oil to China.

Checking Russia's sponsorship of Venezuela and Iran must begin by acknowledging an inconvenient truth: Russia under Putin's control is not a meaningful ally. Arms deals and security alliances formed by the VIRUS now surround key U.S. allies, increasing the likelihood and scale of conflict. Hamas, Hezbollah, the FARC, Quds Force—all would wither on the vine without substantial material support from the VIRUS. Instead, all are thriving, despite the global recession, adding an additional layer of complexity and instability to the schemes of Venezuela, Iran, and Russia.

Russia has benefited geopolitically from the instability it enables. Today Russia has more sway in Latin America than the Soviet Union did at any time, except during the early 1960s. And Russia's support of Iran, UNSCR 1929 notwithstanding, serves to confirm Senator Schumer's sense that "Russia uses Iran [for] leverage over us."[34]

To foil this partnership, the Obama administration should reconsider its decision to amend plans for missile defenses systems in Eastern Europe. Here the United States has a score of foreign policy successes to build upon. In the 1980s America's firm stance against the Soviets contrasted markedly with Western Europe's waffling. More recently, aid and praise endeared "New Europe" to the Bush administration, and many nations committed troops to the wars in Afghanistan and Iraq. Classical deterrence has gone over well for decades. But America's popularity has waned in ex-communist Europe of late, according to the German Marshall Fund.[35] Altering missile defenses to a sea-based platform is widely seen as a strategic capitulation to Russia and is proof-positive to some that the United States is gradually withdrawing from its commitment to Europe.

A decade ago the National Intelligence Council warned that European governments "will use US handling of Russia as a barometer of how well or poorly Washington is exerting leadership and defending European interests."[36] That sentiment is nowhere more valid than in Eastern Europe, where people view Washington as the underwriter of security because of "a historically rooted fear of Russian power and consequently a more American view of the Hobbesian realities."[37] Concessions by Washington to Moscow and a lack of engagement have led prominent voices in the region to air their gripes. Almost two dozen senior figures, including Vaclav Havel and Lech Walesa, wrote a public letter lamenting the erosion of ties under President Obama in July of 2009.

Truth be told, missile defense has never been a narrowly defined security issue. Iran is not considered a direct threat to Eastern Europe, and in any event its missiles could only go as far as Turkey or Ukraine. By contrast, Russia's missile capacity could handily overwhelm or trick the American-installed defenses with decoys. And the missile defense systems would only become operational in 2018 at the earliest. Rather, the decision reflects a strategic message, sent by the Bush administration, that the United States is prepared to defend its allies in Eastern Europe and Israel alike from aerial attack. Given the Russian leadership's sense of realpolitik, any perceived withdrawal by the U.S. government will only be regarded as weakness. Instead of quid pro quo, the United States is likely to gain greater insight into Mr. Putin's soul. An emboldened Russia will more directly threaten Eastern Europe, as foreshadowed by Russia's recent penchant for war games.[38] It could also lead to more loans-for-arms deals in Venezuela and Ecuador without any significant movement on UN sanctions against Iran. Keeping plans alive for a land-based defense would maintain a bargaining chip with little or no actual cost to the U.S. defense budget in the short term.

ROLE OF THE MEDIA

Perhaps the most effective way to stymie the Venezuela-Iran alliance in the short term is investigation by major media outlets. Chapter 3 noted how reports on Conviasa flights by CNN and Fox News in the summer of 2010 were directly responsible for the termination of the Caracas-Damascus-Tehran flights. Media investigations on other sketchy elements of the Venezuela-Iran alliance could produce similar results. For instance:

- Visitation at VenIran production facilities to put an end to zombie factories that are regularly staffed but not regularly turning out products.
- The status of Chávez's "nuclear village" and the participation of Iran in recovering uranium in both Venezuela and Bolivia.
- Coverage of Russia's agreement to help Venezuela launch a nuclear reactor. Interestingly, the day after the thirty-three Chilean miners were safely rescued, the headline story on *bbcmundo.com*, the BBC's Spanish-language website, announced a specific nuclear deal between Medvedev and Chávez. In the United States coverage of the story got consigned to the news ticker at the bottom of the screen.
- Banco Internacional de Desarrollo's day-to-day operations in Caracas and Quito.
- Iranian projects in Bolivia that may be for social development, or may be operations to recover uranium to hand over to Iran.

While U.S. media have been engaged on some topics, reporting has been conspicuously absent when it comes to fleshing out the extent of support that the FARC receives within Venezuela. Several London newspapers such as the *Guardian* and the *Telegraph* track developments on this front, as does the BBC. But major U.S. media rarely cover the ongoing developments between the Colombian government, the FARC, and Venezuela. The *Wall Street Journal* and *Miami Herald* are the main exceptions to this trend. Uninterested American media permit disengaged American policy, and it also feeds the sense in Colombia that the war against the FARC is one without allies, only a financial backer.

POLICY CONCLUSIONS

Disengagement from Latin America is not an option. On the other hand, formulating a regional approach to secure and stabilize Latin America to U.S. interests, and talk of energy independence, are long-term goals that cannot address short-term security threats. To that end, it is important to follow the country-specific recommendations introduced in this chapter in order to keep Latin America from becoming a hotbed of Venezuelan and Iranian influence. In general, public confrontations with Chávez should be avoided, but when Colombia makes public accusations against the Chávez government for its ties to the FARC, the United States should, after weighing the evidence, stand ready to support Colombia in regional forums such as the Organization of American States and the UN. Peru should be supported in its attempt to modernize and integrate into the global economy. And Brazil's rising stardom in Latin America should be encouraged as it can provision security and stability in South American affairs in an unrivaled manner. Supporting these nations can produce mutually beneficial results in a matter of months, and they stand a good chance of boosting U.S ties to the broader region.

At the end of the day, the virility of the Venezuela-Iran alliance—the revolutionary credo—is derived from orienting the pact around anti-Americanism and restoring lost grandeur. Even though the two governments are only nominally democracies, to some degree they still need to account for domestic conditions. Their oil-based economies are always volatile and usually frail, so, absent vibrant economic reforms, trade agreements between them can only provide a mirage of prosperity, offering scant succor for the masses. With time the failure of governance will become apparent as regional neighbors, indeed most nations, reap greater benefits from engaging the West. The United States and its allies should shed light on the chasm between rhetoric and the harshness of day-to-day lives in these countries. In the twenty-first century the appeal for revolutionary opposition or reversion to the security of the past is slain by realization of the nonrevolutionary quality of life.

Inoculation is not the same as eradication, and in order to stem the influence that Chávez and the Islamic Republic have amassed, realistic approaches and trade-offs are necessary.

Conclusion

Eight years ago Venezuela and Iran were essentially isolated on the world stage, Iran shunned and Venezuela ignored. Surging oil prices and a rising tide of anti-American sentiment catalyzed the change. Venezuela and Iran capitalized on these trends, spreading their oil wealth abroad in order to gain allies. Within a few years they had managed to hoist themselves to the status of regional powers with global ambitions.

From 2006 to 2008, with oil prices high and disgust with America's involvement in Iraq and Afghanistan at fever pitch, Venezuela and Iran tried to rouse an anti-American alternative worldview, replete with lavish foreign aid programs and institutions, like ALBA, meant to serve as an alternative to the neoliberal agenda. The jerky advance of democracy in Latin America and the Middle East helped. In Latin America Chávez engendered a series of stalwart allies in Bolivia and Ecuador. In the Middle East Iran reaped the benefit of its longtime allies, Hezbollah and Hamas, becoming major political parties in Lebanon and the Palestinian territories. This effectively legitimized Iran's presence on the far side of the Middle East, right on Israel's borders.

As this political coup unfolded, Venezuela and Iran appeared to be paladins of a new world order, one that either directly worked to America's detriment or, perhaps more benignly, spelled irrelevance for the erstwhile superpower—the "post-American world." To buoy their status, Venezuela and Iran doled out aid packages to their allies on a scale that significantly eclipsed Western aid programs. According to a calculation made by University of California–San Diego professor Richard Feinberg, Chávez's aid pledges rival that of the Marshall Plan in real terms.[1] Even by the most conservative estimates, Chávez's aid to other Latin American nations eclipsed that from the U.S. Agency for International Development and the World Bank combined.

Iran then followed Venezuela's lead in Latin America, promising aid to the newly elected governments that Chávez supported. As the Chávez "bridge" moved into place, Bolivia and Nicaragua, and Ecuador to a lesser degree, were showered with attention from Iran. In 2007 Venezuela and Iran's pledges of aid amounted to more than 25 percent of the GDP for both Bolivia and Nicaragua. During this time Venezuela and Iran could present their machinations as pangs of a new world order that offered concessions, not dictates, to poor nations.

However, a crash in oil prices preceded a deep global recession. From more than $140 a barrel in July 2008, oil prices hit a nadir of $34 a barrel in February 2009. The immediate collapse probably caused less of a problem for Venezuela and Iran than the price level of $65 to $80 a barrel that oil resettled at in 2009 and 2010. For the Islamic Republic, oil at $70 a barrel caused more of a strain than any sanctions passed to that point. For Venezuela it meant giving up lavish oil subsidies and plans for pipelines that could bring nations on the southern tip of South America and the Caribbean closer into Chávez's orbit. Each government had to revise its approach, narrowing ambitions to central objectives. Foreign projects and alliances had to be prioritized, trade-offs had to be made. Although the lyrics of the anti-American "axis of unity" stayed the same, the melody changed.

Nicaragua's Sandinista government became the clearest casualty of the astringency. Coming to office (for the second time) in 2007, President Daniel Ortega of Nicaragua was the most ideologically similar leader to Chávez in the Americas. He had proven his deep anti-American convictions, and he eagerly pursued close relations with Caracas and Tehran. In return Iran promised a spate of development projects totaling some $1 billion to help establish Iran's presence in the country. Venezuela's aid to Nicaragua, which began as a means of supporting Ortega's run for the presidency, added to the sense that Nicaragua occupied a special place in the emerging anti-American bloc in Latin America. Promises of developmental aid and mutual praise continued into 2008.

However, Nicaragua has received almost no assistance from Iran. A $350 million port complex planned on Nicaragua's Caribbean coast is unlikely to be built. Comparing the projects discussed publicly by either Nicaraguan or Iranian officials reveals that only one out of at least twenty ever got started.[2] Venezuela also waffled on its pledges to Nicaragua. As a recipient of Venezuelan oil through Petrocaribe, Ortega's Nicaragua has been forced to pay more up front for crude. Moreover, Venezuela's plans for a large $4 billion oil refinery in Nicaragua were halted in the fall of 2008.[3] Another fact regarding Nicaragua shines light on the Venezuela-Iran calculus: there is no credible evidence of the government's collusion with Iran's nuclear program. No sketchy financial ties, no handover of uranium, only misplaced worries about an embassy that doesn't exist.

By contrast, both Venezuela and Iran's aid pledges to Bolivia have been significantly fulfilled. In the case of Ecuador, Iran did not offer the Correa administration any foreign aid when it came to office in 2007. Bilateral trade between the two nations spiked in 2008, but, interestingly, it was not until 2010 that Iran offered its first foreign aid package to Ecuador. Bolivia and Ecuador demonstrate that recession has not meant an end to foreign aid by Chávez or Iran, only greater discretion.

What, then, makes Bolivia and Ecuador more deserving than Nicaragua? In short, the ability of Correa and Morales to quickly subdue checks to the presidential power, possession of natural resources, and local support—or at least absence of vocal local opposition—for the presence of Iranian contractors. It stretches coincidence that both Bolivia and Ecuador are implicated in aiding Iran's nuclear program—Ecuador for hosting Iranian banks known to finance the country's nuclear program; Bolivia for providing Iran access to its uranium deposits, and, if leaked Israeli intelligence documents are to be believed, providing uranium to Iran.

This summary points to two conclusions. First, the Venezuela-Iran alliance is not chiefly an anti-American crusade; rather, it is a tool to advance and consolidate each state's regional ambitions. Iran's aid pledges to Latin American countries help solidify Chávez's sphere of influence, the Hugo sphere, in the Andes. On the other hand, the channels that Iran has opened up in Latin America allow the Islamic Republic to endure sanctions and preserve its status in the Middle East.

This first conclusion points toward a second: the drop in oil prices since July 2008 has not defanged the Venezuela-Iran alliance. Granted, many bilateral deals between Venezuela and Iran—tractor plants, cars, bicycles, all made in Venezuela with Iranian capital and management—have lumbered to a halt since 2008 or operate on an irregular basis. But instead of weakening the connections between Venezuela and Iran, the recession has merely brushed away the disguise. At the core of their relations is a series of illicit ties, and these ties have either continued or intensified. Cooperation on nuclear issues has become clearer since 2009, when the Chávez government acknowledged that Iran was involved in uranium mining in Venezuela. Joint banking operations have expanded in both Venezuela and Iran, while BID has opened an office in Quito, Ecuador. Furthermore, credible accounts of Hezbollah and the Quds Force's spread into Venezuela have accelerated since 2009. In sum, Venezuela and Iran have given up on intricate foreign aid schemes and development projects to promote a new world order but illicit ties continue. The essence of the Venezuela-Iran alliance is now unmasked.

GAUGING THE THREAT

Rhetorically, Venezuela and Iran's cooperation corners on opposing the United States. Many people either accept the claims at face value, or dismiss them altogether. To give an example of the former, a slew of quotes are invoked to support the following argument: "The cold reality is this: Hugo Chávez, the president of Venezuela, is a much more dangerous individual than the famously elusive leader of al-Qaeda."[4] Similar views are widely held about the Iranian government. Based on the sophistication, precision, and discipline of Iran's proxy forces, some argue that Iran is in fact more dangerous than al Qaeda. Powerful politicians have frequently reinforced these views. Benjamin Netanyahu, both as an opposition politician and now as prime minister of Israel, has been quick to remind U.S. audiences: "You are the Great Satan, we are only the Little Satan." One shortcoming of this view is that it misleads people into emotional reactions, making an effective policy response difficult.

The opposite view is common as well: Venezuela and Iran are not at all a threat to the United States. This view is not held just by foreign policy doves, but also by intelligent observers who simply believe that Chávez and Ahmadinejad are buffoons, and buffoons can't do any real harm. The problem in this case is that the rhetoric Chávez and Ahmadinejad employ is so extreme, even delusional, that the underlying direction of the Venezuela-Iran threat is overlooked. But the "axis of unity" presents real threats to the Western order. In brief, these include the following:

- Conviasa flights transited suspicious passengers and cargo between Caracas, Damascus, and Tehran until the route's curtailment in September 2010.
- Hezbollah and the Quds Force now have an operational base in Venezuela.
- Venezuela cooperates with Iran to advance the Islamic Republic's nuclear program by joint recovery of Venezuela's uranium.
- Iranian-owned banks that operate with permission of the governments of Venezuela and Ecuador are almost certainly financial feeders for the Islamic Republic's nuclear program.
- Venezuela sends oil to Iran expressly in order to help the Islamic Republic endure UN sanctions.

All of these points, except possibly the last, are direct challenges to the national security of Colombia, Israel, or both. Netanyahu's statement, while understandable, implies the United States is the primary threat from Iran's rising power, when in fact Israel is the one most directly threatened. Iran with the bomb poses an existential threat to Israel's security, and thus every machination that moves Iran closer to a nuclear weapon puts Iran's national security in doubt.

To go from the potential to the concrete, Iran's support of Hezbollah and Hamas in recent years has enabled these groups to carry out attacks that kill Israelis. Iran, along with its close ally Syria, supply each group with rockets used to attack Israel. Since each group's separate wars with Israel, they have grown stronger thanks to Iran. In a veiled threat a Hezbollah official and member of Parliament in Lebanon told the *New York Times* in October 2010, "We are not sleeping . . . we are working."[5] Hezbollah's leader Hassan Nasrallah claims the group now has forty thousand missiles—most coming from Iran—compared to the thirteen thousand it had when the group went to war with Israel in 2006.[6] In the Palestinian territories, murders of Israeli civilians carried out by Hamas in September 2010 showed the group's ability to paralyze Israeli-Palestinian peace talks almost at will, acts of terrorism that serve Iran's strategic interests.

Linking the security of Israel, or other states in the Middle East, to Venezuela is not obvious. Venezuela does not appear to contribute any significant military assets to the Islamic Republic. But Iran's growing strength in the Middle East is a direct product of its ability to sidestep UN sanctions, and in this way Venezuela's cooperation feeds Iran's confidence in the Middle East. Intelligence reports also indicate that Iran and Hezbollah have recruited informants working in Venezuela to gather information on Jewish travelers, which, when the reports surfaced in 2008, caused concern over abductions.[7] This hasn't happened, but it points toward the lingering threat that Iran, and Venezuela as Iran's host, pose to security in Latin America.

If any question remains who in Latin American is under threat by the Venezuela-Iran alliance, Hugo Chávez has drawn a clear parallel: "Colombia is the Israel of Latin America."[8] Quds Force operatives and Hezbollah have been involved in training FARC guerillas and groups of the Venezuelan army in guerilla warfare. Also, Iranian military manuals were among the cache recovered from Colombia's 2008 raid on the FARC camp in Ecuador.[9]

This is not to say that Venezuela and Iran do not pose a threat to the United States; the alliance they have created does. But the purpose of their alliance is to befuddle U.S. foreign policy, raising the cost of U.S. action against either of them. This includes the costs of sanctions on Iran, the potential of a U.S. attack or U.S. support for an Israeli attack on Iran, and U.S. support for Colombia. In August of 2010 Iranian state-owned media defended the government's relationship with Venezuela by stating that the purpose was "to dull U.S. pressure."[10] Unfortunately for the United States, this statement not only captures a key rationale for the Venezuela-Iran alliance, it has proven quite successful. As Hugo Chávez grew as a threat to regional stability in Latin America and Colombia in particular, the United States softened its support for the Colombian government. And many of the concrete features of the Venezuela-Iran alliance aim at dulling U.S. pressure on Iran: the token amount of oil Chávez sends to Iran; the financial ties that Iran has created in Venezuela and Ecuador; and the lingering prospect of Hezbollah retaliation against the West.

Regarding the last point, Hezbollah's operational base in Venezuela could become a threat to U.S. national security of the first order. Currently Hezbollah's presence appears to serve as a deterrent to U.S. action against Iran, a not-so-subtle reminder that Iran is capable of retaliating across the globe, even in America's backyard. Viewed in this light, Hezbollah's threat is defensive in nature. But if a phantasmagorical escalation of tensions between America and Iran took place, Hezbollah could move to strike at the United States from Latin America.

The importance of these groups' presence in Venezuela should not be either overstated or understated. Hezbollah is nesting into Venezuela both for commercial reasons—drug trafficking is a growth industry in Venezuela—and in case it is called on to carry out attacks against Western targets. In so doing, Hezbollah would not only risk major reprisals by the United States, but it would blow its cover in Venezuela. Hence, Hezbollah's presence in Venezuela, well known to Western intelligence officials and regularly noted in intelligence reports, appears to serve as a deterrent—a way of keeping Western officials mindful of Iran's global reach and capacity to retaliate against attack outside of the Middle East.

Still, Hezbollah is a terrorist organization, and Venezuela is underappreciated as a breeding ground. Reasonably sophisticated terrorist networks rely on safe havens for incubation. To generalize: Islamic terrorists are recruited in the Middle East, trained in terrorist camps there, and then cells nestle in third-party locales where they can blend in prior to moving into final position for an attack. The most obvious example would be the 9/11 attackers, who planned their operation in Hamburg, Germany, before moving to the United States for the execution phase. Since 2001 Europe has stepped up monitoring of communities where radicalism may spawn terrorists. Venezuela is a promising new haven. It is closer to the United States than Europe, it is poorly monitored, and there is a host community to provide camouflage. This last point requires brief explanation. Although Venezuela and Iran have no history of close ties, a Syrian diaspora has flourished in Venezuela, and vice versa, over several generations. Several of Chávez's cabinet officials, for instance, are second-generation Syrians. And the Syrian town of Sweida is known as "Little Venezuela." Embedded within a vibrant Syrian community in Venezuela, extremists could plot largely outside Western governments' ability to monitor them.

THE VIRUS IS CHRONIC

Venezuela and Iran enjoy the active cooperation of one major stakeholder: Russia. As Russia moved further away from Western norms during Vladimir Putin's second term as president, Venezuela and Iran assumed a higher profile in Russia's strategic posture. The exchanges that make up VIRUS cooperation, especially Russia's arms sales and technical nuclear assistance, are destabilizing to the regional security of Latin America and the Middle East. Conventional arms sales to Venezuela threatened an arms race in Latin America, and this threat may resurface. Iran's nuclear program is stewing all sorts of nuclear contingency plans across the Middle East. In return for Russian support, Venezuela and Iran have become key parts of Moscow's major geostrategic goal: the control of Europe's energy supplies. The Kremlin probably did not envisage the VIRUS as a clear and deadly pact; formal military ties between Russia, Venezuela, and Iran don't currently add up to much, the joint Russo-Venezuelan naval exercises in the Caribbean Sea in November 2008 notwithstanding. Trade between Russia and the two nations has certainly increased, but much of this relates to arms. Venezuela and Iran are not proxies intended to actually attack the United States, they are independent nations with their own ambitions. With Moscow's backing the VIRUS aims to chronically weaken the West, tattering the West's security blanket along its edges by arming and supporting a stronger Venezuela and Iran that have managed to encircle Colombia and Israel. The VIRUS ensures that low-boil diplomatic problems stay on the burner.

Tensions between Russia and the West may have peaked in 2008, with the war between Russia and Georgia.[11] Since the onset of the global recession, the Obama and Medvedev administrations have promulgated a "reset" campaign meant to renew warm relations between the two nations. President Medvedev's support for a fourth round of sanctions against Iran is the most significant indication that Moscow may be rethinking its support for Iran. Other gestures, including the prospect of Russia's membership in the WTO, talk of greater U.S.-Russian bilateral trade, and a deal to limit nuclear stockpiles, the so-called New START Treaty, are further hints that the Russian president seeks more cooperation and less confrontation with the West.

But while Medvedev may not have ultimately blocked sanctions on Iran, he has not turned his back on the country either. For every positive sign of change in Moscow's approach to the West, there is a troubling sign of VIRUS vitality. The inauguration of the Bushehr nuclear plant in August 2010 is one example. Arms sales to Venezuela, on credit because Chávez can no longer afford to pay up front given the drop in oil are prices, are another. Also, talk of a Russian military base off the coast of Venezuela intensified since the "reset" was announced. And in October of 2010, Presidents Medvedev and Chávez announced specific plans for Russia to build Venezuela's first nuclear reactor; the White House reacted coolly, noting that every nation has a right to civilian nuclear energy, but with rights "come responsibilities." The *New York Times* mused, "Venezuela, like Iran, is brimming with energy from oil and natural gas, possibly raising concerns about its motives."[12]

Russia's national security strategy remains obsessed with halting NATO expansion. A spate of elaborate counter-NATO war games carried out since 2009 attest to the Kremlin's preoccupation. One plausible explanation for the mixed signals from Moscow is the lingering influence of Putin. An alternative explanation may be that Moscow is signaling a change of heart only because oil prices are low; should prices rise again it could well be seen as vindication of a confrontational stance toward the West.[13] Given these factors, and the larger continuity of support that Medvedev has extended to Venezuela and Iran, it seems likely that for Russia "reset" does not involve diminishing VIRUS cooperation.

Regarding Iran, where the West most desperately needs Russian cooperation, Moscow seems to prefer stasis: a rogue Iran, shunned by America and Europe, but also without a bomb. This preserves Russia's leverage with both the West and Tehran. Perhaps equally important, it helps run out the clock on the Nabucco project, which challenges Russia's energy dominance over Europe, because Iran under heavy sanctions keeps European investors from flocking there to buy into deals that propose to pipe gas from Central Asia that skirts Russia. Temporizing for too long may eventually cause enough friction to end Russia and Iran's partnership, but that means change will come about because Iran commits itself toward a different path, not because Moscow changes the tone of their relations. The VIRUS is unlikely to be disjointed because Russia sees the light, embraces the West, and stops backing Venezuela and Iran.

ACCEPTING CHINA'S ROLE

Acknowledging Russia's sponsorship of Venezuela and Iran often entails assigning China a status on par with Russia. The tendency to lump China alongside Russia when discussing governments that work against America's interest is a staple of the power politics school of international relations. Robert Kagan provides a good example of this reasoning when he argues:

> In recent years, as the autocracies of Russia and China have risen and the radical Islamists have waged their struggle, the democracies have been divided and distracted by issues both profound and petty. . . . Disunity has weakened and demoralized the democracies at a moment when they can least afford it. History has returned, and the democracies must come together to shape it, or others will shape it for them.[14]

Without a doubt, China is heavily invested in Iran's energy sector (and Venezuela's, too). But in important ways China's interests diverge from Russia's, and this makes Beijing's support for Iran and Venezuela less threatening to Western security. While China, like Russia, brokers contracts to develop oil and gas fields in Venezuela and Iran—despite sanctions—its support skews toward Caracas and Tehran so that these governments do not stir up broad regional conflicts, which could endanger China's investments. China's arms sales to Venezuela have been limited in size and intended for defensive purposes, mainly to help crack down on drug traffickers. It is unclear the exact composition of China's arms dealings with Iran, but most defense analysts corroborate China's insistence that it has "scaled way back" on arms sales over the past decade. And there are no signs of current Chinese involvement in Iran's nuclear program. Finally, China and the United States are oil importers, so their long-term agenda works against the interest of Venezuela and Iran's oil plots. Russia is a stark contrast on all these counts.

Beijing seeks stable partners as it scours the globe in search of natural resources. Iran has a tremendous cache of hydrocarbons that China wants to
make use of; Venezuela is a less promising outlet. China's reluctance to use
its Security Council veto to sanction Iran reflects, chiefly, its need to protect
its investment. In the Security Council, therefore, China and Russia's interests
coincide over Iran. Yet treating Beijing like Moscow risks alienating China
from cooperating with the West diplomatically now and in the future over
an array of issues while further insulating Iran against Western pressure.

DEVISING A RESPONSE

Countering the Venezuela-Iran alliance requires strategies that will coax
their ties back into the realm of proper bilateral relations. The Obama administration, like the Bush administration before it, does not seem interested
in engaging Latin America in a regional manner; doing so would require a
significant diplomatic push and the willingness to propose a series of free
trade deals that would necessitate standing up to powerful lobbies that seek
to protect agri-business from competition. Even if the president were to
countenance such a move, it would require years for such a bounty to take
effect and thereby reduce the influence of Venezuela and Iran.

Given these realities, a selective approach to Latin America is advised,
aimed at key countries in the region, starting with Colombia. U.S. support
for Colombia should extend well beyond the realm of security assistance to
include passage of the U.S.-Colombia free trade agreement that has been
stalled in Congress for years. Diplomatic support should be given to
Colombia when it voices specific concerns over FARC activities in
Venezuela. This is necessary not only because Colombia needs broader support, but because by standing behind its friends in the region, Washington
can once again signal that its alliances with Latin American nations are not
just one-way affairs. Engaging Brazil and Peru more closely could also bring
significant benefits to these countries, and to U.S. interests, at the expense
of Venezuela and Iran.

Meanwhile, Venezuela and its allies in the region should be engaged on
a selective basis. A seeming concession to Chávez, the removal of the U.S.
arms embargo on Venezuela, is also needed. It would probably not lead
Chávez to soften his rhetoric, but it may attenuate Russia's interest in

Venezuela. As the United States does this, the Treasury Department should press the Correa government in Ecuador to more closely monitor its financial system in order to prevent terrorist financing, which, given Ecuador's immense vulnerability to U.S. economic and financial pressure, can reduce the likelihood that Ecuador will play a role in financing the Islamic Republic's nuclear program.

Such policies should not aim to demonize Venezuela or Iran offhand, but narrowly target the illicit features of their cooperation. All the while, independent media outlets can play a vital role in asking pointed questions about Iran's presence in Latin America when things don't add up. By exposing Venezuela and Iran's legerdemain and pushing their ties back toward the realm of legitimate relations, the Venezuela-Iran alliance can be undone.

Acknowledgments

This book would have been impossible but for the assistance of a singular group of family, friends, students and colleagues. Through their boundless curiosity, my students at Coastal Carolina University unwittingly provided encouragement. The editors at Potomac Books have been incredible. Senior editor Hilary Claggett guided me through each step of the publication process, imparting feedback and advice along the way. Amanda Irle and Julie Gutin were nimble copyeditors, helping me to sift the wheat from the chaff.

Writing may be a solitary process, but I never felt lonely. Cliff Willett and the good folks at the Best Pancake House in Little River, SC, kindly hosted my A.M. writing ritual. My friends Amalia Willett, Anant Pradhan, and Ryan Rossi provided much-needed help in scaling the maps and graphs.

This book benefited from a variety of institutions. I am a recent product of the University of North Carolina, and, more recently, the School of Foreign Service at Georgetown University. The two imparted a lifelong interest in politics; I hope to eventually vindicate their decisions to invest in me.

The Foreign Policy Association has been a red thread in my intellectual development. At UNC I had the pleasure of participating in Great Decisions, a program in which a select group of undergraduates works to bring expert speakers to a wide audience of students and others in the community. My great decision came by way of signing up for the class, which steered me toward serious study of world affairs. In 2009, I had the chance to start blogging for the Foreign Policy Association, allowing me regular opportunities to engage Latin American politics. My sincere gratitude goes to Robert Nolan, editor for the Foreign Policy Association. Also, my fellow FPA bloggers do a good job of keeping me in the know about all manner of events—large, small, and odd—in the world.

World Politics Review occupies a unique place in online political analysis. Judah Grunstein, WPR's editor in chief, has both encouraged me in my research and provided helpful feedback on the Introduction of this manuscript.

Finally, a few words on my two special ladies. My mother, to whom this book is dedicated, has provided love and unflinching support. My Duchess of Moldova, Victoria Livinski, gave me the confidence to write my first book. After attentively listening to my musings on Venezuela and Iran, she put together a movie trailer that hit on the salient themes of their cooperation. It became a fixture of her family gatherings, giving me the opportunity to address questions about Hugo Chávez posed by Josh Panos, Victoria's fourteen-year-old cousin. She also read the manuscript more than once, and helped translate several articles from Russian.

Of course, all errors herein are my own.

Notes

Introduction

1 Steven Mufson and Marc Kaufman, "Longtime Foes U.S., Iran Explore Improved Relations," *Washington Post*, October 29, 2001.

2 Greg Barker, "Showdown with Iran," a PBS *Frontline* documentary (aired October 23, 2007), http://www.pbs.org/wgbh/pages/frontline/showdown/view/?utm_campaign=viewpage&utm_medium=grid&utm_source=grid.

3 Francisco Rodríguez, "Venezuela's Empty Revolution," *Foreign Affairs* 87, no. 2 (March/April 2008): 49–62.

4 Victor Flores, "Venezuela-Iran: une alliance anti-Washington," Agence France-Presse, September 17, 2006.

5 IMF Direction of Trade Statistics, Annual Values.

6 Steve Stecklow and Farnaz Fassihi, "Iran's Global Foray Has Mixed Results," *Wall Street Journal*, September 28, 2009, http://online.wsj.com/article/SB125409124052344735.html (accessed October 12, 2009).

Chapter 1. Iran: A Sphere of Influence by Other Means

1 Cited in Daniel Yergin, *The Prize: The Epic Quest for Oil, Money, and Power* (New York: Simon & Schuster, 1991), 566. For an extensive recounting of the Shah's plans for Iran see Part V.

2 Yergin, *The Prize*, 766.

3 Robert C. Baer, *The Devil We Know: Dealing With the New Iranian Superpower* (New York: Crown Publishers, 2008), 41–42.

4 Augustus Richard Norton, *Hezbollah: A Short History* (Princeton, NJ: Princeton University Press, 2007),109–10.

5 Christopher Hitchens, "The Swastika and the Cedar," *Vanity Fair*, May 2009, http://www.vanityfair.com/politics/features/2009/05/christopher -hitchens200905?currentPage=1 (accessed April 10, 2010).

6 Meyrev Wurmser, "The Iran-Hamas Alliance," Hudson Institute, October 4, 2007. Most sources cite approximately $30 million as the amount Iran has provided Hamas from 1993 to 2006. For a detailed accounting see The Israel Project, http://www.theisraelproject.org/site/c.hsJPK0PIJpH/b.2060919/k.753D/Iran _Leading_State_Sponsor_of_Terror.htm. Other sources, such as the Council on Foreign Relations, report that diplomats and other experts believe the amount has varied between $20 and $30 million annually beginning in 1993. See their background report on Hamas: http://www.cfr.org/publication/8968/hamas.html.

7 Cited in Wurmser. "The Iran-Hamas Alliance."

8 Mohammad Hafez, *Manufacturing Human Bombs: The Making of Palestinian Suicide Bombers* (Washington: U.S. Institute of Peace, 2006), 26.

9 Cited in ibid., 26.

10 Jane Adas, "Robert Pastor on the U.S., Hamas, and Middle East Peace," *Washington Report on Middle East Affairs* (May–June 2010): 40–42, http://www.wrmea.com/component/content/article/351-2010-may-june/9051 -mazin-qumsiyeh-on-the-history-and-practice-of-nonviolent-palestinian -resistance-.html.

11 As of this writing the Lebanese government has indicated that Hezbollah members will be indicted. Hezbollah leader Hassan Nasrallah claims to have evidence that Israel was behind Hariri's murder.

12 My thoughts on this topic have been particularly informed by Kenneth Pollack's *A Path Out of the Desert* (New York: Random House, 2008), chapter 17.

13 "Iran Offers Hamas Financial Aid," BBC News, February 22, 2006.

14 Michael Bröning, "Hamas 2.0," *Foreign Affairs*, August 5, 2009, http://www.foreignaffairs.com/articles/65214/michael-bröning/hamas-20 (accessed August 8, 2011).

15 Dennis C. Blair, *Annual Threat Assessment of the Intelligence Community for the Senate Select Committee on Intelligence*, February 12, 2009, 8.

16 Thomas E. Ricks, *Fiasco: The American Military Adventure in Iraq* (New York: Penguin, 2006), 265.

17 Bob Woodward, *State of Denial: Bush at War, Part III* (New York: Simon & Schuster, 2006), 414–15.

18 Ibid., 474.

19 Cited in Michael Ledeen, *The Iranian Time Bomb: The Mullah Zealots Quest for Destruction* (New York: St. Martin's Press, 2007), 110.

20 Michael Slackman, "Iran Gives Hamas Enthusiastic Support, But Discreetly, Just in Case," *New York Times*, January 12, 2009, http://www.nytimes.com/2009/01/13/world/middleeast/13iran.html?_r=1&emc=eta1 (accessed May 25, 2010).

21 For a detailed explanation of Crocker's take on Iran's role in Iraq, see the "Opinion Leaders" roundtable interview with him at US Embassy News, April 11, 2008, http://iraq.usembassy.gov/remarks_04112008.html (accessed July 7, 2010).

22 This statement is inspired by Parag Khanna's sentiment that "power abhors a vacuum," which is in turn a take on a pronouncement by Kenneth Waltz: "As nature abhors a vacuum, so international politics abhors unbalanced power."

Chapter 2. The Hugo Sphere

1 Simon Romero, "Venezuela's Military Ties with Cuba Stir Concerns," *New York Times*, June 14, 2010.

2 The DNI Report for 2009 notes that Raúl Castro is attempting to increase international legitimacy by adopting "a more moderate political image," which puts him slightly at odds with Chávez. DNI Annual Report 2009, www.dni.gov/reports/2009_NIS.pdf (accessed August 8, 2011), 33.

3 José de Cordoba, "Chávez Lets Colombia Rebels Wield Power Inside Venezuela," *Wall Street Journal*, November 25, 2008, http://online.wsj.com/article/SB122721414603545331.html (accessed June 3, 2010).

4 "The FARC Files," *The Economist*, May 22, 2008, http://www.economist.com/node/11412645 (accessed June 12, 2010).

5 Jeremy McDermott, "Colombia's Rebels: A Fading Force," BBC News, February 1, 2008, http://news.bbc.co.uk/2/hi/americas/7217817.stm (accessed July 12, 2010).

6 As an interesting aside, it may well have been Chávez's close ties with the FARC that made the March 1 raid possible. Two days prior Colombian intelligence, possibly in collaboration with the U.S. National Security Agency, was able to track Reyes's position because of a cell phone call he had with President Chávez. In some of the seized communications Chávez is given the code name "Ángel." See, for example, "The FARC Files," *The Economist*.

7 Ibid.

8 "Chavez's FARC Ties May be Insufficient Grounds for US Sanctions," *The Guardian* (London), May 16, 2008.

9 Juan Forero, "FARC Computer Files Are Authentic, Interpol Probe Finds," *Washington Post*, May 16, 2008.

10 Giles Tremlett, "Hugo Chavez 'Terrorist Link' Sparks Diplomatic Row Between Spain and Venezuela," *The Guardian* (London), March 2, 2010, http://www.guardian.co.uk/world/2010/mar/01/hugo-chavez-venezuela-spain-eta (accessed May 25, 2010).

11 Ibid.

12 Ibid.

13 "Colombia Shows Proof of FARC Rebels in Venezuela; Chavez Scoffs," *Latin America Herald Tribune* (date unavailable), http://www.laht.com/article.asp?CategoryId=10717&ArticleId=360547 (accessed July 23, 2010).

14 Tina Rosenberg, "The Perils of Petrocracy," *New York Times Magazine*, November 4, 2007.

15 Javier Corrales, "Using Social Power to Balance Soft Power: Venezuela's Foreign Policy," *Washington Quarterly* 32, 4 (October 2009): 97–114.

16 See, for instance, "Venezuela's Chavez Spends Heavily to Help Allies," Reuters, October 12, 2007, http://www.reuters.com/article/idUSN12220829.

17 Gustavo Fernández, "Bolivian Foreign Policy: Observations on the Bolivia-Iran Relationship," in *Iran in Latin America: Threat or 'Axis of Annoyance'?*, Cynthia J. Arnson, Haleh Esfandiari, and Adam Stubits, eds. (Washington, DC: Woodrow Wilson International Center for Scholars, 2009), 83–99.

18 Conrado Hornos, "Chavez Keeps up South American Energy Diplomacy," Reuters, August 8, 2007, http://www.reuters.com/article/idUSN0835483220070808 (accessed May 10, 2010).

19 Geri Smith, "Chavez: Trading Oil for Influence," *Businessweek*, December 26, 2005, http://www.businessweek.com/magazine/content/05_52/b3965071.htm (accessed June 30, 2010).

20 Tim Rogers, "Chávez Plays Oil Card in Nicaragua," *Christian Science Monitor*, May 5, 2006, http://www.csmonitor.com/2006/0505/p01s04-woam.html (accessed August 12, 2010).

21 Samuel Logan, "Iran's Latin American Inroads," *International Relations and Security Network (ISN)*, April 29, 2009, http://www.isn.ethz.ch/isn/Current-Affairs/Security-Watch/Detail/?page525=6&ots591=4888CAA0-B3DB-1461-98B9-E20E7B9C13D4&lng=en&size525=10&id=99532 (accessed May 12, 2010); "Syria Joined ALBA as an Observer Member," *Venezuelan National Radio (RNV)*, October 22, 2010, http://www.rnv.gob.ve/noticias/index.php?act=ST&f=31&t=140297.

22 Corrales in "Social Power" cites Venezuelan "commitments" as $43 billion, based on figures complied by Gustavo Coronel, see page 99.

23 Simon Romero, "Chavez, Seeking Foreign Allies, Spends Billions," *New York Times*, April 4, 2006, http://www.nytimes.com/2006/04/04/world/americas /04venezuela.html (accessed July 10, 2010); Natalie Obiko Pearson and Ian James, "Venezuela Offers Billions to Countries in Latin America," Associated Press, August 27, 2007.

24 Corrales, "Social Power," 100.

25 Ibid., 101.

26 "Bolivia Withdraws from ICSID," *Latin Lawyer*, May 22, 2007, http://www.americasnet.net/news/Bolivia_ICSID.pdf (accessed July 1, 2010).

27 "ICSID in Crisis," posted by the Bretton Woods Project, July 10, 2009, http://www.brettonwoodsproject.org/art-564878(accessed June 23, 2010). See also Fernando Cabrera Diaz, "Ecuador Continues Exit from ICSID," *International Treaty News*, June 8, 2009, http://www.investmenttreatynews.org/cms/news /archive/2009/06/05/ecuador-continues-exit-from-icsid.aspx.

28 One might make the argument that what I term willful noncompliance is, in fact, a form of "strategic non-cooperation." (For more on this see Judith Kelley, "Strategic Cooperation as Soft Balancing: Why Iraq Was Not Just About Iraq," *International Politics* 42, 2 (2005), 153–73. However, this is unlikely because Bolivia and Ecuador clearly do not appear to be jockeying for better negotiating terms with the United States.

29 For a list, see the Egmont Group's website: http://www.egmontgroup.org/about /list-of-members/by-region/americas (accessed August 2, 2010). For more on this, see also the International Bar Association's Anti-Money Laundering Forum: http://www.anti-moneylaundering.org/southamerica/Bolivia.aspx.

30 U.S. Department of State, Country Reports: Western Hemisphere Overview, April 30, 2008, http://www.state.gov/s/ct/rls/crt/2007/103710.htm.

31 Financial Standards Forum, "Anti-Money Laundering," August 2008, http://www.estandardsforum.org/ecuador/standards/anti-money-laundering -combating-terrorist-financing-standard (accessed June 23, 2010).

32 Including the UN Drug Convention, the UN International Convention for the Suppression of the Financing of Terrorism, the UN Convention Against Transnational Organized Crime, and the UN Convention Against Corruption, among many others.

33 For a more detailed discussion of Ecuador's crackdown on money laundering in the 1990s, see James R. Richards, *Transnational Criminal Organizations, Cybercrime, and Money Laundering* (Boca Raton, FL: CRC Press, 1999): 275–76.

34 "The Andean Laundry," *The Economist*, March 27, 2010.

35 Javier Corrales, "Venezuela: Petropolitics and the Promotion of Disorder," *Undermining Democracy: 21st Century Authoritarians* (Washington, D.C.: Freedom House, June 2009): 66.

36   For an overview of the democratic faults of Ecuador that is surely too concise for professors who study "democratic transitions" in political science, see Tim Padgett, "In Ecuador, A Vote for Change?" *Time*, October 2, 2007, http://www.time.com /time/world/article/0,8599,1667386,00.html?artId=1667386?contType=article ?chn=world (accessed July 23, 2010). For a more thoroughgoing academic analysis of these problems see, for instance, Juan Linz and Alfred Stepan, *Problems of Democratic Transition and Consolidation* (Baltimore: JHU Press, 1996).

37   Transparency International, "Corruption Perceptions Index: 2005," http://www.transparency.org/policy_research/surveys_indices/cpi/2005 (accessed July 5, 2010).

38   Monica Machicau and Eduardo Garcia, "Venezuela's Chavez Spends Heavily to Help Allies," Reuters, October 12, 2007, http://www.reuters.com/article/ idUSN1222082920071012.

39   "Ecuador's New Constitution: In Good Faith," *The Economist*, October 2, 2008, http://www.economist.com/node/12342501 (accessed July 23, 2010).

40   American Society of International Law, Bolivia: Presidential Supreme Decree 28701 (May 1, 2006), http://www.asil.org/ilib060525.cfm#ll (accessed July 1, 2010).

41   Parmy Olson, "Bolivia Has a Gas Problem," *Forbes*, August 14, 2006, http://www.forbes.com/2006/08/14/bolivia-gas-nationalization-cx_po _0814bolivia.html (accessed August 7, 2010).

42   Joshua Partlow and Stephan Kuffner, "Voters in Ecuador Approve New Constitution," *Washington Post*, September 29, 2008.

43   Monte Reel, "Bolivia's Irresistible Reserves," *Washington Post*, February 10, 2008, http://www.washingtonpost.com/wp-dyn/content/article/2008/02/09 /AR2008020901326.html (accessed July 23, 2010).

44   *Regional Surveys of the World: South America, Central and the Caribbean: 2002*, 10th ed. (London: Europa Publications, 2002), 783.

45   Mark Milner, "Chávez Seeks to Peg Oil at $50 a Barrel," *The Guardian*, April 3, 2006, http://www.guardian.co.uk/business/2006/apr/03/venezuela.oilandpetrol (accessed July 23, 2010).

46   "Chavez Calls for New OPEC Members," BBC News, June 1, 2006, http://news.bbc.co.uk/2/hi/business/5035894.stm (accessed July 23, 2010).

47   Lourdes Garcia-Navarro and Alex Chadwick, "Venezuela's Chávez Calls for OPEC Production Cuts," NPR, June 1, 2006, http://www.npr.org/templates/story /story.php?storyId=5444727&ps=rs (accessed July 23, 2010).

48   An estimated one-third of FARC members are female.

49   "Colombia Clashes with Nicaragua Over Guerilla Tie," *Wall Street Journal*, July 28, 2008.

50   Ibid.

51 "Witness Points to Chavez in Argentina Election Case," *Washington Post*, July 7, 2009, http://www.washingtonpost.com/wp-dyn/content/article/2008/07/06 /AR2008070602298.html (accessed July 10, 2010). For more information: see "New Accusation in Argentina Suitcase Scandal," Reuters, December 20, 2007, http://www.reuters.com/article/idUSN2018803520071220.

52 "Argentina Says It Better Off Without IMF Advice," Reuters, April 24, 2010, http://www.reuters.com/article/idUSN2414517920100424 (accessed August 23, 2010).

53 Dennis C. Blair, *Annual Threat Assessment of the U.S. Intelligence Community for the Senate Select Committee on Intelligence: 2010.* February 2, 2010, http://www.dni.gov /testimonies/20100202_testimony.pdf (accessed July 23, 2010).

Chapter 3. "Poisonous Fruit"

1 Robert M. Morgenthau, "The Emerging Axis of Iran and Venezuela," *Wall Street Journal*, September 8, 2009, http://online.wsj.com/article/NA_WSJ_PUB: SB10001424052970203440104574400792835972018.html (accessed May 12, 2010).

2 Those insisting a marriage was predetermined often refer to a promise, scribbled out by Chávez in Tehran in 2000, that the peoples of Venezuela and Iran were "bound together by the new paths of history." See Douglas Schoen and Michael Rowan, *The Threat Closer to Home: Hugo Chávez and the War Against America* (New York: Free Press), 2009.

3 Simon Romero, "Venezuela Strengthens its Relationships in the Middle East," *New York Times*, August 21, 2006, http://www.nytimes.com/2006/08/21/world/americas /21venez.html?emc=eta1.

4 "Venezuela, Iran initial 29 accords," *El Universal*, September 22, 2007 (accessed August 23, 2010).

5 Elide Brun, "Iran's Place in Venezuela's Foreign Policy," *Iran in Latin America: Threat or 'Axis of Annoyance'?*, Cynthia J. Arnson, Haleh Esfandiari, and Adam Stubits, eds. (Washington, DC: Woodrow Wilson International Center for Scholars, 2009), 40.

6 Parisa Hafezi, "Iran, Venezuela in 'Axis of Unity' Against the U.S.," Reuters, July 2, 2007, http://www.reuters.com/article/idUSDAH23660020070702 (accessed July 12, 2010).

7 Ibid.

8 Han Jingjing, ed., "Venezuela, Iran Sign Dozens of New Agreements," *Xinhua*, November 26, 2009, http://news.xinhuanet.com/english/2009-11/26/content _12541972.htm (accessed August 23, 2010).

9 Brun, "Iran's Place in Venezuela's Foreign Policy," 35–50.

10 Steve Stecklow and Farnaz Fassihi, "Iran's Global Foray Has Mixed Results," *Wall Street Journal*, September 29, 2009, http://online.wsj.com/article /SB125409124052344735.html (accessed October 12, 2009).

11 "Venezuela, Iran Have Executed 57 Industrial Agreements," *El Universal* (Caracas), August 26, 2010, http://www.eluniversal.com/2010/08/26/en_eco_esp_venezuela, -iran-have_26A4386931.shtml.

12 Stecklow and Fassihi, "Iran's Global Foray Has Mixed Results."

13 Ibid.

14 Natalie Obiko Pearson, "Iran and Venezuela Plan Anti-US Fund," *USA Today*, January 14, 2007, http://www.usatoday.com/news/world/2007-01-14-iran -venezuela_x.htm (accessed July 23, 2010).

15 Brun, "Iran's Place in Venezuela's Foreign Policy," 37.

16 Javier Corrales, "Venezuela: Petropolitics and the Promotion of Disorder," *Undermining Democracy: 21st Century Authoritarians* (Washington, D.C.: Freedom House, June 2009), 66.

17 The most instructive example of this is "import substitution industrialization," practiced by many Latin American nations between the 1940s and 1970s.

18 Ibid.

19 Morgenthau, "The Emerging Axis of Iran and Venezuela," *Wall Street Journal*.

20 "Iran, Venezuela Launch Joint Development Bank," Agence France-Presse, April 3, 2009, http://www.google.com/hostednews/afp/article/ALeqM5iskmQ6xtdC4 Ebzc799pWYG_RSMXg (accessed July 24, 2010).

21 Ibid.

22 "Venezuelan Bank Penalized for Alleged Link with Iranian Plan," *El Universal*, July 27, 2010, http://english.eluniversal.com/2010/07/27/en_eco_esp_venezuelan -bank-pena_27A4254177.shtml (accessed August 14, 2010).

23 Ibid.

24 Stecklow and Fassihi, "Iran's Global Foray Has Mixed Results."

25 "Military Industries Feature in Iran-Venezuela Cooperation," *UPI*, September 15, 2009, http://www.upi.com/Business_News/Security-Industry/2009/09/15/Military -industries-feature-in-Iran-Venezuela-cooperation/UPI-34011253026800/.

26 "Iran's Quds Force in Venezuela, Latin America: Pentagon," Agence France-Presse, April 22, 2010, http://www.google.com/hostednews/afp/article /ALeqM5jvXOYLKMt3NWFER4xXMlDPSTmhBw (accessed May 14, 2010).

27 U.S. Department of Defense, "Unclassified Report on Military Power of Iran," April 2010. The report can be found through several sources. For example, it can be downloaded from a hyperlink posted by the *Washington Times* in an article from April 21, 2010, by Bill Gertz titled "Iran Boosts Qods Shock Troops in

Venezuela," http://www.washingtontimes.com/news/2010/apr/21/iran-boosts
-qods-shock-troops-in-venezuela/ (accessed May 3, 2010).

28 Charlie Devereux and Andrew Cawthorne, "Chávez Denies Elite Iranian Forces in
Venezuela," Reuters, April 26, 2010, http://www.reuters.com/article
/idUSTRE63Q0B820100427 (accessed May 30, 2010).

29 U.S. Department of Defense, "Unclassified Report on Military Power of Iran." See
also Richard Clarke's interview with ABC News: "Who's Behind Iran's Death
Squad: Iran's Secret Agents Answer to a Higher Power," February 14, 2007,
retrieved August 23, 2010, http://abcnews.go.com/WNT/BrianRoss/story?id
=2876019&page=1 (accessed August 23, 2010).

30 Scott Stewart, "Hezbollah, Radical but Rational," STRATFOR, August 12, 2010.

31 Ibid.

32 Chris Kraul and Sabastian Rotella, "Fears of Hezbollah Presence in Venezuela,"
Los Angeles Times, August 27, 2008, http://articles.latimes.com/2008/aug/27
/world/fg-venezterror27 (accessed July 23, 2010).

33 Ibid.

34 Office of the Coordinator for Counterterrorism, "Country Reports on Terrorism:
Western Hemisphere Overview," April 30, 2008, http://www.state.gov/s/ct/rls
/crt/2007/103710.htm.

35 Ibid.

36 Ibid.

37 National Terror Alert Response Center, "Mexico Thwarts Plans for South
American Network," July 7, 2010, http://www.nationalterroralert.com/
updates/2010/07/06/mexico-thwarts-hezbollah-plana-for-south-american
-network/ (accessed July 18, 2010); Jack Khoury and Haaretz Service, "Mexico
Thwarts Hezbollah Bid to Set up South American Network," *Haaretz*, June 7,
2010, http://www.haaretz.com/news/diplomacy-defense/mexico-thwarts
-hezbollah-bid-to-set-up-south-american-network-1.300360.

38 "Exclusive: Hezbollah Uses Mexican Drug Routes into U.S.," *Washington Times*,
March 27, 2009, http://www.washingtontimes.com/news/2009/mar/27/hezbollah
-uses-mexican-drug-routes-into-us/?page=1 (accessed July 19, 2010).

39 Kraul and Rotella, "Fears of Hezbollah Presence in Venezuela."

40 Ibid.

41 Stewart, "Hezbollah, Radical but Rational."

42 Stecklow and Fassihi, "Iran's Global Foray Has Mixed Results."

43 See, for example, Brun, "Iran's Place in Venezuela's Foreign Policy," 43.

44 Bret Stephens, "The Tehran-Caracas Nuclear Axis," *Wall Street Journal*, December
15, 2009.

45   Office of the Coordinator for Counterterrorism, "Country Reports on Terrorism: Western Hemisphere Overview."

46   Ed Barnes, "Exclusive: Venezuela Cancels Round-Trip 'Terror Flight' to Syria and Iran," Fox News, September 14, 2010, http://www.foxnews.com/us/2010/09/14 /terror-flight-venezuela-iran-illicit-arms-hezbollah-hamas-protest/.

47   Ibid.

48   Dugold McConnell and Brian Todd, "Venezuela Defends Controversial Flights to Iran and Syria," CNN, August 21, 2010, http://www.cnn.com/2010/WORLD/asiapcf /08/21/venezuela.flights.iran/index.html.

49   Ibid.

50   Ibid.

51   Ibid.

52   Ibid.

53   Ibid.

54   "Venezuela Airline Cancels Route to Iran, Syria," Wall Street Journal, September 15, 2010, http://billionaires.forbes.com/article/04xLduX7VY7lW?q=Caracas.

55   McConnell and Todd, "Venezuela Defends Controversial Flights to Iran and Syria."

56   "Venezuela Airline Cancels Route to Iran, Syria."

57   Barnes, "Exclusive: Venezuela Cancels Round-Trip 'Terror Flight' to Syria and Iran."

58   James Sturcke, "Chávez Jokes About Helping Iran Build Nuclear Bomb," The Guardian, October 7, 2009, http://www.guardian.co.uk/world/2009/oct/07/hugo -chavez-iran-nuclear-bomb.

59   Cited in ibid.

60   "Brazil Wary on Nuclear Cooperation With Iran," Reuters, May 23, 2005.

61   Mariela Leon and Marianna Parraga, "Negotiations to Purchase Nuclear Reactor from Argentina Confirmed," El Universal, October 22, 2005, http://www.eluniversal.com /2005/10/11/en_pol_art_11A618849.shtml (accessed October 3, 2010).

62   Simon Romero, "Chávez Aide Says Iran Is Helping It Look for Uranium," New York Times, September 25, 2009, http://www.nytimes.com/2009/09/26/world /americas/26venez.html (accessed August 12, 2010).

63   Ibid.

64   Ibid.

65   John R. Bolton, "The Chavez Threat," Los Angeles Times, September 16, 2010, http://www.latimes.com/news/opinion/commentary/la-oe-bolton-chavez -20100916,0,3843771.story (accessed September 16, 2010).

66   Robert M. Morgenthau. "Caracas-Tehran Axis."

Chapter 4. Iran Infiltrates the Americas

1 Tyler Bridges, "Iran's Unlikely Embrace of Bolivia Builds Influence in U.S. Backyard," *McClatchy*, February 5, 2009, http://www.mcclatchydc.com/2009/02 /05/61600/irans-unlikely-embrace-of-bolivia.html (accessed May 3, 2010).

2 Daniel P. Erikson, "Ahmadinejad Finds It Warmer in Latin America," *Los Angeles Times*, October 3, 2007.

3 IMF Direction of Trade Statistics.

4 Ibid.

5 "Iran Trade Triples," *Latin Business Chronicle* , December 2, 2009, http://www.latinbusinesschronicle.com/app/article.aspx?id=3842 (accessed June 23, 2010).

6 Ibid.

7 Erikson, "Ahmadinejad Finds it Warmer in Latin America."

8 Roni Sofer, "Israel: Ties to South America Aiding Iran's Nuclear Program," *Ynet News*, May 25, 2009, http://www.ynetnews.com/articles/0,7340,L-3721335,00.html (accessed June 7, 2010).

9 Cited in Bridges, "Iran's Unlikely Embrace."

10 Jean Friedman-Rudovsky, "Is Bolivia Cozying Up to Iran?" *Time*, October 9, 2007.

11 Ibid.

12 Steve Stecklow and Farnaz Fassihi, "Iran's Global Foray Has Mixed Results," *Wall Street Journal*, September 29, 2009, http://online.wsj.com/article/ SB125409124052344735.html (accessed October 12, 2009).

13 Félix Maradiaga and Javier Meléndez, "Iranian-Nicaraguan Relations One Year Into the Sandinista Government," *Iran in Latin America: Threat or 'Axis of Annoyance'?*, Cynthia J. Arnson, Haleh Esfandiari, and Adam Stubits, eds. (Washington, DC: Woodrow Wilson International Center for Scholars, 2009), 70.

14 Siobhan Morrissey, "Iran's Romance of Nicaragua," *Time*, September 10, 2007, http://www.time.com/time/world/article/0,8599,1660500,00.html (accessed August 12, 2010).

15 "Nicaragua e Irán: Unión invincible," *BBC Mundo*, June 11, 2007, http://news.bbc.co.uk/hi/spanish/latin_america/newsid_6741000/6741829.stm (accessed July 5, 2010).

16 Anne-Marie O'Connor and Mary Beth Sheridan, "Iran's Invisible Nicaragua Embassy," *Washington Post*, July 13, 2009, http://www.washingtonpost.com/wp -dyn/content/article/2009/07/12/AR2009071202337.html (accessed June 5, 2010).

17 Maradiaga and Meléndez, "Iranian-Nicaraguan Relations One Year Into the Sandinista Government," 75.

18 Fernández in *Iran in Latin America: Threat or 'Axis of Annoyance'?*, Cynthia J. Arnson, Haleh Esfandiari, and Adam Stubits, eds. (Washington, DC: Woodrow Wilson International Center for Scholars, 2009), 86

19 Ibid., 86–87.

20 "Ecuador's Correa: 'US No Longer 'Satan' For Latin America," Deutsche Presse-Agentur, July 18, 2007.

21 Gustavo Fernández, "Bolivian Foreign Policy: Observations on the Bolivia-Iran Relationship," *Iran in Latin America: Threat or 'Axis of Annoyance'?*, Cynthia J. Arnson, Haleh Esfandiari, and Adam Stubits, eds. (Washington, DC: Woodrow Wilson International Center for Scholars, 2009), 86.

22 César Montúfar, "Recent Diplomatic Developments Between Ecuador and Iran: A Gesture of Sovereign Affirmation or Lukewarm Geopolitical Alignment?" in Cynthia J. Arnson, Haleh Esfandiari, and Adam Stubits, eds., *Iran in Latin America: Threat or 'Axis of Annoyance'?*, (Washington, DC: Woodrow Wilson International Center for Scholars, 2009), 101–14

23 Ibid.

24 Ibid., 110.

25 Cited in ibid.

26 "Iran's Unlikely Embrace of Bolivia."

27 Cited in Stecklow and Fassihi, "Iran's Global Foray."

28 Ibid.

29 Meléndez and Maradiaga, "Iranian-Nicaraguan Relations," 75.

30 Stecklow and Fassihi, "Iran's Global Foray."

31 "Ecuador Plans to Buy Arms from Iran," *Tehran Times*, December 15, 2008, http://www.tehrantimes.com/Index_view.asp?code=184841 (accessed May 3, 2010).

32 "Iranian Bank to Open Branch in Ecuador," *Press TV*, September 10, 2009, http://previous.presstv.ir/detail.aspx?id=105831(accessed June 12, 2010).

33 Andrew Cawthorne, "Ecuador Says Iran Ties Landed it on Laundering List," Reuters, February 2, 2010.

34 Ibid.

35 Ibid.

36 "Secret Document: Venezuela, Bolivia Supplying Iran with Uranium," *Haaretz*, May 26, 2009, http://www.haaretz.com/news/bolivia-denies-israel-report-it-supplied-iran-with-uranium-1.276747 (accessed July 1, 2010); "Israel Ties 2 Nations to Iran's Uranium," *New York Times*, May 25, 2009, http://www.nytimes.com/2009/05/26/world/middleeast/26israel.html?_r=2&partner=rss&emc=rss.

37   Ibid.

38   "Iran's Rumored Nicaraguan 'Mega-Embassy' Sets off Alarm Bells," *Washington Post*, July 13, 2009, http://www.washingtonpost.com/wp-dyn/content/article /2009/07/12/AR2009071202337.html (accessed August 7, 2011).

39   U.S. Director of National Intelligence, 2009, 32.

Chapter 5. A VIRUS of Instability

1   David Blair, "Profile: Muammar Gaddafi," *London Telegraph*, August 13, 2009, http://www.telegraph.co.uk/news/uknews/6022449/Profile-Muammar-Gaddafi -Libyan-leader-at-time-of-Lockerbie-bombing.html.

2   This phrase is drawn from an article by Dmitri Trenin, "Russia Leaves the West," *Foreign Affairs* 85, 4 (July/August 2006): 87–96.

3   Yuri Zarakhovich, "NATO: Still a Sore Point with Putin," *Time*, April 1, 2008, http://www.time.com/time/world/article/0,8599,1726902,00.html (accessed July 23, 2010).

4   Scott Peterson. "Broad Backlash to Putin Reforms," *Christian Science Monitor*, January 19, 2005, http://www.csmonitor.com/2005/0119/p01s03-woeu.html.

5   CNN, "Another Look Into Putin's Soul?" February 24, 2005, http://www.cnn.com /2005/WORLD/europe/02/24/summit.russia.dougherty/index.html?iref=allsearch (accessed August 8, 2011).

6   Trenin, "Russia Leaves the West."

7   Cited in Joseph S. Nye, *The Paradox of American Power: Why the World's Superpower Can't Go It Alone* (New York: Oxford University Press, 2002), 27.

8   Quantity should not be taken as quality; America's defense industry is leaps ahead of the rest of the world in sophistication.

9   "Venezuela Threatens to Sell F-16 Fleet to Iran," Fox News, May 16, 2006, http://www.foxnews.com/story/0,2933,195672,00.html (accessed May 12, 2010).

10   Virginia Lopez, "Russia's Venezuela Foray: Tit for Tat," *Time*, September 11, 2008, http://www.time.com/time/world/article/0,8599,1840332,00.html (accessed July 23, 2010). Also see "Russia to Build Two Kalashnikov Factories in Venezuela by 2010," *RIA Novosti*, June 8, 2007, http://en.rian.ru/russia/20070806/70445720.html (accessed July 30, 2010).

11   "Russia Top Arms Supplier to Latin America Thanks to Sales to Venezuela," *El Universal*, February 3, 2010, http://english.eluniversal.com/2010/02/03/en _pol_art_russia,-top-arms-sup_03A3385931.shtml (accessed July 14, 2010).

12   This is the bedrock of what Realist scholars consider to be a "systemic" condition of the international system.

13   Andrew Downie, "A South American Arms Race?" *Time*, December 21, 2007, http://www.time.com/time/world/article/0,8599,1697776,00.html (accessed July 30, 2010).

14   Lionel Beehner, *Backgrounder: Russia-Iran Arms Trade*, Council on Foreign Relations, November 1, 2006.

15   Iran's status as a key Russian arms buyer are detailed by many sources; information in this section is drawn from Janusz Bugajski's *Dismantling the West: Russia's Atlantic Agenda* (Washington, DC: Potomac Books, 2009), 49.

16   Some sources give a later date. Most reports cite a December 2005 deal for five S-300s. See "Russia Vague on S-300 Delivery to Iran," *PressTV*, August 21, 2010, http://www.presstv.ir/detail/139487.html.

17   For example, see "Russia, Iran S-300 Contract Still in Force," *Voice of Russia*, July 15, 2010, http://english.ruvr.ru/2010/07/15/12407962.html.

18   Gregory Feifer, "Russia Finds an Eager Weapons Buyer in Iran," NPR, January 18, 2007, http://www.npr.org/templates/story/story.php?storyId=6906839 (accessed May 4, 2010).

19   Ibid.

20   Simon Shuster, "Russian Support for Iran Sanctions Called into Question," *Time*, July 15, 2010, http://www.time.com/time/world/article/0,8599,2004159,00.html.

21   "Venezuela to Build Stronger Air Defenses with Russian Aid," *RIA Novosti*, September 14, 2009, http://en.rian.ru/mlitary_news/20090914/156118402.html (accessed May 23, 2010).

22   Julie McCarthy, "Venezuela Works on its Defenses," NPR, August 20, 2006, http://www.npr.org/templates/story/story.php?storyId=5678460 (accessed July 12, 2010).

23   Juan Forero, "After Deadly Assault on Guerillas, Chávez Orders Troops to Colombian Border," *Washington Post*, March 3, 2008, http://www.washingtonpost.com/wp-dyn/content/article/2008/03/02/AR2008030200773.html (accessed May 3, 2010).

24   "Russia Will Sell Fighter Jets to Venezuela," *International Herald Tribune*, June 4, 2006, http://www.nytimes.com/2006/06/04/world/europe/04iht-russia.1884852.html?_r=1&scp=1&sq=arms%20embargo%20venezuela&st=cse (accessed July 12, 2010).

25   "Russia Arms Latin America," *Voice of America*, April 27, 2007, http://www.voanews.com/english/news/news-analysis/a-13-2007-05-02-voa4.html (accessed May 23, 2010).

26   Ibid.

27   "The Bear Is Happy to Be Back," *The Economist*, February 8, 2007.

28 Andrew Lee Butters, "Russia Flexes Its Muscles in MidEast," *Time*, August 27, 2008, http://www.time.com/time/world/article/0,8599,1836613,00.html (accessed September 2, 2010).

29 Olga Razumovskaya, "Bushehr Launch Boosts Rosatom," *Moscow Times*, August 23, 2010, http://www.themoscowtimes.com/news/article/bushehr-launch-boosts-rosatom/413450.html.

30 "Tehran Proposes Iran-Russia Nuclear Fuel Production Consortium," *Tehran Times*, August 28, 2010, http://www.tehrantimes.com/index_View.asp?code=225696.

31 "Iran Favors Russia for Nuclear Projects," *Press TV*, August 19, 2010, http://www.presstv.ir/detail/139268.html.

32 Jay Solomon, "Russians to Fuel Iranian Reactor," *Wall Street Journal*, August 14, 2010, http://online.wsj.com/article/SB10001424052748703960004575427851574039466.html.

33 Jamie Fly, "The Real Meaning of Bushehr," *Foreign Policy*'s "Shadow Government" Blog, August 24, 2010, http://shadow.foreignpolicy.com/posts/2010/08/24/the_real_meaning_of_bushehr.

34 Ibid.

35 Ibid.

36 Ibid.

37 "Russia-Venezuela Nuclear Accord," BBC News, November 27, 2008, http://news.bbc.co.uk/2/hi/7751562.stm (accessed October 29, 2010).

38 Javier Corrales, "Using Social Power to Balance Soft Power," *The Washington Quarterly* 32, no. 4 (October 2009): 104.

39 Ellen Barry, "Russia Flexes Muscles in Oil Deal with Chavez," *New York Times*, September 26, 2008.

40 I am grateful to Javier Corrales's essay "Using Social Power to Balance Soft Power" for elucidating the strategic dynamics of Russia's policies vis-à-vis OPEC.

41 John Deutch and James R. Schlesinger, *National Security Consequences of US Oil Dependency*, New York: Council on Foreign Relations, October 2006.

42 Kenneth Pollack, *A Path Out of the Desert* (New York: Random House, 2008), 16.

Chapter 6. Russia's Geostrategic Conundrum

1 Robert Kaplan, "The Geography of Chinese Power," *Foreign Affairs* 89, no. 3 (May/June 2010): 22–41.

2 Cited in Ian Bremmer, *The J Curve: A New Way to Understand Why Nations Rise and Fall* (New York: Simon & Schuster, 2006), 142.

3   Parag Khanna, *The Second World: How Emerging Powers Are Redefining Global Competition in the Twenty-First Century* (New York: Random House, 2008), 73.

4   John J. Mearsheimer, *The Tragedy of Great Power Politics* (New York: Norton, 2001), 135.

5   See, for instance, Dennis C. Blair, "Annual Threat Assessment of the US Intelligence Community for the Senate Select Community on Intelligence," U.S. Director of National Intelligence, February 2010, http://www.dni.gov/testimonies /20100202_testimony.pdf (accessed July 23, 2010).

6   Richard Galpin, "Energy Fuels New 'Great Game' in Europe," BBC News, June 9, 2009, http://news.bbc.co.uk/2/hi/europe/8090104.stm.

7   Galpin, "Energy Fuels New 'Great Game' in Europe."

8   Zbigniew Brzezinski, *The Grand Chessboard: American Primacy and Its Geostrategic Imperatives* (New York: Basic Books, 1997), 130.

9   For a fascinating recounting of these attempts, see chapter 17 in Steve Levine, *The Oil and the Glory: The Pursuit of Empire and Fortune on the Caspian Sea* (Random House: New York, 2007).

10   John W. Parker, *Persian Dreams: Moscow and Tehran Since the Fall of the Shah.* (Washington, DC: Potomac Books, 2009), 156.

11   Ben N. Dunlap, "Divide and Conquer? The Russian Plan for Ownership of the Caspian Sea," *Boston College International and Comparative Law Review* 27, 1, (December 2004): 115–30, http://lawdigitalcommons.bc.edu/iclr/vol27/iss1/4.

12   Parker, *Persian Dreams*, 162.

13   Ibid.

14   Brzezinski, *Grand Chessboard*, 121.

15   Robert Baer, *The Devil We Know: Dealing With the New Iranian Superpower* (New York: Crown Publishers, 2008), 133.

16   Khanna, *The Second World*, 58.

17   Adrian Karatnycky, "Escaping Putin's Energy Squeeze," *Washington Post*, July 1, 2007, http://www.washingtonpost.com/wp-dyn/content/article/2007/06/29 /AR2007062902165.html (accessed June 3, 2010).

18   Adrian Karatnycky and Alexander Motyl, "The Key to Kiev," *Foreign Affairs* 88, no. 3 (May/June 2009): 106–20.

19   U.S. Geological Survey, "Circum-Arctic Resource Appraisal," http://energy.usgs.gov/arctic/ (accessed June 15, 2010).

20   Cited in Scott G. Borgerson, "Arctic Meltdown: The Economic and Security Implications of Global Warming," *Foreign Affairs*, 87, no. 2 (March/April 2008): 63–77.

21 Robin Paxton and Anthony Barker, "Russia's Shtokman Natural Gas Project," Reuters UK, February 5, 2010, http://uk.reuters.com/article/idUSLDE6141PU20100205?sp=true (accessed May 23, 2010).

22 Ibid.

23 Lars Schoultz, *Beneath the United States: A History of U.S. Policy Toward Latin America* (Cambridge, MA: Harvard University Press, 1998), 368.

24 US Military Deployments, 1969–Present, PBS, http://www.pbs.org/wgbh/pages/frontline/shows/pentagon/maps/9.html (accessed June 2, 2010).

25 Tony Halpin, "Russia Challenges US Dominance With Venezuela Naval War Games," *Times Online* (London), November 24, 2008, http://www.timesonline.co.uk/tol/news/world/us_and_americas/article5225275.ece (accessed May 21, 2010).

26 Tom Parfitt, "Chavez Says 'Yes' to Russian Base," *The Guardian*, March 16, 2009, http://www.guardian.co.uk/world/2009/mar/16/chavez-russia-venezuela-nuclear-base (accessed June 6, 2010).

27 Ibid.

28 Ibid.

29 Ibid.

30 Brzezinski, *Grand Chessboard*, 118.

31 Luke Harding, "Energy Conflicts Could Bring Military Clashes, Russian Security Strategy Warns," *The Guardian* (UK), May 13, 2009.

32 Leigh Phillips, "Russia-Norway Pact Eases Arctic Tension," *Bloomberg Business Week*, April 28, 2010.

33 See, for instance, "One Hundred Days of Yanukovich," *The Economist*, June 3, 2010.

34 Keith Smith, *Russian Energy Politics in the Baltics, Poland, and Ukraine* (Washington, D.C.: Center for International and Security Studies, 2004), 9.

35 M. K. Bhadrakumar, "Pipeline Geopolitics: Russia, China, Iran Redraw Energy Map," *Asia Times Online*, January 12, 2010.

36 Ibid.

Chapter 7. A VIRUS Spawns

1 Judy Dempsey, "Iran, Belarus Forge 'Strategic Partnership,'" *New York Times*, May 21, 2007, http://www.nytimes.com/2007/05/21/world/europe/21iht-belarus.4.5810021.html (accessed August 11, 2010).

2 "Belarus, Venezuela Strengthen Energy, Trade Ties During Lukashenko Visit," *Radio Free Europe*, March 18, 2010, http://www.rferl.org/content/Belarus_Venezuela_Strengthen_Energy_Trade_Ties_During_Lukashenka_Visit/1986969.html (accessed July 7, 2010).

3 "Belarus Eyes Latvia as New Route for Venezuelan Oil," *Hurriyet Daily News*, August 23, 2010, http://www.hurriyetdailynews.com/n.php?n=belarus-eyes -latvia-as-new-route-for-venezuelan-oil-2010-08-23.

4 Ibid.

5 "Russia Welcomes Belarus-Venezuela Close Ties," *Belarus Telegraph Agency*, March 31, 2010, http://news.belta.by/en/news/econom?id=510712 (accessed September 3, 2010).

6 Ibid.

7 "Russia Cuts Belarus Gas Supplies Over Debt," BBC News, June 21, 2010, http://www.bbc.co.uk/news/10362731.

8 Ibid.

9 Ibid.

10 Andrew Osborn, "Belarus-Russia 'Gas War' Ends," *The Telegraph*, June 24, 2010, http://www.telegraph.co.uk/news/worldnews/europe/russia/7852161/Russia -Belarus-gas-war-ends.html.

11 Luke Harding, "Belarus Turns Off Flow of Gas to Europe," *The Guardian*, June 22, 2010, http://www.guardian.co.uk/world/2010/jun/22/belarus-gas-row-russia (accessed June 25, 2010).

12 Ibid.

13 "Nothing Can Hurt Belarus-Russia Relations: Lukashenko," *RIA Novosti*, September 14, 2010, http://en.rian.ru/russia/20100914/160587139.html (accessed September 14, 2010).

14 "Iran, Belarus Will Not Succumb to Pressure Exerted by Other States," *Belarus Telegraph Agency*, May 22, 2007, http://news.belta.by/en/news/politics/?id=156369 (accessed July 12, 2010).

15 See, "Iran, Belarus See Jofair Oilfield Operational Soon," *Tehran Times*, February 17, 2010, http://www.tehrantimes.com/index_View.asp?code=214288.

16 Yan, ed., "Iran-Belarus Determined to Expand Relations: Ahmadinejad," *Xinhua*, December 17, 2009, http://news.xinhuanet.com/english/2009-12/17/content _12658615.htm; "Treasury Identifies 21 Entities Determined to be Owned or Controlled by the Government of Iran," September 3, 2010, http://useu.usmission.gov/treasury_080310.html.

17 "Selling Guns to Terrorists from the 'Heart of Europe,'" *Wall Street Journal* (Europe), April 26, 2002.

18 Moisés Naím, *Illicit: How Smugglers, Traffickers, and Copycats Are Hijacking the Global Economy* (New York: Doubleday, 2005), 62–63.

19 H.R. 4436: Belarus Arms Transfers Accountability Act of 2009. Text available online at http://www.opencongress.org/bill/111-h4436/text?version=ih&nid=t0:ih:25.

20 Michael Ledeen, *The Iranian Time Bomb: The Mullah Zealots' Quest for Destruction* (New York: St. Martin's Press, 2007), 120.

21 "Belarus Selling Iran M-Iskander Missiles," *Press TV*, May 1, 2009, http://www.presstv.ir/detail.aspx?id=93244&sectionid=351020101 (accessed May 15, 2010).

22 "Belarus Denies Sales of S-300 to Iran," *RIA Novosti*, April 8, 2010, http://en.rian.ru/mlitary_news/20100804/160070974.html (accessed June 5, 2010).

23 "Venezuelan Seeks Another Anti-U.S. Ally in Syria," *New York Times*, August 31, 2006, http://www.nytimes.com/2006/08/31/world/middleeast/31chavez.html (accessed September 12, 2010).

24 "Chavez Meets with Syria's Assad in Venezuela," *CBS News*, June 27, 2010.

25 Daniel Williams, "Syria, Venezuela Sign Olive Oil Trade Agreement," *Olive Oil Times*, June 21, 2010, http://www.oliveoiltimes.com/olive-oil-business/africa-middle-east/syria-venezuela/3721.

26 "Syria's Assad Seeks Investment in Latin America," *Al Arabiya*, June 25, 2009, http://www.alarabiya.net/articles/2010/06/25/112260.html.

27 *The Sean Hannity Show*, "Interview with Álvaro Vargas Llosa," Fox News, July 18, 2010.

28 Claire Duffet, "Why Russia's Dmitry Medvedev is Visiting Syria," *Christian Science Monitor*, May 11, 2010, http://www.csmonitor.com/World/Middle-East/2010/0511/Why-Russia-s-Dmitry-Medvedev-is-visiting-Syria (accessed May 14, 2010).

29 Dmitry Solovyov, Ori Lewis, and Jon Boyle, "Russia to Sell Syria Warplanes, Air Defense Systems," Reuters, May 14, 2010, http://www.reuters.com/article/idUSTRE64D35S20100514 (accessed May 14, 2010).

30 Ibid.

31 Janusz Bugajski, *Dismantling the West: Russia's Atlantic Agenda* (Washington, DC: Potomac Books, 2009), 48.

32 Ibid.

33 Fernando Coronil, *The Magical State: Nature, Money, and Modernity in Venezuela* (Chicago: University of Chicago Press, 1997), 292.

34 Ibid.

35 Venezuelan Constitution, Title VI: Article 305, 1999, accessed online from the Venezuelan Embassy, http://www.embavenez-us.org/constitution/title_vi.htm (accessed July 7, 2010).

36 "Agricultural Statistics: Machinery: Tractors," Nationmaster.com, http://www.nationmaster.com/time.php?stat=agr_agr_mac_tra&country=ve (accessed May 25, 2010).

37   Chris Kraul, "U.S. Eyes Venezuela-Iran Commercial Alliance," *Los Angeles Times*, June 24, 2006, http://articles.latimes.com/2006/jun/24/world/fg-veniran24 (accessed July 7, 2010). For discussion of the various nuclei of endogenous development see Betsy Bowman and Bob Stone, "Venezuela's Cooperative Revolution," *Dollars & Sense*, http://www.dollarsandsense.org/archives/2006/0706bowmanstone.html (accessed July 7, 2010).

38   M. Ghadiryanfar, et al., "A Pattern for Power Distribution Based on Tractor Demand in Iran," *CIGR Ejournal*, manuscript MES 1294, XI, July 2009.

39   "VenIran Tractors, Agricultural Tanks," *Iran Daily*, September 9, 2008.

40   Norman Bailey, "Iranian Penetration into the Western Hemisphere Through Venezuela," House Subcommittee Testimony, October 27, 2009.

41   "Venezuela Returns Chinese Tractors on Mechanical Defects," *El Universal*, September 13, 2006, http://english.eluniversal.com/2006/09/13/en_eco_art_13A777631.shtml (English translation) (accessed July 7, 2010).

42   Robert M. Morgenthau, "The Emerging Axis of Iran and Venezuela," *Wall Street Journal*, September 9, 2009.

43   Bailey, "Iranian Penetration into the Western Hemisphere Through Venezuela."

44   Cited in Robert Baer, *The Devil We Know: Dealing With the New Iranian Superpower* (New York: Crown Publishers, 2008), 107–8.

45   See Joseph Nye and Robert Keohane, *Power and Interdependence* (New York: Longman, 2001), chapter 2.

46   Naím, *Illicit*, 62–64.

Chapter 8. "Going Out" with China

1   See Ross Terrill, *The New Chinese Empire: And What It Means for the United States* (New York: Basic Books, 2003), 260; also, "China's Missile Exports and Assistance to Iran," Nuclear Threat Initiative (NTI), http://www.nti.org/db/china/miranpos.htm (accessed July 20, 2010).

2   Cited in Robert Baer, *The Devil We Know: Dealing With the New Iranian Superpower* (New York: Crown Publishers, 2008), 110.

3   "China's Missile Exports and Assistance to Iran," Nuclear Threat Initiative (NTI), http://www.nti.org/db/china/miranpos.htm (accessed July 20, 2010).

4   Stephanie Lieggi, "From Proliferator to Model Citizen? China's Recent Enforcement of Nonproliferation-Related Trade Controls and its Potential Positive Impact in the Region," *Strategic Studies Quarterly* 4, no. 2 (Summer 2010): 39–62.

5   "US Warns China Over Weapons Links in Iran, Iraq, and Afghanistan," *AFP*, May 15, 2008, http://afp.google.com/article/ALeqM5jJfF5GYxlLMZyjHJamD90XWZytiA (accessed July 7, 2010).

6   Lieggi, "From Proliferator to Model Citizen?" 44.

7   Robin Wright, "Iran's New Alliance with China Could Cost U.S. Leverage," *Washington Post*, November 17, 2004, http://www.washingtonpost.com/wp -dyn/articles/A55414-2004Nov16.html (accessed July 6, 2010)

8   Ibid.

9   "World Oil Chokepoints," U.S. Energy Information Administration, updated January 2008, http://www.eia.doe.gov/cabs/world_oil_transit_chokepoints/pdf.pdf (accessed July 18, 2010).

10   For an insightful discussion of China's energy strategy, see: David Zweig and Bi Jianhai, "China's Global Hunt for Energy," *Foreign Affairs* (September/October 2005), http://www.foreignaffairs.com/articles/61017/david-zweig-and-bi-jianhai /chinas-global-hunt-for-energy?page=4.

11   Ibid.

12   Data drawn from OPEC, "Annual Statistics Bulletin 2008," http://www.opec.org/library/Annual%20Statistical%20Bulletin/pdf/ASB2008.pdf. For more on Chinese interest in Iran because of underproduction of its energy sector, see: Wen-Sheng Chen, "China's Oil Strategy: 'Going Out' to Iran," *Asian Politics and Policy* 2, no. 1: 39–54.

13   S.W. Chien, *The Oil and Gas in the Middle East and Caspian Sea and China's Energy Security Strategy* (Beijing: Shishi Press, 2007), 650. Cited in Chen, "China's Oil Strategy: 'Going Out' to Iran," 46.

14   Wang Guanqun, "China, Venezuela Sign Agreements on Oil, Hydropower Projects," *Xinhua*, April 18, 2010, http://www.gov.cn/misc/2010-04/18/content _1585628.htm (accessed July 20, 2010).

15   "Country Analysis Briefs: Venezuela," U.S. Energy Information Association, http://www.eia.doe.gov/cabs/venezuela/Full.html (accessed July 19, 2010).

16   Javier Corrales and Michael Penfold, *Dragon in the Tropics: Hugo Chavez and the Political Economy of Revolution in Venezuela* (Washington: Brookings Institution Press, 2010), chapter 5.

17   Andy Webb-Vidal and Doug Cameron, "US Mulls Losing Oil Supplies from Venezuela," *Financial Times* (found online on MSNBC), January 14, 2005, http://www.msnbc.msn.com/id/6826081/ (accessed July 6, 2010).

18   Ibid.

19   Peter Wilson, "Chavez Visits China as Venezuela Curbs U.S. Oil Ties," *Bloomberg*, August 21, 2006, http://www.bloomberg.com/apps/news?pid=newsarchive& sid=aKxotAMwY_D8 (accessed July 6, 2010).

20   US EIA. "World Oil Chokepoints."

21   Cited in ibid.

22 Simon Hall, "Venezuela, China in Oil Talks," *Wall Street Journal*, February 2, 2010, http://online.wsj.com/article/NA_WSJ_PUB:SB100014240527487040228045750 40431689856008.html (accessed July 6, 2010).

23 Simon Romero, "Chávez Says China to Lend Venezuela $20 Billion," *New York Times*, April 18, 2010, http://www.nytimes.com/2010/04/19/world/americas /19venez.html (accessed July 28, 2010).

24 Chris Kraul, "Venezuela Deepens Trade, Military Ties to China," *Los Angeles Times*, January 12, 2009, http://articles.latimes.com/2009/jan/12/world/fg-venezuela -china12 (accessed July 30, 2010).

25 Tamsin Carlisle, "China-Venezuela Oil Deal Bad for the Environment," National Blogs, "The Grid," April 19, 2010, http://blogs.thenational.ae/the_grid/2010/04 /for-the-middle-east-and.html (accessed July 30, 2010).

26 Frank Jack Daniel, Eyanir Chinea, and Jackie Frank, "China Delivers Venezuela Jets for Anti-Drugs Fights," Reuters, March 13, 2010, http://www.reuters.com /article/idUSTRE62C1IY20100313.

27 Ibid.

28 Dennis C. Blair, "Annual Threat Assessment of the Intelligence Community for the Senate Select Committee on Intelligence," Unclassified Report of the Director of National Intelligence, February 12, 2009, 29.

29 Chávez and Venezuela's military leaders have repeatedly said the explicit purpose of Chinese arms is to aid in the country's fight against drug traffickers, unlike most Russian arms procurements. See "Venezuela's Chávez Receives Chinese Planes Armed with Missile, Rockets and Bombs," *Latin American Herald Tribune* (date unavailable), http://laht.com/article.asp?ArticleId=353675&CategoryId=10718.

30 This idea comes an article by Javier Corrales, "Using Social Power to Balance Soft Power," *Washington Quarterly* (October 2009): 97–110.

31 Corrales, "Using Social Power," 106.

32 Saudi Arabia's response would heavily impact the price of oil.

33 Ibid.

34 Shai Oster, "China's Oil Needs Affect its Iran Ties," *Wall Street Journal*, September 28, 2009, http://online.wsj.com/article/SB125408502540944481.html (accessed July 21, 2010).

35 Robert Kagan, *The Return of History and the End of Dreams* (New York: Knopf, 2008), 68.

36 See, for instance, Amir Taheri, "Iran Has Started a Mid East Arms Race," *Wall Street Journal*, March 23, 2009, http://online.wsj.com/article/NA_WSJ_PUB :SB123776572203009141.html.

37 "China Investment in Iran Worries US," *Press TV* (Iran), July 29, 2010, http://www.presstv.ir/detail.aspx?id=136724&sectionid=351020101.

Chapter 9. Cracks in the Facade

1 "Saudi Arabia Eager to Replace Iran," *Kommersant* (Moscow), February 15, 2008, http://www.kommersant.com/p853111/r_527/Saudi_Arabia_cooperation/ (accessed September 3, 2010).

2 Robert C. Baer, *The Devil We Know: Dealing With the New Iranian Superpower* (New York: Crown Publishers, 2008), 254.

3 "Saudi Arabia Eager to Replace Iran," *Kommersant*.

4 "An Axis in Need of Oiling," *The Economist*, October 25, 2008, 71–72.

5 Ibid.

6 Ibid.

7 "Oil Hits New Highs on Iran Fears," BBC News, July 11, 2008, http://newsvote.bbc.co.uk/2/hi/business/7501939.stm (accessed September 12, 2010).

8 Simon Romero, Michael Slackman and Clifford Levy, "3 Oil-Rich Countries Face a Reckoning," *New York Times*, October 21, 2008.

9 "Dreams of a Different World," *The Economist*, September 17, 2009, 49.

10 See, for instance, David Hearst, "Dangerous Proxy War Gains an International Dimension," *The Guardian*, August 9, 2008, http://www.guardian.co.uk/world /2008/aug/09/georgia.russia1; also, "A Discussion About the Escalating Conflict Between Georgia and Russia," *The Charlie Rose Show*, August 11, 2008.

11 Reuel Marc Gerecht, "Iran's Hamas Strategy," *Wall Street Journal*, January 7, 2009, http://online.wsj.com/article/SB123128812156759281.html (accessed June 2, 2010).

12 "Chávez's Base Rebukes Him at Polls," *Wall Street Journal*, November 25, 2008, online.wsj.com/article/SB122748432718751705.htm (accessed July 7, 2010).

13 James Bone, Tony Halpin, and Michael Theodoulou, "'Axis of Diesel' Forced to Change Its Ways by Plummeting Oil Price," *The Sunday Times* (London), October 18, 2008, http://business.timesonline.co.uk/tol/business/industry_sectors/natural _resources/article4965242.ece (accessed May 13, 2010).

14 Julian Evans, "Medvedev Ups the Tempo of Change," *Wall Street Journal*, July 1, 2010, http://online.wsj.com/article/SB100014240527487045753045752963437993651 82.html?mod=WSJ_WSJ_News_JOURNALREPORTS7_4.

15 Dmitry Medvedev, "Go Russia!" RT, September 10, 2009, http://rt.com/Politics /2009-09-11/dmitry-medvedev-program-document.html (accessed July 21, 2010).

16 Ibid.

17 Charles King and Rajan Menon. "Prisoners of the Caucuses: Russia's Invisible Civil War," *Foreign Affairs*, 89, 4 (July/August 2010): 20–34.

18 "Losing Power," *The Economist*, November 5, 2009,
    http://www.economist.com/node/14803155.

19 "Iran GDP: Real Growth Rate," Index Mundi, retrieved May 12, 2010,
    http://www.indexmundi.com/iran/gdp_real_growth_rate.html.

20 Joseph A. Christoff, "Iran Sanctions: New Act Underscores Importance of
    Comprehensive Assessment of Sanctions' Effectiveness," U.S. Government
    Accountability Office, July 29, 2010, http://www.gao.gov/new.items/d10928t.pdf.

21 "Still Sitting Pretty," *The Economist*, June 12, 2010, 51–53.

22 "Ahmadinejad Warns Medvedev of Joining 'U.S. Plot' Against Iran," *Haaretz*, July
    23, 2010, http://www.haaretz.com/news/diplomacy-defense/ahmadinejad-warns
    -medvedev-of-joining-u-s-plot-against-iran-1.303718.

23 Robin Pomeroy and Guy Faulconbridge, "Iran and Russia Clash in Worst Row for
    Years," Reuters, May 26, 2010, http://www.reuters.com/article
    /idUSLDE64P0VV20100526.

24 Pavel Felgenhauer, "The 'Unraveling Relationship' Between Russia and Iran," BBC
    News, July 24, 2010, http://www.bbc.co.uk/news/world-europe-10684110.

25 Ibid.

26 "No Talk of Reducing Ties with Russia at Parliamentary Committee: MP," in
    Tehran Times, June 28, 2010, http://www.tehrantimes.com/index_View.asp?code
    =222068 (accessed July 24, 2010).

27 Simon Shuster, "Russian Support for Iran Sanctions Called into Question," *Time*,
    July 15, 2010, http://www.time.com/time/world/article/0,8599,2004159,00.html.

28 Ibid.

29 Ibid.

30 "Russia's Nuclear Help to Iran Stirs Questions About Its 'Improved' Relations with
    U.S.," Fox News, August 14, 2010, http://www.foxnews.com/politics/2010/08/14
    /russias-nuclear-help-iran-stirs-questions-improved-relations/.

31 "Russia Vague on S-300 Delivery to Iran," *Press TV*, August 21, 2010,
    http://www.presstv.ir/detail/139487.html.

32 David E. Sanger and Andrew E. Kramer, "U.S. Lauds Russia on Barring Arms for
    Iran," *New York Times*, September 23, 2010, http://www.nytimes.com/2010
    /09/23/world/europe/23prexy.html?_r=1&emc=eta1.

33 "Iran, Afghanistan, Tajikistan's Interests Interlinked," *Tehran Times*, August 7,
    2010, http://www.tehrantimes.com/index_View.asp?code=224314.

34 "Iran and Turkey Sign Pipeline Deal," *Al Jazeera*, July 23, 2010,
    http://english.aljazeera.net/business/2010/07/201072314455840549.html.

35 "Russia Boosts Military Cooperation with Israel," Hurriyet Daily News, September 6, 2010, http://www.hurriyetdailynews.com/n.php?n=russia-boosts-military-cooperation-with-israel-2010-09-06.

36 Moshe Arens, "F-35-Take It or Leave It," Haaretz, July 27, 2010, http://www.haaretz.com/print-edition/opinion/f-35-take-it-or-leave-it-1.304297.

37 "Russia Boosts Military Cooperation with Israel," Agence France-Press.

38 Ibid.

39 "An Axis in Need of Oiling," The Economist.

40 Luis Fleischman, "Brazil Tilts Toward Chávez and Iran," The Cutting Edge, October 12, 2009, http://www.thecuttingedgenews.com/index.php?article=11652 (accessed September 3, 2010).

41 "An Axis in Need of Oiling," The Economist.

42 "Venezuela-Russia Arms Deals Release Turbulence in the Region," El Universal, April 5, 2010, http://english.eluniversal.com/2010/04/09/en_ing_esp_venezuela-russia-arm_09A3718293.shtml (accessed June 8, 2010).

43 Simon Romero et al., "3 Oil-Rich Countries Face a Reckoning," New York Times, October 21, 2008.

44 "An Unconventional Glut," The Economist, March 13, 2010, 72–74.

45 "US Surpasses Russia as Top Gas Producer," Upstream Online, January 12, 2010, http://www.upstreamonline.com/live/article203335.ece (accessed June 3, 2010).

46 "An Unconventional Glut," The Economist, 72–74.

47 Ibid.

48 Ibid.

49 U.S. DNI Annual Report, 2009, 3.

50 "Falling Oil Prices Squeeze Chavez Diplomacy," MSNBC, January 6, 2009, http://www.msnbc.msn.com/id/28527787/ (accessed July 2, 2010).

51 Simon Romero, "Venezuela's Hope of More Sway Dim as Riches Dip," New York Times, May 16, 2009, http://www.nytimes.com/2009/05/20/world/americas/20venez.html (accessed July 24, 2010).

52 Anne-Marie O'Connor and Mary Beth Sheridan, "Iran's Invisible Nicaragua Embassy," Washington Post, July 13, 2009, http://www.washingtonpost.com/wp-dyn/content/article/2009/07/12/AR2009071202337.html.

53 "Iran Loans More than $250 Million to Bolivia," Voice of America News, August 31, 2010, http://www.voanews.com/english/news/americas/Iran-Loans-More-than-250-Million-to-Bolivia-101913708.html.

54 "Iran to Loan $200 Million to Ecuador," Latin American Herald Tribune, September 6, 2010, http://laht.com/article.asp?CategoryId=14089&ArticleId=325760.

55 Anne Applebaum, "Russia's Caribbean Farce," *Washington Post*, December 2, 2008,http://www.washingtonpost.com/wp-dyn/content/article/2008/12/01/AR2008120102406.html (accessed September 1, 2010).

56 Cited in Lionel Beehner, *Backgrounder: Russia-Iran Arms Trade*, Council on Foreign Relations, November 1, 2006.

Chapter 10. Inoculation

1 The term "benign neglect," coined in 1970 by then-counselor to the president for urban affairs Daniel P. Moynihan, was later also used by Gustav Petersen in "Benign Neglect Is Not Enough" in April 1973. For discussions relating to recent policies, see, for instance, Makram Haluani, "Benign Neglect: Cooperation in the Western Hemisphere," *Harvard International Review* (Winter 2003): 50–54.

2 Fernando Henrique Cardoso, *The Accidental President of Brazil: A Memoir* (New York: Public Affairs, 2006), 261.

3 Anne-Marie O'Connor and Mary Beth Sheridan, "Iran's Invisible Nicaragua Embassy," *Washington Post*, July 13, 2009, http://www.washingtonpost.com/wp-dyn/content/article/2009/07/12/AR2009071202337.html.

4 Ibid.

5 "Obama Urges 'Equal' Ties in Hemisphere," *Washington Post*, April 18, 2009, http://www.washingtonpost.com/wp-dyn/content/article/2009/04/17/AR2009041700389.html (accessed September 24, 2010).

6 Larry Rohter, "Venezuela Wants Trade Group to Embrace Anti-Imperialism," *New York Times*, January 19, 2007, http://www.nytimes.com/2007/01/19/world/americas/19latin.html (accessed September 12, 2010).

7 "A Discussion with Sebastián Piñera," *The Charlie Rose Show*, September 23, 2010, 9.

8 "The Caribbean Basin Security Initiative: A Shared Regional Partnership," Department of State Fact Sheet, May 20, 2010, http://www.state.gov/r/pa/scp/fs/2010/142088.htm.

9 John Deutch and James R. Schlesinger, *National Security Consequences of US Oil Dependency* (New York: Council on Foreign Relations, October 2006), 6.

10 Simon Romero, "Venezuela Still Aids Colombia Rebels, New Material Shows," *New York Times*, August 3, 2009.

11 Jorge Castañeda, "It's Time to Confront Hugo Chávez," Project Syndicate, September 29, 2009, http://www.project-syndicate.org/commentary/castaneda26/English (accessed August 2, 2010).

12 Conservative columnist Robert Novak made this a focal point in one commentary, insisting that not passing a free trade agreement would "humiliate Colombian President Alvaro Uribe, a free-trader and a bulwark against the spreading influence in Latin America of Venezuela's leftist strongman, President Hugo Chavez." Op-ed

found online: "Our Man in the Andes Won't Publicly Confront Hugo Chavez," Union Leader, June 29, 2006. http://www.unionleader.com/article.aspx?headline =Robert+D.+Novak%3A+Will+Democrats+heed+labor's+demand+on+trade+pact %3F&articleId=222edf7d-c5e7-4b69-8769-6b274296f715.

13 Michael Shifter, *Hugo Chávez: A Test for U.S. Policy*, a Special Report of the Inter-American Dialogue, Washington, D.C. (March 2007): 6.

14 "Speak Softly and Carry a Blank Cheque," *The Economist*, July 15, 2010, http://www.economist.com/node/16592455?story_id=16592455.

15 Ibid.

16 Total calculated based on information in "Speak Softly and Carry a Blank Cheque."

17 Larry Rohter, "Argentina's New Role Model: It's Old Rival, Brazil," *New York Times*, September 5, 2002, http://www.nytimes.com/2002/08/05/world/argentina-s-new -role-model-its-old-rival-brazil.html?scp=9&sq=argentina%20rather%20be%20a %20star&st=cse&pagewanted=2 (accessed August 2, 2010).

18 The most authoritative work on this topic is Jorge Castañeda's *Utopia Unarmed: The Latin American Left After the Cold War* (New York: Vintage Paperback, 1994).

19 Simon Romero, "Venezuela's Hope of More Sway Dims as Riches Dip," *New York Times*, May 19, 2009, http://www.nytimes.com/2009/05/20/world/americas /20venez.html (accessed July 24, 2010).

20 Ibid.

21 For example, see: "Lula to Rich Nations: 'Stop Your Hypocrisy,' Buy Brazil Biofuel," AFP, April 27, 2008, http://afp.google.com/article/ALeqM5h2uh668bubJikiI0j8wYhWFfrmlg (accessed September 24, 2010).

22 "Brazil's Victory in Cotton Trade Case Exposes America's Wasteful Subsidies," *Washington Post*, June 3, 2010, http://www.washingtonpost.com/wp-dyn/content /article/2010/06/02/AR2010060204228.html.

23 "Brazil and Peacekeeping: Policy, Not Altruism," *The Economist*, September 25, 2010, 50–52.

24 Javier Corrales and Michael Penfold, *Dragon in the Tropics: Hugo Chavez and the Political Economy of Revolution in Venezuela* (Washington: Brookings Institution Press, 2010), see chapter 5.

25 Ibid.

26 "EE.UU critica lazos de Irán con America Latina," *BBC Mundo*, May 8, 2008, http://news.bbc.co.uk/hi/spanish/latin_america/newsid_7389000/7389197.stm (accessed July 4, 2010).

27 See, for example, Douglas Schoen and Michael Rowan, *The Threat Closer to Home: Hugo Chávez and the War Against America* (New York: Free Press, 2009), chapter 10.

28 Ibid., 174.

29 Phillip R. Cuccia, "Something Brewing in Venezuela," *Strategic Studies Institute,* op-ed., January 2010, 31.

30 "Russia, Ecuador Ink Strategic Partnership Declaration," *RIA Novosti,* October 29, 2009, http://en.rian.ru/russia/20091029/156637189.html; Hugh Bronstein, "Ecuador Wants You to Smell the Roses, and Eat Them," Reuters, September 13, 2010, http://www.reuters.com/article/idUSTRE68C57A20100913?pageNumber=2.

31 Bronstein, "Ecuador Wants You to Smell the Roses, and Eat Them."

32 Reuel Marc Gerecht and Mark Dubowitz, "To Pressure Iran, Squeeze Russia and China," *Wall Street Journal,* September 13, 2010.

33 Ibid.

34 See, for example, Charles Schumer's, "Confronting Iran," *Wall Street Journal,* op-ed, June 3, 2008, http://schumer.senate.gov/new_website/opeds/WSJ6_3_08oped.htm (accessed September 2, 2010).

35 German Marshall Fund of the United States, *Transatlantic Trends: 2010,* http://trends.gmfus.org/doc/2010_English_Key.pdf.

36 "Global Trends, 2015," National Intelligence Council, 75, http://www.dni.gov/nic/NIC_globaltrend2015.html (accessed August 6, 2011).

37 Robert Kagan, *Of Paradise and Power* (New York: Vintage, 2003), 6.

38 Ibid.

Conclusion

1 Richard Feinberg, "Chávez's Conditionality," *Latin Business Chronicle,* June 4, 2007, http://www.latinbusinesschronicle.com/app/article.aspx?id=1296 (accessed October 2, 2010).

2 Steve Stecklow and Farnaz Fassihi, "Iran's Global Foray Has Mixed Results," *Wall Street Journal,* September 29, 2009, http://online.wsj.com/article/SB125409124052344735.html (accessed October 12, 2009).

3 Simon Romero et al., "3 Oil-Rich Countries Face a Reckoning," *New York Times,* October 21, 2008.

4 Douglas Schoen and Michael Rowan, *The Threat Closer to Home: Hugo Chávez and the War Against America* (New York: Free Press), 2009, 2.

5 Thanassis Cambanis, "Stronger Hezbollah Emboldened for Fights Ahead," *New York Times,* October 6, 2010.

6 Ibid.

7   Chris Kraul and Sebastian Rotella, "Fears of Hezbollah Presence in Venezuela," *Los Angeles Times*, August 27, 2008, http://articles.latimes.com/2008/aug/27/world/fg-venezterror27.

8   Jeremy McDermott, "Hugo Chavez: Colombia Is 'Israel of Latin America," *Telegraph*, July 24, 2009, http://www.telegraph.co.uk/news/worldnews/southamerica/venezuela/5901163/Hugo-Chavez-Colombia-is-Israel-of-Latin-America.html (accessed September 12, 2009).

9   Presentation by Dr. David Myers before the Center of Security and International Studies, October 1, 2010, http://csis.org/event/outlook-venezuela's-foreign-policy (accessed August 8, 2011).

10 "Iran-Venezuela ties dull U.S. pressure," *Press TV*, August 30, 2010, http://www.presstv.ir/detail/140579.html.

11 Jeffrey Mankoff, "Changing Course in Moscow," *Foreign Affairs*, September 7, 2010, http://www.foreignaffairs.com/articles/66743/jeffrey-mankoff/changing-course-in-moscow (accessed August 8, 2011).

12 Andrew E. Kramer, "Russia Says It Will Build Nuclear Plant for Venezuela," *New York Times*, October 15, 2010, http://www.nytimes.com/2010/10/16/world/americas/16venez.html?partner=rss&emc=rss.

13 Ibid.

14 Robert Kagan, *The Return of History and the End of Dreams* (New York: Knopf, 2008), 4.

Selected Bibliography

Agence France-Presse. "Iran, Venezuela Launch Joint Development Bank." April 3, 2009, http://www.google.com/hostednews/afp/article/ALeqM5iskmQ6xtdC4Ebzc799pW YG_RSMXg (accessed July 24, 2010).

———. "Iran's Quds Force in Venezuela, Latin America: Pentagon." April 22, 2010, http://www.google.com/hostednews/afp/article/ALeqM5jvXOYLKMt3NWFER4xX MlDPSTmhBw (accessed May 14, 2010).

———. "Lula to Rich Nations: 'Stop Your Hypocrisy,' Buy Brazil Biofuel." April 27, 2008, http://afp.google.com/article/ALeqM5h2uh668bubJikiI0j8wYhWFfrmlg (accessed September 24, 2010).

———. "Russia Boosts Military Cooperation with Israel." September 6, 2010, http://news.yahoo.com/s/afp/20100906/wl_mideast_afp/russiaisraelmilitarydiplom acy (accessed September 6, 2010).

———. "US Warns China Over Weapons Links in Iran, Iraq, and Afghanistan." May 15, 2008, http://afp.google.com/article/ALeqM5jJfF5GYxlLMZyjHJamD90XWZytiA (accessed July 7, 2010).

———. "Venezuela-Iran: une alliance anti-Washington." September 17, 2006.

Applebaum, Anne. "Russia's Caribbean Farce." *Washington Post*, December 2, 2008, http://www.washingtonpost.com/wp-dyn/content/article/2008/12/01/ AR2008120102406.html (accessed September 1, 2010).

Al Arabiya. "Syria's Assad Seeks Investment in Latin America." June 25, 2009, http://www.alarabiya.net/articles/2010/06/25/112260.html (accessed July 8, 2010).

Arens, Moshe. "F-35-Take It or Leave It." *Haaretz*, July 27, 2010, http://www.haaretz.com/print-edition/opinion/f-35-take-it-or-leave-it-1.304297 (accessed July 27, 2010).

Arnson, Cynthia, Haleh Esfandiari, and Adam Stubits, eds. *Iran in Latin America: Threat of 'Axis of Annoyance'?* Washington: Woodrow Wilson International Center for Scholars, 2009.

Associated Press. "Bolivia denies Israel report it supplied Iran with uranium." *Haaretz*, May 25, 2009, http://www.haaretz.com/news/bolivia-denies-israel-report-it -supplied-iran-with-uranium-1.276747 (accessed July 1, 2010).

——. "Israel Ties 2 Nations to Iran's Uranium." *New York Times*, May 25, 2009, http://www.nytimes.com/2009/05/26/world/middleeast/26israel.html?_r=2 &partner=rss&emc=rss(accessed July 10, 2010) .

——. "Venezuela Offers Billions to Countries in Latin America." August 27, 2007.

——. "Venezuela Threatens to Sell F-16 Fleet to Iran." Fox News, May 16, 2006, http://www.foxnews.com/story/0,2933,195672,00.html (accessed May 12, 2010).

Baer, Robert C. *The Devil We Know: Dealing With the New Iranian Superpower*. New York: Crown Publishers, 2008.

Barnes, Ed. "Exclusive: Venezuela Cancels Round-Trip 'Terror Flight' to Syria and Iran." Fox News, September 14, 2010. http://www.foxnews.com/us/2010/09 /14/terror-flight-venezuela-iran-illicit-arms-hezbollah-hamas-protest/ (accessed September 14, 2010).

Barry, Ellen. "Russia Flexes Muscles in Oil Deal with Chavez." *New York Times*, September 26, 2008.

BBC Mundo. "EE.UU critica lazos de Irán con America Latina." May 8, 2008, http://news.bbc.co.uk/hi/spanish/latin_america/newsid_7389000/7389197.stm (accessed July 4, 2010).

———. "Nicaragua e Irán: Unión invincible." June 11, 2007, http://news.bbc.co.uk/hi /spanish/latin_america/newsid_6741000/6741829.stm (accessed July 5, 2010).

BBC News. "Chavez Calls for New OPEC Members." June 1, 2006, http://news.bbc.co.uk /2/hi/business/5035894.stm (accessed July 23, 2010).

———. "Energy Fuels New 'Great Game' in Europe." September 24, 2009.

———. "Iran Offers Hamas Financial Aid." February 22, 2006.

———. "Oil Hits New Highs on Iran Fears." July 11, 2008, http://newsvote.bbc.co.uk /2/hi/business/7501939.stm (accessed September 12, 2010).

———. "Russia Cuts Belarus Gas Supplies Over Debt." June 21, 2010, http://www.bbc.co.uk/news/10362731 (accessed June 28, 2010).

————. "Russia-Venezuela Nuclear Accord." November 27, 2008, http://news.bbc.co.uk/2/hi/7751562.stm (accessed October 29, 2010).

Beehner, Lionel. *Backgrounder: Russia-Iran Arms Trade*. Council on Foreign Relations, November 1, 2006.

Belarus Telegraph Agency. "Iran, Belarus Will Not Succumb to Pressure Exerted by Other States." May 22, 2007, http://news.belta.by/en/news/politics/?id=156369 (accessed July 12, 2010).

————. "Russia Welcomes Belarus-Venezuela Close Ties." March 31, 2010, http://news.belta.by/en/news/econom?id=510712 (accessed September 3, 2010).

Bhadrakumar, M.K. "Pipeline Geopolitics: Russia, China, Iran Redraw Energy Map." *Asia Times Online*, January 8, 2010, http://www.atimes.com/atimes/Central _Asia/LA08Ag01.html (accessed June 24, 2010).

Blair, David. "Profile: Muammar Gaddafi, Libyan leader at time of Lockerbie bombing." *Telegraph* (London), August 13, 2009, http://www.telegraph.co.uk/news/uknews/6022449/Profile-Muammar-Gaddafi -Libyan-leader-at-time-of-Lockerbie-bombing.html (accessed June 3, 2010).

Blair, Dennis C. "Annual Threat Assessment of the Intelligence Community for the Senate Select Committee on Intelligence: 2010." February 2010, http://www.dni.gov /testimonies/20100202_testimony.pdf (accessed July 23, 2010).

————. "Annual Threat Assessment of the U.S. Intelligence Community for the Senate Select Committee on Intelligence: 2009." February 2009.

Blomfield, Adrian. "Israel Humbled by Arms from Iran." *The Telegraph*, August 15, 2006, http://www.telegraph.co.uk/news/1526407/Israel-humbled-by-arms-from -Iran.html (accessed July 4, 2010).

Bolton, John R. "The Chavez Threat." *Los Angeles Times*, September 16, 2010, http://www.latimes.com/news/opinion/commentary/la-oe-bolton-chavez -20100916,0,3843771.story (accessed September 16, 2010).

Bone, James, Tony Halpin, and Michael Theodoulou. "'Axis of Diesel' Forced to Change Its Ways by Plummeting Oil Prices." *Sunday Times* (London), October 18, 2008, http://business.timesonline.co.uk/tol/business/industry_sectors/natural_resources /article4965242.ece (accessed May 13, 2010).

Borgerson, Scott G. "Arctic Meltdown: The Economic and Security Implications of Global Warming." *Foreign Affairs* 87, no. 2, (March/April 2008): 63–77.

Bremmer, Ian. *The J Curve: A New Way to Understand Why Nations Rise and Fall*. New York: Simon & Schuster, 2006.

Bretton Woods Project. "ICSID in Crisis." July 10, 2009,
   http://www.brettonwoodsproject.org/art-564878 (accessed June 23, 2010).

Bridges, Tyler. "Iran's Unlikely Embrace of Bolivia Builds Influence in U.S. Backyard."
   McClatchy, Feburary 5, 2009, http://www.mcclatchydc.com/2009/02/05/61600
   /irans-unlikely-embrace-of-bolivia.html (accessed May 3, 2010).

Bronstein, Hugh. "Ecuador Wants You to Smell the Roses, and Eat Them," Reuters,
   September 13, 2010, http://www.reuters.com/article/idUSTRE68C57A20100913?
   pageNumber=2 (accessed September 13, 2010).

Brzezinski, Zbigniew. *The Grand Chessboard: American Primacy and Its Geostrategic
   Imperatives.* New York: Basic Books, 1997.

Bugajski, Janusz. *Dismantling the West: Russia's Atlantic Agenda.* Washington, DC:
   Potomac Books, 2009.

Butters, Andrew Lee. "Russia Flexes Its Muscles in MidEast." *Time*, August 13, 2008,
   http://www.time.com/time/world/article/0,8599,1836613,00.html (accessed
   September 2, 2010).

Cambanis, Thanassis. "Stronger Hezbollah Emboldened for Fights Ahead." *New York
   Times*, October 6, 2010.

Cameron, Doug, and Andy Webb-Vidal. "US Mulls Losing Oil Supplies from
   Venezuela." *Financial Times* (found online on MSNBC), January 14, 2005,
   http://www.msnbc.msn.com/id/6826081/ (accessed July 6, 2010).

Cancel, Daniel. "Russia to Finance $2.2 Billion for Venezuelan Arms." Bloomberg
   News, September 13, 2009, http://www.bloomberg.com/apps/news?pid
   =newsarchive&sid=agFcOwD.Kdz8.

Cardoso, Fernando Henrique. *The Accidental President of Brazil: A Memoir.* New York:
   Public Affairs, 2006.

Castañeda, Jorge. "It's Time to Confront Hugo Chávez." *Project Syndicate*, September
   29, 2009, http://www.project-syndicate.org/commentary/castaneda26/English
   (accessed August 2, 2010).

———. *Utopia Unarmed: The Latin American Left After the Cold War.* New York: Vintage
   Paperback, 1994.

Cawthorne, Andrew. "Ecuador Says Iran Ties Landed It on Laundering List." Reuters,
   February 2, 2010.

Chadwick, Alex, and Lourdes Garcia-Navarro. "Venezuela's Chávez Calls for OPEC Production Cuts." *National Public Radio*, June 1, 2006, http://www.npr.org /templates/story/story.php?storyId=5444727&ps=rs (accessed July 23, 2010).

The Charlie Rose Show. "A Discussion About the Escalating Conflict Between Georgia and Russia." August 22, 2008.

———. "A Discussion with Sebastián Piñera." September 23, 2010.

Chen, Wen-Sheng. "China's Oil Strategy: 'Going Out' to Iran." *Asian Politics and Policy* 2, no. 1: 39–54.

Chien, S. W. *The Oil and Gas in the Middle East and Caspian Sea and China's Energy Security Strategy*. Beijing: Shishi Press, 2007.

Coronil, Fernando. *The Magical State: Nature, Money, and Modernity in Venezuela*. Chicago: University of Chicago Press, 1997.

Corrales, Javier. "Using Social Power to Balance Soft Power: Venezuela's Foreign Policy." *The Washington Quarterly* 32, no. 4. (October 2009): 97–114.

———. "Venezuela: Petropolitics and the Promotion of Disorder." *Undermining Democracy: 21st Century Authoritarians*. Washington, DC: Freedom House, June 2009.

———, and Michael Penfold. *Dragon in the Tropics: Hugo Chavez and the Political Economy of Revolution in Venezuela*. Washington, DC: Brookings Institution Press, 2010.

Daniel, Frank Jack, Eyanir Chinea, and Jackie Frank. "China Delivers Venezuela Jets for Anti-Drugs Fights." Reuters, March 13, 2010, http://www.reuters.com/article /idUSTRE62C1IY20100313 (accessed June 8, 2010).

De Cordoba, José. "Chávez Lets Colombia Rebels Wield Power Inside Venezuela." *Wall Street Journal*, November 25, 2008, http://online.wsj.com/article /SB122721414603545331.html (accessed June 3, 2010).

Dempsey, Judy. "Iran, Belarus Forge 'Strategic Partnership.'" *New York Times*, May 21, 2007,http://www.nytimes.com/2007/05/21/world/europe/21iht-belarus .4.5810021.html (accessed August 11, 2010).

Deutch, John, and James R. Schlesinger. *National Security Consequences of US Oil Dependency*. New York: Council on Foreign Relations, October 2006.

Devereux, Charlie, and Andrew Cawthorne. "Chávez Denies Elite Iranian Forces in Venezuela." Reuters, April 26, 2010, http://www.reuters.com/article /idUSTRE63Q0B820100427 (accessed May 30, 2010).

Downie, Andrew. "A South American Arms Race?" *Time*, December 21, 2007, http://www.time.com/time/world/article/0,8599,1697776,00.html (accessed July 30, 2010).

Duffet, Claire. "Why Russia's Dmitry Medvedev Is Visiting Syria." *Christian Science Monitor*, May 11, 2010, http://www.csmonitor.com/World/Middle-East/2010/0511/Why-Russia-s-Dmitry-Medvedev-is-visiting-Syria (accessed May 14, 2010).

The Economist. "The Andean Laundry." March 27, 2010.

———. "An Axis in Need of Oiling." October 25, 2008.

———. "The Bear Is Happy to Be Back." February 8, 2007.

———. "Brazil and Peacekeeping: Policy, Not Altruism." September 25, 2010.

———. "Dreams of Different World." September 19, 2009.

———. "Ecuador's New Constitution: In Good Faith." October 2, 2008, http://www.economist.com/node/12342501 (accessed July 23, 2010).

———. "The FARC Files." May 22, 2008, http://www.economist.com/node/11412645 (accessed June 12, 2010).

———. "Losing Power." November 5, 2009, http://www.economist.com/node/14803155 (June 12, 2010).

———. "One Hundred Days of Yanukovich." June 3, 2010.

———. "Speak Softly and Carry a Blank Cheque." July 15, 2010, http://www.economist.com/node/16592455?story_id=16592455 (July 24, 2010).

———. "Still Sitting Pretty." June 12, 2010.

———. "An Unconventional Glut." March 13, 2010.

Ellings, Richard. Foreword to "Going Out." NBR 17, no. 3 (September 2006), http://www.nbr.org/publications/analysis/pdf/Preview/vol17no3_preview.pdf.

Erikson, Daniel P. "Ahmadinejad Finds It Warmer in Latin America." *Los Angeles Times*, October 3, 2007.

Evans, Julian. "Medvedev Ups the Tempo of Change." *Wall Street Journal*, July 1, 2010, http://online.wsj.com/article/SB10001424052748704575304575296343799365182.html?mod=WSJ_WSJ_News_JOURNALREPORTS7_4 (accessed July 1, 2010).

Feifer, Gregory. "Russia Finds an Eager Weapons Buyer in Iran." NPR, January 18, 2007, http://www.npr.org/templates/story/story.php?storyId=6906839 (accessed May 4, 2010).

Feinberg, Richard. "Chávez's Conditionality." *Latin Business Chronicle*, June 4, 2007, http://www.latinbusinesschronicle.com/app/article.aspx?id=1296 (accessed October 2, 2010).

Felgenhauer, Pavel. "The 'Unraveling Relationship' Between Russia and Iran," BBC News. July 24, 2010, http://www.bbc.co.uk/news/world-europe-10684110 (accessed July 24, 2010).

Fleischman, Luis. "Brazil Tilts Toward Chávez and Iran." *The Cutting Edge*, October 12, 2009, http://www.thecuttingedgenews.com/index.php?article=11652 (accessed September 3, 2010).

Forero, Juan. "After Deadly Assault on Guerillas, Chávez Orders Troops to Colombian Border." *Washington Post*, March 3, 2008, http://www.washingtonpost.com/wp-dyn/content/article/2008/03/02/AR2008030200773.html (accessed July 31, 2010).

———. "Chavez, Seeking Foreign Allies, Spends Billions." *New York Times*, April 4, 2006, http://www.nytimes.com/2006/04/04/world/americas/04venezuela.html (accessed July 10, 2010).

———. "FARC Computer Files Are Authentic, Interpol Probe Finds." May 16, 2008.

Fox News. "Russia's Nuclear Help to Iran Stirs Questions About Its 'Improved' Relations with U.S." August 14, 2010, http://www.foxnews.com/politics/2010/08/14/russias-nuclear-help-iran-stirs-questions-improved-relations/ (accessed August 14, 2010).

Friedman-Rudovsky, Jean. "Is Bolivia Cozying Up to Iran?" *Time*, October 9, 2007.

Gerecht, Reuel Marc. "Iran's Hamas Strategy." *Wall Street Journal*, January 7, 2009, http://online.wsj.com/article/SB123128812156759281.html (accessed June 2, 2010).

———, and Mark Dubowitz. "To Pressure Iran, Squeeze Russia and China." *Wall Street Journal*, September 13, 2010.

Gray, Kevin, Damian Wroclavsky, and Xavier Briand. "New Accusation in Argentina Suitcase Scandal." Reuters, December 20, 2007,http://www.reuters.com/article/idUSN2018803520071220 (accessed June 2, 2010).

Guanqun, Wang, ed. "China, Venezuela Sign Agreements on Oil, Hydropower Projects." *Xinhua*, April 18, 2010, http://www.gov.cn/misc/2010-04/18/content_1585628.htm (accessed July 20, 2010).

The Guardian. "Chavez's FARC Ties May be Insufficient Grounds for US Sanctions."
May 16, 2008. http://www.guardian.co.uk/world/2008/may/16/venezuela.usa
(accessed June 18, 2010).

Haaretz. "Ahmadinejad Warns Medvedev of Joining 'U.S. Plot' Against Iran." July 23,
2010, http://www.haaretz.com/news/diplomacy-defense/ahmadinejad-warns
-medvedev-of-joining-u-s-plot-against-iran-1.303718 (accessed July 23, 2010).

Hafez, Mohammed. *Manufacturing Human Bombs: The Making of Palestinian Suicide
Bombers*. Washington, DC: U.S. Institute of Peace Press, 2006.

Hafezi, Parisa. "Iran, Venezuela in 'Axis of Unity' Against the U.S." Reuters, July 2,
2007, http://www.reuters.com/article/idUSDAH23660020070702 (accessed July
12, 2010).

Hall, Simon. "Venezuela, China in Oil Talks." *Wall Street Journal*, February 2, 2010,
http://online.wsj.com/article/NA_WSJ_PUB:SB1000142405274870402280457504
0431689856008.html (accessed July 6, 2010).

Halpin, Tony. "Russia Challenges US Dominance With Venezuela Naval War Games."
Sunday Times (London), November 24, 2008, http://www.timesonline.co.uk/tol
/news/world/us_and_americas/article5225275.ece (accessed May 21, 2010).

Haluani, Makram. "Benign Neglect: Cooperation in the Western Hemisphere."
Harvard International Review (winter 2003): 50–54.

Harding, Luke. "Belarus Turns Off Flow of Gas to Europe." *The Guardian*, June 22,
2010, http://www.guardian.co.uk/world/2010/jun/22/belarus-gas-row-russia
(accessed August 6, 2010).

———."Energy Conflicts Could Bring Military Clashes, Security Strategy Warns." *The
Guardian*, May 13, 2009.

Hearst, David. "Dangerous Proxy War Gains an International Dimension." *The Guardian*,
August 9, 2008, http://www.guardian.co.uk/world/2008/aug/09/georgia.russia1
(accessed June 30, 2010).

Heller, Fernando. "Ecuador's Correa: 'US No Longer Satan For Latin America.'"
Deutsche Presse-Agentur, July 18, 2007.

Hitchens, Christopher. "The Swastika and the Cedar." *Vanity Fair*, May 2009,
http://www.vanityfair.com/politics/features/2009/05/christopher-hitchens200905
?currentPage=1 (accessed April 10, 2010).

Hobbes, Thomas. *Leviathan*. London: Penguin, 1985.

Hornos, Conrados. "Chavez Keeps up South American Energy Diplomacy." Reuters, August 8, 2007, http://www.reuters.com/article/idUSN0835483220070808 (accessed June 1, 2010).

Hurriyet Daily News. "Belarus Eyes Latvia as New Route for Venezuelan Oil." August 23, 2010, http://www.hurriyetdailynews.com/n.php?n=belarus-eyes-latvia-as-new -route-for-venezuelan-oil-2010-08-23 (accessed August 26, 2010).

Index Mundi. "Iran GDP: Real Growth Rate." March 11, 2010, http://www.indexmundi.com/iran/gdp_real_growth_rate.html (accessed May 12, 2010).

Al Jazeera. "Iran and Turkey Sign Pipeline Deal." July 23, 2010, http://english.aljazeera.net/business/2010/07/201072314455840549.html (accessed July 23, 2010).

Jingjing, Han, ed."Venezuela, Iran Sign Dozens of New Agreements." *Xinhua*, November 26, 2009, http://news.xinhuanet.com/english/2009-11/26/content _12541972.htm (accessed August 23, 2010).

Kagan, Robert. *Of Paradise and Power: America and Europe in the New World Order.* New York: Vintage, 2003.

———. *The Return of History and the End of Dreams.* New York: Knopf, 2008.

Kaiser, Emily, and Patrick Grahame. "Argentina Says It Better Off Without IMF Advice." Reuters, April 24, 2010, http://www.reuters.com/article /idUSN2414517920100424 (accessed August 23, 2010).

Kaplan, Robert. "The Geography of Chinese Power." *Foreign Affairs* 89, no. 3, (May/June 2010): 22–41.

Karatnycky, Adrian. "Escaping Putin's Energy Squeeze." *Washington Post*, July 1, 2007, http://www.washingtonpost.com/wp-dyn/content/article/2007/06/29 /AR2007062902165.html (accessed June 3, 2010).

———, and Alexander Motyl. "The Key to Kiev." *Foreign Affairs* 88, no. 3, (May/June 2009): 106–120.

Khanna, Parag. *The Second World: How Emerging Powers Are Redefining Global Competition in the Twenty-First Century.* New York: Random House, 2008.

Khoury, Jack, and Haaretz Service. "Mexico Thwarts Hezbollah Bid to Set up South American Network." *Haaretz*, June 7, 2010, http://www.haaretz.com/news/diplomacy -defense/mexico-thwarts-hezbollah-bid-to-set-up-south-american-network -1.300360 (accessed June 12, 2010).

King, Charles, and Rajan Menon. "Prisoners of the Caucuses: Russia's Invisible Civil War." *Foreign Affairs* 89, no. 4 (July/August 2010): 20–34.

Kommersant. "Saudi Arabia Eager to Replace Iran." February 15, 2008, http://www.kommersant.com/p853111/r_527/Saudi_Arabia_cooperation/ (accessed September 3, 2010).

Kramer, Andrew E. "Russia Plans Nuclear Plant in Venezuela." *New York Times*, October 15, 2010, http://www.nytimes.com/2010/10/16/world/americas /16venez.html?partner=rss&emc=rss (accessed October 15, 2010).

———, and David E. Sanger. "U.S. Lauds Russia on Barring Arms for Iran." *New York Times*, September 23, 2010, http://www.nytimes.com/2010/09/23/world/europe /23prexy.html?_r=1&emc=eta1 (accessed September 23, 2010).

Kraul, Chris. "U.S. Eyes Venezuela-Iran Commercial Alliance." *Los Angeles Times*, June 24, 2006, http://articles.latimes.com/2006/jun/24/world/fg-veniran24 (accessed July 7, 2010).

———. "Venezuela Deepens Trade, Military Ties to China." *Los Angeles Times*, January 12, 2009, http://articles.latimes.com/2009/jan/12/world/fg-venezuela-china12 (accessed July 30, 2010).

———, and Sebastian Rotella. "Fears of Hezbollah Presence in Venezuela." *Los Angeles Times*, August 27, 2008, http://articles.latimes.com/2008/aug/27/world/fg -venezterror27 (accessed July 23, 2010).

Latin American Herald Tribune. "Colombia Shows Proof of FARC Rebels in Venezuela; Chavez Scoffs." http://www.laht.com/article.asp?CategoryId=10717&ArticleId= 360547 (accessed July 23, 2010).

———. "Iran to Loan $200 Million to Ecuador." September 6, 2010, http://laht.com/article.asp?CategoryId=14089&ArticleId=325760 (accessed September 6, 2010).

———. "Venezuela's Chávez Receives Chinese Planes Armed with Missile, Rockets and Bombs." http://laht.com/article.asp?ArticleId=353675&CategoryId=10718 (accessed June 3, 2010).

Latin Business Chronicle. "Iran Trade Triples." December 2, 2009, http://www.latinbusinesschronicle.com/app/article.aspx?id=3842 (accessed June 23, 2010).

Latin Lawyer. "Bolivia Withdraws from ICSID." May 22, 2007, http://www.latinlawyer.com/lawfirms/article/24123/bolivia-withdraws-icsid/ (accessed June 14, 2010).

Ledeen, Michael A. *The Iranian Time Bomb: The Mullah Zealots' Quest for Destruction.* New York: St. Martin's Press, 2007.

Leon, Mariela, and Marianna Parraga. "Negotiations to Purchase Nuclear Reactor from Argentina Confirmed." *El Universal*, October 11, 2005, http://www.eluniversal.com /2005/10/11/en_pol_art_11A618849.shtml (accessed October 3, 2010).

LeVine, Steve. *The Oil and the Glory: The Pursuit of Empire and Fortune on the Caspian Sea.* New York: Random House, 2007.

Lieggi, Stephanie. "From Proliferator to Model Citizen? China's Recent Enforcement of Nonproliferation-Related Trade Controls and its Potential Positive Impact in the Region." *Strategic Studies Quarterly* 4, no. 2 (Summer 2010): 39–62.

Logan, Samuel. "Iran's Latin American Inroads." International Relations and Security Network (ISN), April 29, 2009, http://www.isn.ethz.ch/isn/Current-Affairs/Security-Watch/Detail/?page525=6&ots591=4888CAA0-B3DB-1461-98B9 -E20E7B9C13D4&lng=en&size525=10&id=99532 (accessed May 12, 2010).

Lopez, Virginia. "Russia's Venezuela Foray: Tit for Tat." *Time*, September 11, 2008, http://www.time.com/time/world/article/0,8599,1840332,00.html (accessed July 23, 2010).

Luhnow, David, and Dan Molinski. "Inflation and Recession Deal Venezuela a Double Blow." *Wall Street Journal*, June 25, 2010, http://online.wsj.com/article /SB10001424052748704911704575326881209373378.html (accessed June 25, 2010).

Mankoff, Jeffrey. "Changing Course in Moscow." *Foreign Affairs: Snapshot.* September 7, 2010.

Marcano, Cristina, and Alberto Barrera Tyszka. *Hugo Chávez.* New York: Random House, 2006.

McCarthy, Julie. "Venezuela Works on its Defenses." NPR, June 20, 2006, http://www.npr.org/templates/story/story.php?storyId=5678460 (accessed July 12, 2010).

McConnell, Dugald, and Todd, Brian. "Venezuela Defends Controversial Flights to Iran and Syria." *CNN*, August 21, 2010, http://www.cnn.com/2010/WORLD/asiapcf /08/21/venezuela.flights.iran/index.html (accessed August 21, 2010).

McDermott, Jeremy. "Colombia's Rebels: A Fading Force." BBC News, February 1, 2008, http://news.bbc.co.uk/2/hi/americas/7217817.stm (accessed July 12, 2010).

————. "Hugo Chavez: Colombia is 'Israel of Latin America." *Telegraph*, July 24, 2009, http://www.telegraph.co.uk/news/worldnews/southamerica/venezuela/5901163/Hugo -Chavez-Colombia-is-Israel-of-Latin-America.html (accessed September 12, 2010).

Mearsheimer, John J. *The Tragedy of Great Power Politics*. New York: Norton, 2001.

Medvedev, Dmitry. "Go Russia!" *RT*, September 11, 2009, http://rt.com/Politics/2009- 09-11/dmitry-medvedev-program-document.html (accessed July 21, 2010).

Milner, Mark. "Chávez Seeks to Peg Oil at $50 a Barrel." *The Guardian*, April 3, 2006, http://www.guardian.co.uk/business/2006/apr/03/venezuela.oilandpetrol (accessed July 23, 2010).

Morgenthau, Robert M. "The Emerging Axis of Iran and Venezuela." *Wall Street Journal*, September 8, 2009, http://online.wsj.com/article/NA_WSJ_PUB: SB10001424052970203440104574400792835972018.html (accessed May 12, 2010).

Morrissey, Siobhan. "Iran's Romance of Nicaragua." *Time*, September 10, 2007, http://www.time.com/time/world/article/0,8599,1660500,00.html (accessed August 12, 2010).

MSNBC. "Falling Oil Prices Squeeze Chavez Diplomacy." January 6, 2009, http://www.msnbc.msn.com/id/28527787/ (accessed July 2, 2010).

Naím, Moisés. *Illicit: How Smugglers, Traffickers, and Copycats Are Hijacking the Global Economy*. New York: Doubleday, 2005.

National Terror Alert Response Center. "Mexico Thwarts Plans for South American Network." July 6, 2010, http://www.nationalterroralert.com/updates /2010/07/06/mexico-thwarts-hezbollah-plana-for-south-american-network/ (accessed July 18, 2010).

New York Times. "Russia Will Sell Fighters to Venezuela." June 4, 2006, http://www.nytimes.com/2006/06/04/world/europe/04iht-russia.1884852.html ?_r=1&scp=1&sq=arms%20embargo%20venezuela&st=cse (accessed July 12, 2010).

————. "Venezuelan Seeks Another Anti-U.S. Ally in Syria." August 31, 2006, http://www.nytimes.com/2006/08/31/world/middleeast/31chavez.html (accessed September 12, 2010).

Norton, Augustus Richard. *Hezbollah: A Short History*. Princeton, NJ: Princeton University Press, 2007.

Nuclear Threat Initiative (NTI). "China's Missile Exports and Assistance to Iran," http://www.nti.org/db/china/miranpos.htm (accessed July 20, 2010).

Nye, Joseph S. *The Paradox of American Power: Why the World's Only Superpower Can't Go It Alone*. New York: Oxford University Press, 2002.

————, and Robert O. Keohane. *Power and Interdependence*, 3rd ed. New York: Longman, 2001.

O'Connor, Anne-Marie, and Mary Beth Sheridan. "Iran's Invisible Nicaragua Embassy." *Washington Post*, July 13, 2009, http://www.washingtonpost.com/wp-dyn/content/article/2009/07/12/AR2009071202337.html (accessed June 5, 2010).

Olson, Parmy. "Bolivia Has a Gas Problem." *Forbes*, August 14, 2006, http://www.forbes.com/2006/08/14/bolivia-gas-nationalization-cx_po_0814bolivia.html (accessed August 7, 2010).

Organization of Petroleum Exporting Countries (OPEC). "Annual Statistics Bulletin 2008." http://www.opec.org/opec_web/static_files_project/media/downloads/publications/ASB2008.pdf.

Osborn, Andrew. "Belarus-Russia 'Gas War' Ends." *Telegraph*, June 24, 2010, http://www.telegraph.co.uk/news/worldnews/europe/russia/7852161/Russia-Belarus-gas-war-ends.html (accessed June 24, 2010).

Oster, Shai. "China's Oil Needs Affect Its Iran Ties." *Wall Street Journal*, September 28, 2009, http://online.wsj.com/article/SB125408502540944481.html (accessed July 21, 2010).

Padgett, Tim. "A New Cold War in the Caribbean." *Time*, July 24, 2008.

————. "In Ecuador, a Vote for Democracy?" *Time*, October 2, 2007, http://www.time.com/time/world/article/0,8599,1667386,00.html?artId=1667386?contType=article?chn=world (accessed July 23, 2010).

Parfitt, Tom. "Chavez Says 'Yes' to Russian Base." *The Guardian*, March 16, 2009, http://www.guardian.co.uk/world/2009/mar/16/chavez-russia-venezuela-nuclear-base (accessed June 6, 2010).

Parker, John W. *Persian Dreams: Moscow and Tehran Since the Fall of the Shah*. Washington, DC: Potomac Books, 2009

Partlow, Joshua, and Stephan Küffner. "Voters in Ecuador Approve New Constitution," *Washington Post*, September 29, 2008.

Paxton, Robin, and Anthony Barker. "Russia's Shtokman Natural Gas Project." Reuters, February 5, 2010, http://uk.reuters.com/article/idUSLDE6141PU20100205?sp=true (accessed May 23, 2010).

PBS Frontline. "The Hugo Chávez Show." November 25, 2008, http://www.pbs.org/wgbh/pages/frontline/hugochavez/view/?utm_campaign=viewp age&utm_medium=grid&utm_source=grid (accessed June 20, 2010).

———. "Showdown with Iran." October 23, 2007, http://www.pbs.org/wgbh/pages/frontline/showdown/view/?utm_campaign=viewpa ge&utm_medium=grid&utm_source=grid (accessed June 6, 2010).

Pearson, Natalie Obiko. "Iran and Venezuela Plan Anti-US Fund." *USA Today,* January 14, 2007, http://www.usatoday.com/news/world/2007-01-14-iran-venezuela_x.htm (accessed July 23, 2010).

Phillips, Leigh. "Russia-Norway Pact Eases Arctic Tension." *Bloomberg Business Week,* April 28, 2010, http://www.businessweek.com/globalbiz/content/apr2010 /gb20100428_055010.htm (accessed May 24, 2010).

Pollack, Kenneth M. *A Path Out of the Desert: A Grand Strategy for America in the Middle East.* New York: Random House, 2008.

Pomeroy, Robin, and Guy Faulconbridge. "Iran and Russia Clash in Worst Row for Years." Reuters, May 26, 2010, http://www.reuters.com/article /idUSLDE64P0VV20100526 (accessed May 28, 2010).

Press TV (Tehran). "Belarus Selling Iran M-Iskander Missiles." May 1, 2009, http://www.presstv.ir/detail.aspx?id=93244&sectionid=351020101 (accessed May 15, 2010).

———. "China Investment in Iran Worries US." July 29, 2010, http://www.presstv.ir /detail.aspx?id=136724&sectionid=351020101 (accessed July 30, 2010).

———. "Iran Favors Russia for Nuclear Projects." August 19, 2010, http://www.presstv.ir/detail/139268.html (accessed August 19, 2010).

———. "Iranian Bank to Open Branch in Ecuador." September 10, 2009, http://presstv.ir/detail.aspx?id=105831&sectionid=3510213 (accessed June 12, 2010).

———. "Iran-Venezuela Ties Dull U.S. pressure." August 30, 2010, http://www.presstv.ir/detail/140579.html (accessed August 30, 2010).

———. "Russia Vague on S-300 Delivery to Iran." August 21, 2010, http://www.presstv.ir/detail/139487.html (accessed August 21, 2010).

Radio Free Europe. "Belarus, Venezuela Strengthen Energy, Trade Ties During Lukashenko Visit." March 18, 2010, http://www.rferl.org/content/Belarus_Venezuela_Strengthen _Energy_Trade_Ties_During_Lukashenka_Visit/1986969.html (accessed July 7, 2010).

Razumovskaya, Olga. "Bushehr Launch Boosts Rosatom." *Moscow Times*, August 23, 2010, http://www.themoscowtimes.com/news/article/bushehr-launch-boosts -rosatom/413450.html (accessed August 24, 2010).

Reel, Monte. "Bolivia's Irresistible Reserves." *Washington Post*, February 10, 2008, http://www.washingtonpost.com/wp-dyn/content/article/2008/02/09 /AR2008020901326.html (accessed July 23, 2010).

Regional Surveys of the World: South America, Central and the Caribbean: 2002, 10th ed. London: Europa Publications, 783.

Reuters. "Brazil Wary on Nuclear Cooperation With Venezuela." May 23, 2005.

———. "Venezuela's Chavez Spends Heavily to Help Allies." October 12, 2007, http://www.reuters.com/article/idUSN12220829 (accessed August 2, 2010).

RIA Novosti (Moscow). "Belarus Denies Sales of S-300 to Iran." April 8, 2010, http://en.rian.ru/mlitary_news/20100804/160070974.html (accessed June 5, 2010).

———. "Nothing Can Hurt Belarus-Russia Relations: Lukashenko." September 14, 2010, http://en.rian.ru/russia/20100914/160587139.html (accessed September 14, 2010).

———."Russia, Ecuador Ink Strategic Partnership Declaration." October 29, 2009, http://en.rian.ru/russia/20091029/156637189.html (accessed August 8, 2010).

———."Russia to Build Two Kalashnikov Factories in Venezuela by 2010." June 8, 2007, http://en.rian.ru/russia/20070806/70445720.html (accessed July 30, 2010).

———."Venezuela to Build Stronger Air Defenses with Russian Aid." September 14, 2009, http://en.rian.ru/mlitary_news/20090914/156118402.html (accessed May 23, 2010).

Ricks, Thomas E. *Fiasco: The American Military Adventure in Iraq*. New York: Penguin, 2006.

Rodríguez, Francisco. "Venezuela's Empty Revolution." *Foreign Affairs* 87, no. 2 (March/April 2008): 49–62.

Rogers, Tim. "Chávez Plays Oil Card in Nicaragua." *Christian Science Monitor*, May 5, 2006, http://www.csmonitor.com/2006/0505/p01s04-woam.html (accessed August 12, 2010).

Rohter, Larry. "Argentina's New Role Model: Its Old Rival, Brazil," *New York Times*, September 5, 2001, http://www.nytimes.com/2002/08/05/world/argentina-s-new-role-model-its-old-rival-brazil.html?scp=9&sq=argentina%20rather%20be%20a%20star&st=cse&pagewanted=1 (accessed August 2, 2010).

———. "Venezuela Wants Trade Group to Embrace Anti-Imperialism." *New York Times*, January 19, 2007, http://www.nytimes.com/2007/01/19/world/americas/19latin.html (accessed September 12, 2010).

Romero, Simon. "Chávez Aide Says Iran is Helping it Look for Uranium." *New York Times*, September 25, 2009, http://www.nytimes.com/2009/09/26/world/americas/26venez.html (accessed August 12, 2010).

———. "Chávez Says China to Lend Venezuela $20 Billion." *New York Times*, April 18, 2010, http://www.nytimes.com/2010/04/19/world/americas/19venez.html (accessed July 28, 2010).

———. "Venezuela's Hope of More Sway Dims as Riches Dip." *New York Times*, May 16, 2009, http://www.nytimes.com/2009/05/20/world/americas/20venez.html (accessed July 24, 2010).

———. "Venezuela's Military Ties with Cuba Stir Concerns." *New York Times*, June 14, 2010.

———. "Venezuela Still Aids Colombia Rebels, New Material Shows." *New York Times*, August 2, 2009.

———. "Venezuela Strengthens its Relationships in the Middle East." *New York Times*, August 21, 2006, http://www.nytimes.com/2006/08/21/world/americas/21venez.html?emc=eta1 (accessed August 23, 2010).

———, Michael Slackman, and Clifford J. Levy. "Three Oil-Rich Countries Face a Reckoning." *New York Times*, October 21, 2008.

Rosenberg, Tina. "The Perils of Petrocracy." *New York Times Magazine*, November 4, 2007.

Schoen, Douglas, and Michael Rowan. *Threat Closer to Home: Hugo Chávez and the War Against America*. New York: Free Press, 2009.

Schoultz, Lars. *Beneath the United States: A History of U.S. Policy Toward Latin America*. Cambridge, MA: Harvard University Press, 1998.

Schumer, Charles. "Confronting Iran." *Wall Street Journal*, June 3, 2008, http://schumer.senate.gov/new_website/opeds/WSJ6_3_08oped.htm (accessed September 2, 2010).

————. "Iran's President Recruits Terror Master." *Sunday Times* (London), April 23, 2006, http://www.timesonline.co.uk/tol/news/world/article708342.ece (accessed July 4, 2010).

The Sean Hannity Show. "Interview with Álvaro Vargas Llosa." July 18, 2010.

Shifter, Michael. *Hugo Chávez: A Test for U.S. Policy.* A Special Report of the Inter-American Dialogue, Washington, DC. March 2007.

Shuster, Simon. "Russian Support for Iran Sanctions Called into Question." *Time*, July 15, 2010, http://www.time.com/time/world/article/0,8599,2004159,00.html (accessed September 5, 2010).

Slackman, Michael. "Iran Gives Hamas Enthusiastic Support, But Discreetly, Just in Case." *New York Times*, January 12, 2009.

Smith, Geri. "Chavez: Trading Oil for Influence." *Businessweek*, December 26, 2005, http://www.businessweek.com/magazine/content/05_52/b3965071.htm (accessed June 30, 2010).

Smith, Keith. *Russian Energy Politics in the Baltics, Poland, and Ukraine.* Washington, DC: Center for Strategic and International Studies, 2004.

Sofer, Roni. "Israel: Ties to South America Aiding Iran's Nuclear Program." *Ynet News*, May 25, 2009, http://www.ynetnews.com/articles/0,7340,L-3721335,00.html (accessed June 7, 2010).

Solomon, Jay. "Russians to Fuel Iranian Reactor." *Washington Post*, July 14, 2010, http://online.wsj.com/article/SB10001424052748703960004575427851574039466.html (accessed July 14, 2010).

Solovyov, Dmitry, Ori Lewis, and Jon Boyle. "Russia to Sell Syria Warplanes, Air Defense Systems." Reuters, May 14, 2010, http://www.reuters.com/article/idUSTRE64D35S20100514 (accessed May 14, 2010).

Stecklow, Steve, and Farnaz Fassihi. "Iran's Global Foray Has Mixed Results." *Wall Street Journal*, September 29, 2009, http://online.wsj.com/article/SB125409124052344735.html (accessed July 5, 2010).

Stephens, Bret. "The Tehran-Caracas Nuclear Axis," *Wall Street Journal*, December 15, 2009.

Stewart, Scott. "Hezbollah, Radical but Rational." STRATFOR, August 12, 2010.

Sturcke, James. "Chávez Jokes About Helping Iran Build Nuclear Bomb." *The Guardian*, October 7, 2009, http://www.guardian.co.uk/world/2009/oct/07/hugo-chavez-iran-nuclear-bomb (accessed June 24, 2010).

Taheri, Amir. "Iran Has Started a Mid East Arms Race." *Wall Street Journal*, March 23, 2009, http://online.wsj.com/article/NA_WSJ_PUB:SB123776572203009141.html (accessed July 22, 2010).

Tehran Times. "Ecuador Plans to Buy Arms from Iran." December 15, 2008, http://www.tehrantimes.com/Index_view.asp?code=184841 (accessed May 3, 2010).

———. "Iran, Afghanistan, Tajikistan's Interests Interlinked." August 7, 2010, http://www.tehrantimes.com/index_View.asp?code=224314 (accessed August 7, 2010).

———. "Iran, Belarus See Jofair Oilfield Operational Soon." February 17, 2010, http://www.tehrantimes.com/index_View.asp?code=214288 (accessed July 9, 2010).

———. "No Talk of Reducing Ties with Russia at Parliamentary Committee: MP." June 28, 2010, http://www.tehrantimes.com/index_View.asp?code=222068 (accessed July 24, 2010).

———. "Tehran Proposes Iran-Russia Nuclear Fuel Production Consortium." July 28, 2010, http://www.tehrantimes.com/index_View.asp?code=225696 (accessed July 29, 2010).

Terrill, Ross. *The New Chinese Empire: And What it Means for the United States*. New York: Basic Books, 2003.

Transparency International. *Corruption Perceptions Index: 2005.* http://www.transparency.org/policy_research/surveys_indices/cpi/2005 (accessed July 5, 2010).

Trenin, Dmitri. "Russia Leaves the West." *Foreign Affairs* 85, 4, (July/August 2006): 87–96.

El Universal. "Russia Top Arms Supplier to Latin America Thanks to Sales to Venezuela." February 3, 2010, http://english.eluniversal.com/2010/02/03/en _pol_art_russia,-top-arms-sup_03A3385931.shtml (accessed July 14, 2010).

———. "Venezuela, Iran Have Executed 57 Industrial Agreements." August 26, 2010, http://www.eluniversal.com/2010/08/26/en_eco_esp_venezuela,-iran-have _26A4386931.shtml (accessed August 26, 2010).

———. "Venezuela, Iran Initial 29 Accords." September 22, 2007.

———. "Venezuelan Bank Penalized for Alleged Link with Iranian Plan." July 27, 2010, http://english.eluniversal.com/2010/07/27/en_eco_esp_venezuelan-bank -pena_27A4254177.shtml (accessed August 14, 2010).

———. "Venezuela Returns Chinese Tractors on Mechanical Defects." September 13, 2006, http://english.eluniversal.com/2006/09/13/en_eco_art_13A777631.shtml (accessed July 7, 2010).

———. "Venezuela-Russia Arms Deals Unleash Turbulence in the Region." April 5, 2010, http://english.eluniversal.com/2010/04/09/en_ing_esp_venezuela-russia -arm_09A3718293.shtml (accessed June 8, 2010).

United Press International (UPI). "Military Industries Feature in Iran-Venezuela Cooperation." September 15, 2009, http://www.upi.com/Business_News/Security -Industry/2009/09/15/Military-industries-feature-in-Iran-Venezuela-cooperation /UPI-34011253026800/ (accessed September 4, 2010).

Upstream Online. "US Surpasses Russia as Top Gas Producer." January 12, 2010, http://www.upstreamonline.com/live/article203335.ece (accessed June 3, 2010).

U.S. Department of Defense. "Unclassified Report on Military Power of Iran." April 2010, http://www.scribd.com/doc/31398368/DoD-Unclassified-Report-on- Military-Power-of-Iran (accessed July 28, 2011).

U.S. Energy Information Administration. "Country Analysis Briefs: Venezuela," http://www.eia.doe.gov/cabs/venezuela/Full.html (accessed July 19, 2010).

———. "World Oil Chokepoints." January 2008, http://www.eia.doe.gov/cabs/world _oil_transit_chokepoints/pdf.pdf (accessed July 18, 2010).

U.S. Geological Survey. "Circum-Arctic Resource Appraisal." http://energy.usgs.gov/arctic/ (accessed June 15, 2010).

U.S. Government Accountability Office. "Iran Sanctions: New Act Underscores Importance of Comprehensive Assessment of Sanctions' Effectiveness." July 29, 2010, http://www.gao.gov/new.items/d10928t.pdf (accessed August 23, 2010).

U.S. State Department. "The Caribbean Basin Security Initiative: A Shared Regional Partnership." Fact Sheet. May 20, 2010, http://www.state.gov/r/pa/scp/fs/2010 /142088.htm (accessed May 20, 2010).

Venezuelan Constitution, Title VI: Article 305. 1999, http://www.embavenez -us.org/constitution/title_vi.htm (accessed July 7, 2010).

Venezuelan National Radio (RNV). "Syria Joined Alba as an Observer Member." October 22, 2010, http://www.rnv.gob.ve/noticias/index.php?act=ST&f=31&t =140297 (accessed October 24, 2010).

Voice of America. "Chavez Meets with Syria's Assad in Venezuela." June 27, 2010. http://www.voanews.com/english/news/middle-east/Venezuelas-Chavez-Meets -With-Syrias-Assad-in-Caracas-97258574.html (accessed June 27, 2010).

———. "Iran Loans More than $250 Million to Bolivia." August 31, 2010, http://www.voanews.com/english/news/americas/Iran-Loans-More-than-250-Million-to-Bolivia-101913708.html (accessed September 5, 2010).

———. "Russia Arms Latin America." April 27, 2007, http://www.voanews.com/english/news/news-analysis/a-13-2007-05-02-voa4.html (accessed May 23, 2010).

Voice of Russia. "Russia, Iran S-300 Contract Still in Force." July 15, 2010, http://english.ruvr.ru/2010/07/15/12407962.html (accessed July 15, 2010).

Wall Street Journal. "Chávez's Base Rebukes Him at Polls," November 25, 2008. online.wsj.com/article/SB122748432718751705.html (accessed July 28, 2011).

———. "Colombia Clashes with Nicaragua Over Guerilla Tie." July 28, 2008, http://online.wsj.com/article/SB121720907667488883.html (accessed July 28, 2011).

———. "Venezuela Airline Cancels Route to Iran, Syria." September 15, 2010, http://billionaires.forbes.com/article/04xLduX7VY7lW?q=Caracas.

Washington Post. "Brazil's Victory in Cotton Trade Case Exposes America's Wasteful Subsidies." June 3, 2010, http://www.washingtonpost.com/wp-dyn/content/article/2010/06/02/AR2010060204228.html (accessed June 3, 2010).

———. "Longtime Foes U.S., Iran Explore Improved Relations." October 29, 2001. http://pqasb.pqarchiver.com/washingtonpost/access/86761665.html?FMT=ABS&FMTS=ABS:FT&date=Oct+29%2C+2001&author=Steven+Mufson+and+Marc+Kaufman&desc=Longtime+Foes+U.S.%2C+Iran+Explore+Improved+Relations (accessed July 28, 2011). This is an archived preview. Viewers must pay to read the full article.

———. "Witness Points to Chavez in Argentina Election Case." July 7, 2008, http://www.washingtonpost.com/wp-dyn/content/article/2008/07/06/AR2008070602298.html (accessed July 10, 2010).

Washington Times. "Exclusive: Hezbollah Uses Mexican Drug Routes into U.S." March 27, 2009, http://www.washingtontimes.com/news/2009/mar/27/hezbollah-uses-mexican-drug-routes-into-us/?page=1 (accessed July 19, 2010).

Williams, Daniel. "Syria, Venezuela Sign Olive Oil Trade Agreement." Olive Oil Times, June 21, 2010, http://www.oliveoiltimes.com/olive-oil-business/africa-middle-east/syria-venezuela/3721 (accessed September 4, 2010).

Wilson, Peter. "Chavez Visits China as Venezuela Curbs U.S. Oil Ties." Bloomberg News, August 21, 2006, http://www.bloomberg.com/apps/news?pid=newsarchive&sid=aKxotAMwY_D8 (accessed July 6, 2010).

Wilson, Scott, and Karen DeYoung. "Obama Urges 'Equal' Ties in Hemisphere." *Washington Post*, April 18, 2009, http://www.washingtonpost.com/wp-dyn/content/article/2009/04/17/AR2009041700389.html (accessed September 24, 2010).

Woodward, Bob. *State of Denial: Bush at War, Part III*. New York: Simon & Schuster, 2006.

Wright, Robin. "Iran's New Alliance with China Could Cost U.S. Leverage." *Washington Post*, November 17, 2004, http://www.washingtonpost.com/wp-dyn/articles/A55414-2004Nov16.html (accessed July 6, 2010).

Yan, ed. "Iran-Belarus Determined to Expand Relations: Ahmadinejad." *Xinhua*, December 17, 2009, http://news.xinhuanet.com/english/2009-12/17/content_12658615.htm (accessed July 3, 2010).

Yergin, Daniel. *The Prize: The Epic Quest for Oil, Money, and Power*. New York: Simon & Schuster, 1991.

Zharakovich, Yuri. "NATO: Still a Sore Point with Putin." *Time*, April 1, 2008, http://www.time.com/time/world/article/0,8599,1726902,00.html (accessed July 23, 2010).

Zweig, David, and Bi Jianhai. "China's Global Hunt for Energy." *Foreign Affairs*, 84, no. 5, September/October 2005, http://www.foreignaffairs.com/articles/61017/david-zweig-and-bi-jianhai/chinas-global-hunt-for-energy?page=4 (accessed July 28, 2011).

Index

About the Author

Sean Goforth teaches world politics and international political economy at Coastal Carolina University in Conway, South Carolina. He blogs for the Foreign Policy Association and is a regular contributor to *World Politics Review*. His writings have appeared on NYTimes.com, the *London Telegraph* (online), realclearworld.com, and have also been cited by the Congressional Research Service. Goforth is a graduate of the University of North Carolina–Chapel Hill and the School of Foreign Service at Georgetown University. He lives in Calabash, North Carolina.